Professor Lepsius
with the Author's compliments.
July 19. 1856

THE WILL

DIVINE AND HUMAN

BY

THOMAS SOLLY

BARRISTER-AT-LAW OF THE MIDDLE TEMPLE, AND LECTURER ON THE ENGLISH LANGUAGE AND LITERATURE AT THE UNIVERSITY OF BERLIN, LATE OF CAIUS COLLEGE, CAMBRIDGE.

The Will is the last thing in the soul, and the ultimate resolution of all others.

CUDWORTH.

CAMBRIDGE:
DEIGHTON, BELL AND CO.
LONDON: BELL AND DALDY.
1856.

PREFACE.

IN the following Essay I have endeavoured to give a systematic solution of the principal problems connected with the Will. For the manner in which I have treated the subject, I must refer the reader to the work itself. A cursory glance at its general scope is all that can be attempted within the limits of a preface.

In the conviction that Necessarianism is as unsound in Philosophy as it is fatal to Religion, I have sought for some strong and unassailable position for the doctrine of liberty. This, however, I have not been able to find in the opinions of those Libertarians who make liberty to consist in a power of choosing in opposition to the net result of the motives. Arbitrarianism, as this theory may be called, considered merely as a convulsive effort to escape from an irksome bondage, is laudable enough in its intentions, but when carried out to its legitimate results is even more objectionable than Necessarianism. For as all the motives are exhausted in arriving at the net result, the act determining against it, is absolutely unmotived, and neither reason nor feeling contribute anything towards it. The assumption therefore of such an act is equivalent to converting the merely negative conception of the absolutely fortuitous into a positive element in human conduct. But low indeed would be man's vocation, and no less thankless the task of philosophy, if the only alternative it could present for his choice were, whether he should acknowledge himself the slave of necessity or the sport of chance.

There is, however, another doctrine of liberty which to the best of my knowledge was originally propounded by Kant, and afterwards adopted by Schelling in its essential features. The doctrine in question makes liberty to consist in a single act, establishing once for all the character of the individual. This view is in so far preferable to Arbitrarianism, as it saves at least a reasonable liberty. But it stands in such direct contradiction with numerous moral phenomena, that its acceptance would involve a degree of scepticism in the deliverances of our consciousness, absolutely fatal to all philosophy whatever. If the crime and the repentance that succeeds it are merely different objective manifestations in time of the same transcendental act of freedom, our whole moral life becomes one gross illusion, and our consciousness utterly mendacious and untrustworthy. Hence the Kantian solution has appeared to me as untenable as the others, for it is equivalent to felling the whole tree in order to lop off an unseemly branch.

The above objections to the arbitrarianism of Reid and the doctrine of Kant, are merely stated here as a general explanation of the course of the following argument. The proof that these positions may be logically deduced from the respective theories is given in the work itself.

Finding, then, no satisfaction in the solutions either of Priestley, Reid, or Kant, I have endeavoured to strike out a rather different path from any of them. To accomplish this, it has been necessary to enter into a somewhat long investigation respecting the nature of an act of consciousness in general, *à priori* conceptions and judgments, the conception of causality, and the grounds of our belief in it. This analysis is essentially Kantian in its principles, and has been all the more necessary on that very account. For as it is only in the last stage of my deduction of liberty that I have diverged from the views of that philosopher, I could only explain my reasons for doing so by examining the previous steps. The desultory reader who opens the book in the middle, and finds a long disquisition on causality and *à priori* reasoning, may probably be inclined to regard it as a digression from the avowed subject of the work. Should he, however, retain this opinion after reading the whole of it, I can assure him that he has not understood my argument, to which the above-mentioned disquisition is absolutely essential.

The problems connected with the relation of the will to the intellect, and the will of God, as also the solutions of them offered in the following pages, are not of such a character as to admit of being briefly stated, and I must therefore refer the reader to the work itself, respecting them.

In the course of the Essay I have repeatedly had occasion to employ mathematical illustrations. To prevent, however, the possibility of a misunderstanding respecting the light in which I regard them, I will observe shortly, that they are only introduced as a means of conveying the idea thus symbolised, with a greater precision and sharpness of outline than is attainable by other means. They are not therefore employed as an organum for the discovery of a truth, or as a method of arriving at a result beyond the grasp of an immediate intuition, as is the case with the ordinary mathematical analysis. In the explanations that accompany them, the positions they are intended to exemplify are made perfectly comprehensible to those who are not acquainted with that science. But the symbolical forms have this advantage, that they render any misunderstanding of the argument they illustrate almost impossible, and greatly facilitate the detection of fallacy. In short, the symbols are employed as the simplest vehicle for the expression of the mutual relations among the various elements of a problem, and this office they accomplish by divesting these relations of all extraneous matter.

With regard to style, it has been my constant endeavour to make my meaning as clear and intelligible as the subject permits—sometimes indeed at the risk of being accused of a puerile diffuseness. I have preferred, however, to err on this side rather than on the other. For the intelligent reader can hurry on more rapidly if he likes; whereas if any one step in a consecutive argument should not be perfectly understood, the stringency of the conclusion is of course no longer felt, and only a general and vague impression left on the student's mind.

It has been with the same object that I have avoided the use of all peculiarly philosophical terms, where I could find others of daily use which would express my meaning with equal precision. Where however this was not the case, I have not hesitated to sacrifice popularity to accuracy, as I should otherwise have conveyed other ideas than those I intended. For instance, I know of no generic term in the English language signifying the act of the mind in knowing an object in general without reference to its nature, besides *cognition,* and consequently, at the risk of offending the ears of those persons who demand that abstract ideas shall be conveyed in comparatively concrete language, I have employed this term wherever the sense required it. To take another instance, if the reader open the book at the chapter on the Relation of the Will to the Intellect, and the expressions, first objective, first subjective, second objective, &c., meet his eye, he may be inclined to object to such terms as harsh and unintelligible. But I have fully explained at the proper place, the sense in which I have employed them, and to express my meaning without them, it would have been necessary to introduce so many long periphrases, that obscurity, and not popularity, would have been the inevitable result. And I would here remark, that while no objection is raised to the use of technical language in the treatment of scientific subjects generally, an exception is frequently made in the case of metaphysics. But this is surely very unreasonable. Words are necessary to express ideas, and if the latter are of such a character as not to occur in every-day life, every-day language will not be sufficient to convey them, and technical terms must be employed.

Perhaps, however, modern philosophy has itself chiefly to blame for any undue jealousy with which its language may be regarded. I think it would require an extraordinary amount of faith to believe of many a German writer that he had a perfectly clear conception of his meaning himself, but could not have made it clearer to others if he had wished. But he who does not write as clearly as he can, is either purposely obscure, or obscure through carelessness, regarding it as a matter of little consequence whether thinkers less profound than himself comprehend his speculations. Either alternative however evinces a supercilious indifference towards the reader, which it is difficult to reconcile with an earnest desire for the promulgation of truth; and the writer who is guilty of it has no just cause of complaint, if the amount of effort he makes to communicate his meaning be regarded as a measure of the importance he attaches to it. Far be it from me however to deny either the profundity or the earnestness of these writers; I believe indeed that the works of modern German philosophers contain greater treasures of deep thought than the English generally have any conception of. But both the profundity and the earnestness are lamentably wasted if they are mainly employed in keeping truth at the bottom of the well when once they have found it there, instead of drawing it up, and placing it in such a light that men may gaze on it, and grow the wiser as they gaze.

Before leaving this subject, I would suggest as a question not quite unworthy consideration, whether it is not possible that extreme obscurity of style may eventually lead to obscurity in a different sense, —one neither contemplated nor desired by the author himself. Contemporaries may for a time be imposed upon by this sort of esotericism; but is there not considerable risk that posterity may grow refractory, that such works will be described in catalogues as "curious and very scarce," and consigned to the same venerable dust which envelops the countless host of the Great Unread? Some symptoms of such fate are already beginning to shew themselves, and it is no uncommon observation, that philosophy is going out of fashion in Germany. If this be really the case in a country so justly preeminent for its speculation, I believe the somewhat forbidding garb which philosophy has assumed is alone in fault. Men perhaps are beginning to be tired of naming themselves after a philosopher, when they are conscious of having comprehended a bare tenth of the one-fifth of his works which they have had the time and energy to read, and they accordingly abandon the study to those who pursue it as a profession.

The foregoing observations must not be understood to imply that philosophy can ever be made a light dilettante study, adapted for leisure reading in an easy chair. On the contrary, I am convinced that a large proportion of mankind can never be made to comprehend abstract speculations, and that they can only profit by the results, when conveyed to them in more concrete forms, through minds of various intermediate gradations between the extreme speculative and the extreme practical. But surely if the great end of philosophy is to purify and ennoble men's thoughts and lives by giving them truer views of their own nature and thus of their relations to God and to each other, it has but ill accomplished its task, if it speaks in a language which earnest thinkers pore over at the rate of half a page a day, closing the book at last with a dim consciousness of having thoroughly misunderstood it. The study of philosophy is like the ascent of a lofty mountain. The summit is often enveloped in clouds; but he who ascends it to obtain a more glorious view of earth or to feel himself nearer Heaven, will do wisely to choose a clear day when the sun is shining warm and bright, and even distant objects stand out distinctly in the blue horizon.

BERLIN,
May 16, 1856.

CONTENTS.

PART II.

PART III.

THE RELATION OF THE WILL TO GOD

BOOK II. THE DIVINE WILL.

APPENDIX A.

APPENDIX B.

INTRODUCTION.

General Outline of the Subject.

SINCE the earliest ages of the world the Forum of the Human Consciousness has been the scene of a mighty suit between the principles of Liberty and Necessity. Many great philosophers have been the advocates on either side,—many generations have successively occupied the judgment-seat; but advocates and judges have alike passed away, and no final decree has as yet been entered on the record. Some men—Englishmen perhaps more especially—have in these latter times become wearied by the long protraction of the cause, have turned away from it in disgust, and in the belief that it concerns no practical interest, have hastened to disclaim their judicial functions. They have argued that the pleadings are but a vain wrangling, for ever revolving round the same point but never approaching it, and that there is no hope of man's arriving at a clear result on this side the grave. But the indomitable perseverance with which the thinkers of all ages have ever returned to the same problem, must be regarded as a sufficient answer to such desponding views, for it is an evidence of an instinctive faith in the powers of the intellect far too strong and too universal to be regarded as a mere illusion. And, indeed, it may be seen from a mere glance at the past history of human opinions, that the successive solution of the subordinate questions has gradually determined the respective provinces of these two principles with an ever-increasing accuracy, and that the subject of controversy has thus been reduced to a far narrower compass than it originally occupied.

The circumstances of an early stage of civilisation call much more frequently for energetic action than profound speculation, and thus excite in man a far livelier consciousness of his liberty than he is likely to retain in a more contemplative age. This disposes him to regard the claims of liberty with peculiar partiality, and to assign to its sphere not only all the changes of which he is conscious that his own will is the immediate cause, but all others also which he observes in the world around him. Not, however, sufficiently acquainted with nature to recognise a greater degree of harmony between its parts than between the actions of different men, he attributes to the former not only the liberty, but also the caprices and idiosyncracies of the latter. In this manner the presumed want of unity in the processes of nature is explained on the ground of the multiplicity of the agents producing them; and every striking phenomenon is regarded as the individual and personal act of the higher intelligence presiding over the element in which it occurs. That the religious sentiment, therefore, should ever assume the form of polytheism, is owing to man's fancied recognition of the reflection of his own passions in the various aspects which the elements present. To effect their private ends Jupiter hurls his lightning, and Æolus unchains the winds, and a wild liberty reigns from one end of nature to the other. Lest, however, under such mad guidance the universe should founder in its voyage through the infinite, and sink into the abyss of primæval chaos, a blind fatalism is thrown in as a ballast to keep the vessel right.

This, then, is man's first attempt to find a clue to the mysteries of nature. But in the course of time the ever-accumulating evidence of his senses and his understanding forces upon him the conviction of the omnipresence of Law; and those fancies of the night, the higher spirits with their casual interferences, are gradually dispelled by the increasing light of day. The universal harmony of nature becomes apparent, and one simple unvarying law of causality is recognised as the actual form of government throughout the external world.

The discovery of a truth is sometimes perverted to the furtherance of an error; and so it was in the present instance. Some men, conscious of the capricious use they made of their own liberty, were unable to imagine any other kind of use of it in another being; for the conception of a free agent who should employ his liberty in maintaining law was above their comprehension. As soon, therefore, as they became aware that their theory was but an illusion—a mere reflection of their own caprices in the operations of nature—they gave it up; but with it they gave up the liberty also. Atheism argued: There is no caprice in the energy producing the changes in nature, therefore there is no liberty; but everything is resolvable into an impersonal, inexorable Law. But the difficulty of conceiving a law without a law-giver has fortunately given the predominance to Theism, which replied: There is no caprice, it is true; but there is a liberty beyond the law,—a liberty which imposed the law, and is therefore superior to it.

The recognition of the dominion of law over the whole external world was a great step, but it was not the last that Philosophy has taken in the same direction. The subjection to law of man's physical nature was already included in that of the external world, of which it forms a part. This fact once acknowledged, suggested another and far deeper question, namely, whether the internal world also—that of man's spiritual nature—does not equally fall under the same iron rule. The two answers to this question coincide for a short distance, and then break off in exactly opposite directions. Both Libertarians and Necessarians are agreed that there is such a thing as human nature,—in other words, that men's emotions and intellects are subject to certain laws,—but beyond this point their opinions diverge. For while the Necessarian maintains the subjection to law of the whole of man's faculties, the Libertarian asserts an exemption in favour of the faculty of the will. It appears from this that Necessarianism and Polytheism arrive at their respective results by precisely opposite operations; for while the Polytheist recognises his own caprice reflected in external nature, the Necessarian recognises the uniformity of external nature reflected in his own[1].

[1] About six months after I had written the above observations I met with a very interesting article entitled Mesmeric Atheism, in which similar views to those in the text are expressed in the following clear and forcible language.

"The *first* impression we have of the government of the universe is, that it is *all free*—the fresh dictate of ever-varying emotion. The *second*, arising on the detection of widening law,

That the progress already made may fairly warrant our entertaining hopes for the future, is, I trust, sufficiently evident from the foregoing sketch of the past history of the case. Perhaps, indeed, this progress is all the less appreciated on account of that very certainty which constitutes its chief merit. So firm are our modern convictions on this point, that we can hardly conceive the ancient Greek's misty notion of the boundary line between Law and Liberty, or realise to ourselves that the title of the former to the realm of external nature has ever been seriously disputed. Yet such was not only the fact, but precisely the primary fact of all Polytheism. Notwithstanding, however, all that has been done, the last issue between Law and Liberty,—the claim of each to be recognised as the ultimate principle in human conduct,—has still to receive its final award. Thus, according to the Necessarians, every human volition is the inevitable product of the character of the man and the circumstances in which he is placed; and the will is absolutely determined in all its acts by psychological laws. They apply the same doctrine to the Deity, and argue, that God being omniscient, must always have known what was absolutely the best, and being infinitely good, must always have chosen it. Thus the acts both of God and man are made to fall under the same unyielding necessity,

is the scientific reaction from the former, and reverses its error by declaring that *all is necessary*. The *third* restricts the universality of both, and neutralises their contradiction, by providing a realm for each, assigning the necessary to physical nature, the free to the human soul; and assuring us that even where an immutable order has become fixed, it is by the resolve of a spontaneous fidelity, not by the decree of a dead fatalism." *Prospective Review*, May 1851, p. 257.

and the whole universe material and spiritual through all time past and future, is represented as one vast machine, every movement of which is regulated by absolute law.

These doctrines are invariably rejected by the understanding in its natural and unsophisticated state. The man who has not entered into any philosophical investigation of the subject never hesitates to assert, that he can choose what actions he will, and that this choice is determined, at least in great measure, by something independent of fixed law, and not merely by the circumstances in which he is placed or the opinions in which he has been educated. Where, however, the powers of philosophical reflection have been developed, and the attempt is made to reconcile this assumed freedom with the known facts of the consciousness, the Divine government of the world, and the Divine character generally, several startling and apparently insuperable difficulties arise, and shake the inquirer's confidence in the convictions he had previously entertained.

When, for instance, we speak of the nature of a thing, we mean the laws according to which it acts; and whatever has a nature is therefore subject to law. How then is a knowledge of human nature possible as far as human conduct is concerned, or rather, how is that nature itself possible, if human actions are not subject to law? Man's conduct is governed by motives suggested by the circumstances with which he is surrounded, and the strongest motive will determine his choice. What then becomes of his freedom?

Again, God foreknows the future. If then He knows that I shall perform any particular action on some future occasion, how is it left to my choice when the occasion arises, to perform it or not? Can I act in contradiction to God's foreknowledge, and make Him to have erred? But, unless the Divine government of the world be a fable, God not only foreknows the future, He plans it too; and the event of all that happens rests in His hands. And yet this seems hardly possible, if human wills are able to do or leave undone, and are subject to no compulsion, either direct or indirect, in the choice of their actions.

These difficulties, which here are but glanced at, have coerced many an understanding to seek a refuge in the doctrine of Necessarianism. But few of those who have been urged to speculate on such subjects by that restless striving after inward harmony between their feelings and conceptions, which constitutes the philosophical impulse, will find peace here. They may be so convinced of the difficulties attending every theory of free-will, as to adopt Necessarianism as their theoretical creed, but they will hardly embrace it from any deep conviction that it answers all the demands of their moral nature. It will be accepted as a choice of evils rather than as a positive good. Its brightest side is the resignation and trust which it may inspire in the course of events; but few will feel perfectly satisfied with the place assigned by it to human conduct.

For if men's actions are determined by laws, and are thus subject to a strict necessity, in what way do they differ from the phenomena of external nature, or with what propriety indeed can they be called actions at all? How can the idea of virtue or vice be attached to an action which is entirely determined by laws, with any greater propriety than to a trade-wind or a hurricane? With what justice can either

God or man condemn or punish an action which all the circumstances of the actor, internal as well as external, made an absolutely necessary link in the great chain of events? And to all these difficulties may be added the ever-recurring instinctive conviction, that there is something within us essentially different from inanimate nature, and that we are governed by an active principle above all law, and subject to no necessity.

Besides these questions respecting the freedom of the will, there is another, also involving some difficulty, respecting the relation in which it stands to the intellect. If the will can choose an object, it must itself possess the faculty of distinguishing various objects from each other; in other words, it must possess an understanding, and is therefore, not only a practical but also an intellectual faculty. Neither is understanding alone sufficient for its purposes, as it frequently has to make its choice between future events which require an act of the imagination to realise them. The hypothesis, that the will does not contain either of these intellectual faculties within itself, but is absolutely blind, and merely derives the knowledge necessary for choice, from the aid of the separate faculties of the understanding and imagination, is open to similar objections. For it is the essence of an intellectual nature, to be able to convey its results only to a similar intellectual nature. Thus the understanding cannot convey its conceptions of objects and their nature to another faculty, unless this latter is also adapted by its nature to receive such conceptions, in other words, is itself intellectual. If then we admit that the will can choose between objects both present and future, we cannot escape the conclusion, that it must in some sense or other be itself both understanding and imagination.

But there is another question of yet deeper import than any I have yet mentioned. I allude to the question of priority between the Divine Will and Moral Law. Is the moral law such as it is because the Deity has so willed it, or has the Deity conformed His will to an antecedent moral law? Is there, in short, any law for the Divine will exterior to it, or is such will the only fountain-head of all law, as it undoubtedly is of all fact?

Notwithstanding the very important place which these questions must necessarily occupy in every comprehensive system, either of religious or philosophical belief, the investigation of them has fallen, more especially of late years, into considerable disrepute, and those who engage in it are often regarded as metaphysical dreamers rather than as earnest inquirers after truth. The objections assume various forms, but they all spring originally from the same root, namely, that scepticism in the powers of the human intellect which is the offspring of indolence and egotism. A man may not be conscious of such motives, but when he has found his own intellect unequal to the solution of a problem, his vanity will certainly dispose him to give a favourable consideration to the opinion, that it lies beyond the province of the human intellect generally; and this conclusion is also calculated to gratify his love of ease by exempting him from further effort.

The first reproach which has been cast at this controversy is its inability to establish any doctrine on grounds sufficiently unimpeachable to command universal assent. Now there may be some force in the objection, as long as we regard the speculations concerning human liberty as constituting the whole question at issue, and not merely as the principal point in a great cause involving many others. To form, however, a fair judgment of the future progress of philosophy, we must look at the successes of the past as well as its failures. If then we compare the whole problem of law and liberty, as originally presented to mankind, with the far narrower limits to which the modern controversy has been reduced, I believe we shall find that so much has been already accomplished as to justify the opinion that the remaining difficulties are not wholly insuperable.

It must be confessed that the progress of knowledge has suggested new problems, and that where some questions have been answered, others have started up in their place. But these difficulties really existed just as much in ancient times as they do now. And, indeed, the progress which is necessary in order to establish on some secure basis the respective limits of the two principles throughout the universe, may, perhaps, be hardly greater than that which the natural philosopher has actually made, since the times when the ancient Greek heard the dreaded Pan's approach in the rustle of every tree, or saw the darkened brow of Jove in every thunder-cloud.

Sometimes an objection is taken to all inquiry into this subject, on the grounds of the character of the reasoning employed. The arguments are considered as a species of sleight of intellect, offering the sophist a brilliant opportunity for the display of his metaphysical acumen, but involving no deep practical human interest. The true but unknown answer, which is supposed to satisfy all the apparent contradictions suggested by our reason, is conceived as resembling an ingenious enigma, escaping the intellect by its complication and subtlety, rather than as the problem of the universe, overpowering the imagination by the infinitude and sublimity of the conceptions necessary to its solution. But surely this is not so; for whatever may be the nature of some of the arguments employed, they can never derogate from the dignity of the question in itself. Besides, the complicated, the enigmatical, is the multifarious before it has been knit together by that unity which serves as its key. It is the phenomena without their law. The higher we rise in our approach to first principles, the simpler and the grander do we find them. Now, the great complex of all this universe, in all time and all eternity, is made up of nothing more than the will of the Creator, and the wills of his creatures. What is all this solid frame of sun, earth, and stars, as far as we can know anything of it, but the projection of the will of God upon the mind of man? What is all history but the action of the will of man within the limits imposed by the will of God? Will, in some form, either Divine or human, is the first principle of all existing things. Surely then, God has not constructed it upon such a pattern, that all its various relationships should present us with nothing higher than a lawyer's quibbles or a sophist's conceits! It is the vastness of the problem and its solution, rather than its cunning texture, that occasions these bewildering difficulties; and the doubts which man's half-knowledge has thrown about the subject are but as cobwebs defiling the base of the heavenward pointing column of God's eternal truth.

To us, however, who in this life at least, stand too near the base to survey the whole at one view, these meshes seem as strong as they are finely spun. We must, then, at first, content ourselves with the endeavour to unravel them by the same instrument which formed them, and find in our understanding the subtle answer to the subtle doubt. For not till these doubts have been cancelled by their answers, and have left our vision unobscured by any film of scepticism, can we hope to gain a glimpse of that simple principle lying at the centre of our being, by virtue of which man is said to be created in the image of God.

But if it be true that the problem of the will is no petty riddle intended for men to exercise their ingenuity upon by way of recreation, but rather one demanding their highest faculties to grasp its true solution in any satisfactory form, it is equally true that this solution involves no trivial passing interest, but rather the most central question of man's whole life and vocation. The speculative and practical elements in human nature stand in such intimate mutual relations, that whatever affects the one is felt to vibrate through the whole length and breadth of the other. That all speculative error has its corresponding practical sin, is a proposition almost susceptible of direct proof. Man's duties arise from his relationship to God on the one hand, and to man on the other; and a false conception of the Deity or of human nature, by altering one of the members of the relationship, will give a false view of the relationship itself, just as we alter the value of a ratio by a change in one of its terms.

We need not search long for a striking instance of the bearing of speculative philosophy on daily practice, and one referring to the Divine government of the world, a very important branch of my subject. Whether, for instance, we should pray to God for temporal blessings is a tolerably practical question, and yet it is one involving deep metaphysical consequences. When we pray to God to keep pestilence from our doors, do we believe that He will work a miracle for our especial benefit? If we do not,—if, on the contrary, we believe that the laws of nature will not swerve from their appointed course, and that outward blessings will come or stay away, according to such laws and without regard to our prayers,—why should we pray for them? Why should we thank God as if for a peculiar act, when there is *no* such peculiar act; when, in short, He has done nothing but leave nature uninterrupted, whether she work for our destruction or our preservation?

Perhaps it may be said, we pray for these outward blessings while our real object is to produce a change in our own hearts. But upon what an unworthy principle does such a supposition base the practice of prayer! According to this view of it, we pray to God for one thing while we are really hoping to obtain another. We ask for some outward good in the conviction that His granting or withholding it is entirely uninfluenced by the prayer, but in the expectation that this mere asking will produce some beneficial effect upon our minds. I do not for an instant mean to deny this beneficial effect; but if we regard it as the whole good to be gained, and come to God with such an equivocation as this in our hearts, prayer becomes a mere cabala, a mockery of Heaven, and nothing more.

Few will deny that the laws of nature are valid for all men, that they are no respecters of persons, and that, in these latter days at least, God does not step forth from the mystery of His sanctuary to violate them even in favour of His own people. The philanthropist who spends his days and nights in the poisoned atmosphere of a fever hospital will probably catch the infection and die. The worldly man who breathes pure air, subsists on wholesome food, and never watches by the bed of sickness, will probably escape the contagion and live. And yet if we believe that God does not interfere with a miraculous act either for our weal or our woe, but leaves all things to follow regularly the laws He has imposed upon nature, why should we address ourselves to Him either by way of prayer or thanksgiving, as if there were any connexion between our words and His acts?

For my own part, I firmly believe in the duty and efficacy of prayer, and that the seeming contradiction between the various elements of the problem,—the human will, the laws of nature, and the Divine government of the world,—admits a complete solution. But I do not believe that such solution lies at the surface, nor do I find any satisfaction in popular explanations, slurring over the real difficulties of the question, and deprecating the rigour of the logician on account of the piety and moral excellence of their tendencies.

Now, to give an honest answer to such sceptical problems, one that shall not shrink from going to the root of the matter and looking the difficulties in the face, is the practical province of the metaphysician. The human mind, however, is so constituted that the majority of mankind cannot comprehend philosophical inquiries. These need not on that account cease to pray; but they must pray in faith alone, thanking God if they are allowed to preserve that faith unscathed by a scepticism which they cannot refute. But how much firmer would be their position if they not only had faith, but were able to give a reason for the faith that is in them; if instead of answering the sceptic with the mere subjective fact, 'I believe,' they were able to shew why the sceptic should believe also!

And this brings me to the consideration of the last form assumed by scepticism in the intellect,—a form which is the most dangerous because it is the most specious, and is only found in connexion with strong religious feeling. Men of ardent faith will sometimes regard it as a sin against their faith to search after a reason for it. They will also treat all the other difficulties in which man's will is involved in a similar manner, and deem it rather meritorious than otherwise to abandon themselves to a species of pious ignorance. Faith, they say, is sufficient for us. Why should we puzzle our brains with intricate philosophical questions, when our faith tells us it is all right, if we could but comprehend it? This is the extinguisher they would put upon all metaphysical speculation connected with religious subjects, in short, upon the highest use of our reason. Let us consider for a moment if the nature of faith is such as to justify this sweeping abnegation of our intellectual powers.

Faith is the general result of the sentiments and affections of the whole man, where the parts that compose it have not been brought to distinct and separate acts of consciousness. To do this, is the province of reason; and when at first she fails—a case which human infirmity renders by no means uncommon—faith may still feel justified in retaining her own, though she cannot produce all her title-deeds. The whole province of faith belongs *objectively* to reason too; for if faith made us believe what is unreasonable *in itself*, it would be an unreasonable, and therefore a false faith, and one we should be better without. Faith is but the advanced guard, marching onward through the territory really belonging to reason, though not actually occupied by it; and the broader the basis of operations covered by reason, the farther may faith itself advance without danger of stumbling upon the outposts of error. Art will supply us with the most fitting illustration of our subject, as it bears the same relation to criticism, that faith does to reason. The man who is born with the genius of a sculptor will begin by modelling the clay under the feeling of the beautiful alone. By degrees, his own experience, or the instructions of older artists, will shew him why this posture is more graceful, that expression more suitable to his subject, than any other. In a word, what was at first a blind instinct will have risen to the surface of his consciousness, and having there assumed a definite and distinct form, will become a rule of art. But the more this blind feeling falls under the dominion of his reason, the loftier will be the starting-point for fresh flights in the field of pure impulse, and the greater the confidence with which the artist will venture upon them. Having attained to a certain height by knowledge, he can rise to a greater height by feeling than he ever could have aspired to by the latter alone.

Now the relation between faith and reason is precisely analogous to that between the primary instinct of the artist and the rules of art which subsequent reflection has based upon it. Faith is the first blind feeling resulting from the æsthetic side of our moral and religious nature. Reason comes afterwards, brings each æsthetic impulse to its separate consciousness, transmutes the uncertain haze that had hung around it into living light, and enables us to carry on our faith into regions still more elevated and sublime. We are all of us sculptors of our destiny. At first, following our blind faith and our æsthetic impulses, we model our circumstances and our characters as best we may. But at length reason speaks, and demands sight for our faith, and order and method for our impulses, that at least a part of our being may fall under her dominion. Then it is that we begin to assume all the privileges of our manhood in their most perfect form. Faith itself is a glorious attribute, and throws a bright halo far beyond the distinctly marked circle of the noonday sun of reason. But he who endeavours to read life's problems by the light of a faith unguided by reason, has forgotten that the orb is antecedent to the halo, and that the same God has made them both. He has mistaken a childish ignorance for a childlike innocence, and by shutting his eyes to the light of Heaven, has practically abjured his faith in Him who gave that light for his guidance and his consolation.

BOOK I.

THE HUMAN WILL.

PART I.

THE HUMAN WILL IN RELATION TO NATURE.

CHAPTER I.

The Point at issue between the Libertarians and Necessarians.

I HAVE endeavoured to shew in the Introduction that the will involves manifold questions of deep interest for the philosopher, and practical importance for the rest of mankind. The problem, however, which has attracted the greatest degree of attention, as that in which all others ultimately merge, is the possibility of human liberty. Both Necessarians and Libertarians assert their belief in it, but they attach such extremely different meanings to the words, that there is in reality but little if any common ground between them. If the Necessarian be right, the whole of the will—in the sense in which the word is used by those who believe in its freedom—is a mere product of the imagination. If, on the other hand, the Libertarian be right, man possesses a faculty, the very existence—and not merely the nature—of which is denied by the Necessarian. The results of these opposed systems are no less divergent. The man who is accustomed to systematise his opinions and follow them out consistently to their logical conclusions, cannot possibly change sides in this question without an entire revolution in his conception of the relations between God and man. From whichever side therefore we view the controversy, it cannot be regarded as a mere affair of outposts, but rather as one in which the whole main body of our religious and philosophical opinions is engaged.

The simplest form of the problem is the following: What is the relation of the Will to Nature? In other words: Is the Will a part of Nature, or is it not? The entire controversy depends ultimately upon the manner in which this question is answered.

For the purpose of identification, the Will may be defined as the faculty of which we are conscious as the immediate cause of our action; this word *action* being understood in the widest sense, and as comprising thought as well as motion.

Nature may be defined as the complex of all phenomena whether physical or mental which are connected together either contemporaneously or successively in the bonds of law.

Now not only does law render nature finite by surrounding it with an impassable barrier, but it also pervades every part of it from the centre to the circumference. It does not execute the functions alone of a coast-guard watching the frontiers of nature's dominions, but rather of an internal police, regulating and preserving the entire organisation of the interior. Wherever there is phenomenon, there is a something not only positive, but also absolutely fixed in its nature by the negative which confines it, and determines it to be no other than the thing which it is. If, for example, a log of wood be floating on the sea, the log itself and every individual particle of it occupy at any one instant precisely that position which is assigned to them by the laws of gravitation and the resolution of the forces of wind and wave acting upon the surface, and cannot possibly occupy any other. Thus the positive which says, *thus far*, is not only circumscribed by, but also ever in the immediate presence of, and in indissoluble connexion with, the negative, which adds, *no farther*. Now the will has at least so much in common with nature, that it is finite as well as positive. It is limited in the first place by the laws of external nature, for otherwise it would exercise that infinite sway over the elements which belongs to Omnipotence alone. It is also limited by certain laws of its own nature. For if we were to assume that it was an absolute monarch within the kingdom of the mind, subject to no control from psychological laws, it would have no nature,—inasmuch as the nature of a thing is nothing more than the complex of the laws which determine its modes of being and acting. But the very fact that we can in any way distinguish it in our consciousness from our other faculties, shews that it has a nature, and consequently that it is subject to such limitations. Thus the positive of the will is also finite, and bounded by a negative prescribing a certain sphere, beyond which its action is prohibited. Up to this point all parties are necessarily agreed; for every inquirer into the nature of the will, must at least presume that the will has a nature to be inquired into. If however we go beyond this, and ask whether no room be left for Liberty, whether law not only limits the sphere of will but also determines every part of its conduct within that sphere, we enter a disputed territory. For this finite nature does not *necessarily* exclude the possibility of there being a certain room for free action within these limits, where the negative does not reach, and where therefore the will may be unshackled. The question then before us is, whether the positive in the will is only a part of the positive in nature, and thus absolutely permeated by law, or whether it is of the character above described, having its circumference only prescribed by law, but enjoying free action within it.

In the present chapter I shall not enter upon the problem itself, but shall confine myself to an attempt at bringing the conflicting opinions into the form of a simple contradiction, and thus arriving at the kernel of the controversy.

Both Libertarians and Necessarians are agreed in considering the will as the immediate cause of our actions, but differ as to the nature of its causality. It will therefore be necessary to distinguish between two senses in which the word cause is employed, accordingly as it expresses the cause which is again the effect of a prior cause, or a cause which is itself uncaused, and unconditioned.

Causality is either phenomenal and conditioned or transcendental and unconditioned, accordingly as we seek in the cause either some partial phenomenon forming one link in the causal chain, and therefore itself dependent on prior causes, or the complex of all the conditions necessary to the production of the effect[1]. This distinction may be made more intelligible by an example. The concussion of flint and steel is succeeded by a spark, which falling upon gunpowder instantly ignites it. In this case the concussion is the cause, and the spark the effect, which again considered as a cause is followed by an explosion. The explosion may also become a cause and propel a cannon-ball, which may knock down a house; and in the same manner the series may be continued *ad infinitum.* Now in the above example, the word cause is employed in conformity with popular language, and signifies nothing more than the particular antecedent phenomenon, which again is itself conditioned or determined by prior causes; and the relation between the members of the phenomenal series is what I understand by conditioned causality. But if we adopt the other signification of the word cause, and regard it as the complex of the conditions necessary to the production of the effect, it is clear that the spark is not the cause of the explosion. For in the first place, the spark is itself the result of preceding phenomena, which form just as strictly part of the conditions, though not the immediate conditions to the production of the effect; and in the second place, there must be some law, and therefore some energy maintaining such law and determining generally that a spark shall be succeeded by an explosion. In this manner the search after an unconditioned cause carries us back along an infinite phenomenal series longitudinally,

[1] In the former case any phenomenon may be a cause, whereas in the latter there is always an element which is not phenomenal, but which is required to complete the whole circle of causal conditions, and this element is the unconditioned cause.

if I may be allowed the expression, and moreover refers us at every step to some collateral energy which maintains the law connecting every successive pair of phenomena in the series. But in both directions our search has this in common, that it never rests contented with anything for a cause, that is itself conditioned or extrinsically determined. For as the cause which we now seek is to complete the *whole* of the conditions, it follows necessarily, that there can be no conditions prior and therefore exterior to it; in other words, by the very hypothesis, the cause is unconditioned. We must then continue our search until we arrive at an initiating cause, or one which is itself not caused. And on the other hand, precisely the same reasons are valid in our search for the collateral energy. For any power or energy determining such relations of phenomena, which is again itself determined, obliges us to look still farther for some other deeper energy determining such determination. The whole complex of conditions thus evidently excludes the conception of another condition exterior to it, and must therefore itself be unconditioned.

Now the unconditioned cause is necessarily free. For were it not so, it would be subject to a condition, a supposition which is excluded by the hypothesis.

The conditioned cause, on the other hand, is necessarily not free, for otherwise it would not be limited by a condition, which is equally excluded by the hypothesis. If however we take the whole of nature, and seek for its cause, inasmuch as it comprises all conditioned causes within itself, the cause in question must clearly be unconditioned and free.

While therefore the causality *in* nature is conditioned, the cause *of* nature itself is unconditioned[1].

[1] In the article in the *Prospective Review* for May 1851, entitled Mesmeric Atheism, to which I have already alluded, there are some remarks on the subject of causation in which I should have entirely concurred, had the reviewer expressly confined them to unconditioned causality alone. The account, however, there given of causality in general is manifestly only applicable to the unconditioned, and thus leads to the inevitable conclusion, that the reviewer recognises no other causality, and denies that the conditioned or phenomenal cause has any claim to the name. But as long as the practice of the vulgar and the general language of philosophers are in favour of a more extended use of the word, I hardly think the restriction either useful or justifiable. The passage in question is as follows: "The consciousness of personal energy is the source and type of our idea of causation; and directs us exactly to what we *mean* by causation. That energy being *free*,—that is, able *ex se* to determine into existence any one of several given possibilities,—nothing possesses a proper *causal* character which is destitute of this attribute. A cause is a power which settles an alternative: and no one ever asks after a cause without the preconception of such alternative. Beside the actual phenomenon there stands in his mind a potential phenomenon, which has been excluded in favour of the realised event: and he wants to know what it is that has decided on the thing that *is*, rather than the thing that *might have been*. This ascription to all causality of a preferential function is a manifest transcript from our own Will, and shews the ultimate identity of the ideas of *volition* and *power*," p. 248.

To this I would reply, that we certainly do consider a spark to be the cause of the explosion of gunpowder, without attaching to it any idea of preference whatever. The potential phenomenon, or that which might have been had not the cause determined otherwise, is simply considered as possible, not from any option being left to the spark, but from the possibility of its never having existed at all, or never having come into contact with the powder. Now, unless I have quite misunderstood the writer's meaning, he would deny the name of cause to the exploding spark, because the ultimate cause of the explosion is the will of God, who determined the law according to which the phenomenon takes place. One thing at least is certain,—we meet in such a phenomenon with no liberty, (which, in the Reviewer's opinion, is essential to all causality,) until we refer it to the will of God, who chose the explosion out of all possibilities as the result which was to follow upon the contact of the spark.

I have employed the word causality in the sense in which Kant employed it in his system of the categories, and in which Brown

Here then we find two sorts of causes, first the cause uncaused, or absolute commencement of an acting or being,—as for instance, that free and unconditioned causal act of the Almighty by which He maintains the laws of nature,—secondly, the partial cause, the cause caused, or absolutely and externally determined cause,—as for instance, the spark that explodes a magazine.

It must not however be supposed that I am contending here for two distinct species of causality. The same ultimate conception lies at the foundation of both the conditioned and the unconditioned. But the former bears to the latter the relation of a part to a whole. In every-day thought and language we are not concerned with the consideration of the entire cause, and therefore give that name to one of the principal conditions which, from its dependence on the other supplementary conditions for its efficacy, is called the conditioned cause. Directly, however, we seek for the entire cause, and would complete the conditions, we must crown them with that unconditioned which is alone conceivable as free.

has employed the word causation in his Treatise on *Cause and Effect*, namely, to express conditioned causality, or the causality in natural laws, without reference to that unconditioned upon which it alone ultimately rests. My difference with the Reviewer is, for the most part, one of names alone, as I should have entirely agreed with his remarks on causality, if he had expressly restricted them to the unconditioned, and had followed the thought and language of daily life, by not rejecting all phenomenal causes as unworthy of the name.

The objections I have raised to the language of the above extract do not, however, apply to the following statement of the liberty of the cause to be found in the same article, as the Reviewer has introduced a few words of qualification to the ultimate or unconditioned cause: "We should not hesitate to maintain that the idea of Cause, in the last logical resort, so far from being identical with that of Necessity, totally excludes it; and instead of rendering liberty of choice inconceivable, is itself inconceivable without it," p. 241.

Now the Necessarians assert that the cause of human actions is to be found in motives determined by laws of human nature imposed on it by some power external to man. Thus, according to them, all human conduct is absolutely determined by laws of conditioned causality alone, and the supplementary unconditioned element is to be sought in the will of the Creator. The Libertarians, on the other hand, believing that human actions find some absolute beginning in the human soul, attribute them to some unconditioned cause in the human soul itself as their first principle, though of course acknowledging certain limitations to the sphere in which this unconditioned cause is able to exert itself.

The language of the Necessarians on this point, is for the most part clear and explicit. All human conduct, according to them, is entirely dependent on the law of cause and effect. Anthony Collins, in his tract entitled *A Philosophical Inquiry concerning Human Liberty,* has endeavoured to establish the doctrine of Necessity, of which he gives the following definition :—" Man is a necessary agent if all his actions are so determined by the causes preceding each action, that not one past action could possibly not have come to pass, or have been otherwise than it hath been ; nor one future action can possibly not come to pass, or be otherwise than it shall be."

" I maintain," says Priestley, " that there is some *fixed law of nature respecting the will,* as well as the other powers of the mind, and everything else in the constitution of nature ; and consequently, that it is never determined without some real or apparent *cause* foreign to itself ; *i. e.* without some *motive of choice,* or that motives influence us in some definite and invariable manner; so that every volition, or choice, is constantly regulated and determined by what precedes it. And this *constant* determination of mind, according to the motives presented to it, is all that I mean by its *necessary determination.* This being admitted to be the fact, there will be a necessary connexion between all things past, present, and to come, in the way of proper *cause and effect,* as much in the intellectual as in the natural world; so that, how little soever the bulk of mankind may be apprehensive of it, or[1] staggered by it, according to the established laws of nature, no event could have been otherwise than it *has been, is,* or *is to be,* and therefore, all things past, present, and to come, are precisely what the Author of nature really intended them to be, and has made provision for[2]?"

These passages, but more especially that from Priestley, are as clear and fair statements of Necessarian doctrine as are to be found in any of the writings of that school. They contain two positions of which the one is a psychological law, the other, its cosmological consequence. They assert in the first place, that the human will is absolutely determined by fixed law in the manner of cause and effect, and in the second place, they conclude from this, that all things past, present, and to come, are absolutely necessary. As, however, my present object is merely to bring the psychological fact into as short a formula as possible, without reference to its cosmological consequences, I would propose the following proposition as the formula of Necessarianism, in the

[1] The passage is correctly quoted in the text; but the sense evidently requires the insertion of the words "how much soever" between "or" and "staggered."

[2] *The Doctrine of Philosophical Necessity,* Sect. I.

belief that it would receive the unqualified assent of the writers above quoted :

The whole human soul is subject to the law of causality.

Our next object must be to arrive at some equally concise form for the doctrine of Liberty. Now the theory of Priestley and Collins, which has merely been condensed in the above formula, is absolutely incompatible with any form of liberty whatever. The universal dominion of law is an hypothesis with which the Libertarian can enter into no compromise ; and whatever may be his positive doctrine of liberty, his formula must contain the most unconditional contradiction of that of Necessarianism. Liberty, however, possesses certain attractions which even the Necessarian is not disposed to surrender without a struggle; and to this I must ascribe the fact, that the most doughty assailants of the thing have endeavoured to give their theory a rather less forbidding appearance, by a very superficial attempt at retaining the name. I say, superficial, for if we examine what this Necessarian liberty really is, we find that when taken in connexion with the rest of the doctrine it is a *vox et præterea nihil,* and that there is not a clod upon a ploughed field which does not enjoy an equal degree of it with man.

Collins says in his preface to tho work already quoted—" Though I deny *liberty* in a certain meaning of that word, yet I contend for *liberty* as it signifies *a power in man to do as he wills or pleases,* which is the notion of *liberty* maintained by Aristotle, Cicero, Mr Locke, and several other philosophers, both ancient and modern." Again, Priestley says in the section already quoted, "I allow to man all the liberty or power that is *possible in itself*, and to which the ideas of mankind in general ever go, which is the *power of doing whatever they will or please*, both with respect to the operations of their minds, and the motions of their bodies, uncontrolled by any foreign principle or cause. Thus every man is at liberty to turn his thoughts to whatever subject he pleases, to consider the reasons for or against any scheme or proposition, and to reflect upon them as long as he shall think proper; as well as to walk wherever he pleases, and to do whatever his hands and other limbs are capable of doing[1]."

Locke has expressed himself in very different language, and with far less precision than the above-mentioned writers; but as far as it is possible to deduce any regular scheme from his very loosely written chapter on Power, he must be considered as advocating the same doctrines.

He tells us, that "the will is determined by

[1] Hobbes was another advocate of this Necessarian liberty. He has given the following illustration of his theory, which Priestley considers particularly happy. "Liberty and Necessity are consistent. As in the water that hath not only liberty, but a necessity of descending in the channel, so likewise, in the actions which men voluntarily do, which, because they proceed from their will, proceed from liberty; and yet, because every act of man's will, and every desire, and inclination, proceedeth from some cause, and that from another cause in a continual chain (whose first link is in the hand of God, the first of all causes) proceed from necessity." *Leviathan*, p. 108. Jonathan Edwards, in his work on the will, gives a similar definition of liberty. "The plain and obvious meaning of the words *freedom* and *liberty*, in common speech, is *power, opportunity or advantage, that any one has to do as he pleases.*" "Let the person come by his volition or choice how he will, yet if he is able, and there is nothing in the way to hinder his pursuing and executing his will, the man is fully and perfectly free, according to the primary and common notion of freedom." Edwards *On the Will*, 4th ed. London, 1775, pp. 38, 40.

something without it[1]," that this something is, "some (and for the most part the most pressing) uneasiness a man is at present under[2]," that "the question is not proper, whether the will be free, but whether the man be free;" and after avowing his belief in the liberty of the latter, but not of the former, asks, "how can we think any one freer, than to have the power to do what he will[3]?" But his idea of liberty appears still more clearly in the following extract, in which he makes it to consist of no property of the mind, but to refer only to the certainty with which the desired result follows upon the volition. "First, then," he says, "it is carefully to be remembered, that freedom consists in the dependence of the existence or not existence of any action, upon our volition of it, and not in the dependence of any action, or its contrary, on our preference. A man standing on a cliff is at liberty to leap twenty yards downwards into the sea, not because he has a power to do the contrary action, which is to leap twenty yards upwards, for that he cannot do; but he is therefore free, because he has a power to leap or not to leap. But if a greater force than his either holds him fast or tumbles him down, he is no longer free in that case; because the doing or forbearance of that particular action is no longer in his power. He that is a close prisoner in a room twenty feet square, being at the north side of his chamber, is at liberty to walk twenty feet southward, because he can walk or not walk it; but is not at the same time at liberty to do the contrary, *i.e.* to walk twenty feet northward. In this then consists

[1] Locke *On the Human Understanding*, Book II. Ch. XXI. § 25.

[2] Ibid. § 31.

[3] Ibid. § 21.

freedom, viz. in our being able to act or not to act, according as we shall choose or will[1]."

This is evidently the definition of liberty which might be expected from a philosophical turnkey; it refers solely to the absence of external restraint, and corresponds entirely with the opinions of Hobbes, Collins, Priestley and Edwards. All these philosophers concurred in maintaining the doctrine, that man's liberty consists in his being able to do what he wills, but that his willing it does not depend on himself, but on the strength of motives, the state of his mind, and the circumstances in which he is placed, all of which are again dependent on the laws of nature, human or physical[2].

[1] Locke *On the Human Understanding*, Book II. Ch. XXI. § 27.

[2] There is one point in which Locke seems to admit of some other liberty. After having said that the will is determined by "some (and for the most part the most pressing) uneasiness a man is at present under," (§ 31) he explains the exception intended in the parenthesis, in the following words :—

"There being in us a great many uneasinesses always soliciting, and ready to determine the will, it is natural, as I have said, that the greatest and most pressing should determine the will to the next action; and so it does for the most part, but not always. For the mind having, in most cases, as is evident in experience, a power to suspend the execution and satisfaction of any of its desires, and so all, one after another, is at liberty to consider the objects of them, examine them on all sides, and weigh them with others. In this lies the liberty man has; and from the not using of it right, comes all that variety of mistakes, errors, and faults, which we run into in the conduct of our lives, and our endeavours after happiness; whilst we precipitate the determination of our wills, and engage too soon before due examination. To prevent this, we have a power to suspend the prosecution of this or that desire, as every one daily may experience in himself. This seems to me the source of all liberty; in this seems to consist that which is (as I think, improperly,) called free-will." (§ 47).

In a later paragraph (§ 52), Locke calls this power of suspending the judgment "the hinge on which the liberty of intellectual beings turns." The shallowness of the fallacy has been easily exposed by the bolder and more consistent Priestley. He observes,

Some persons who feel unable to disentangle themselves from the toils of Necessarianism may

that "a determination to suspend a volition is, in fact, *another volition*, and therefore, according to Mr Locke's own rule, must be determined by the most pressing uneasiness, as well as any other. If any man voluntarily suspends his determination, it is not without some motive or reason; as, for instance, because he is apprehensive of some ill consequence arising from a hasty and inconsiderate resolution. On the other hand, if he determines immediately, it is because he has no such apprehension. In fact, all the liberty that Mr Locke contends for, is perfectly consistent with the doctrine of philosophical necessity, though he does not seem to have been aware of it."

Though this answer of Priestley's is substantially sufficient, yet it is not quite logically complete: for by Locke's own theory "the will is *not* always determined by the greatest uneasiness, as it may suspend the execution of its desires." Consequently, granting with Priestley, that this act of suspension is itself a volition, it still need not, according to Locke, be prompted by the greatest uneasiness, as he has made an especial exception in favour of such volitions. But where does this lead us to? Manifestly to the conclusion, in the first place, that there is a class of volitions (those of the suspension of the judgment), which without proceeding from the greatest uneasiness or strongest motive, can upset other determinations which do proceed from it; and secondly, that the volitions of this exceptional class are subject to no law, and are not, from their nature, capable of being gauged, or having any particular proportion of strength attributed to them, with reference to the strength of the motives they overcome. For suppose it were possible. We know by the hypothesis that the uneasiness prompting the suspension of judgment is not so great as that prompting the action, for otherwise it would follow the general law of the greatest uneasiness, and would not have required a particular exception to be made in its favour. Let us assume then, for argument sake, that whenever the uneasiness prompting the suspension of judgment becomes one half as strong as the motive prompting the action, the former prevails, and the judgment is suspended. This hypothesis would at once involve a contradiction. For the only criterion of the relative strength of the two motives or uneasinesses, (*i. e.* of their strength as moving powers) is the fact as to which prevails; and the only way of stating the above assumed law, would be to say, that whenever the one motive was half as strong as the other, it would be quite as strong; a proposition which is only true where the strength of each = 0, or in other words, where there is no motive at all. These suspension-of-judgment volitions would therefore be an element in all our actions, reducible to no law, and would render the existence of any law in the actions themselves an impossibility; just in the same way as the presence of an unknown quantity in an algebraical

perhaps accept with gratitude such a doctrine as the above, under the impression that it reserves at least a shew of human liberty. It does not, however, require any very deep investigation to expose the fallaciousness of this hope. In the first place, man's liberty is confined within certain limits by the laws of physical nature. He cannot, for instance, either walk through a mountain, or leap to the top of the church-steeple. But if he seek a sphere for his liberty within the limits prescribed by these laws, according to the above theory, he simply finds himself handed over from one form of necessity to another[1]. *Absolute laws,* under the form of motives,

expression, reduced to its simplest form, renders the value of the whole expression unknown. In order to support the theory of these abnormal volitions, Locke ought to have been able to point to some marked distinction between the act of suspending the judgment and every other mental act. This he has neither done, nor attempted to do; and indeed he hardly appears aware of the fact mentioned by Priestley in the above quotation,—that this suspension of judgment is itself a volition.

If then we reject this part of Locke's doctrine as inconsistent with the rest, we shall find that his account of liberty, as explained by the instance of a person confined in prison, is essentially the same as that of Collins and Priestley.

It appears, from the following passage, that Leibnitz entertained a similar opinion to that of Locke: "J'ai fait voir aussi, que notre volonté ne suit pas toujours precisement l'entendement practique, parcequ'elle peut avoir ou trouver des raisons pour suspendre sa resolution jusqu'à une discussion ulterieure." *Cinquième écrit de M. Leibnitz à M. S. Clarke.* To this Clarke answered in the same manner that Priestley has done to Locke: "It may here be observed, by the way," says Clarke, "that this learned author contradicts his own hypothesis, when he says that the will does not always precisely follow the practical understanding, because it may sometimes find reasons to suspend its resolution. For are not those very reasons the last judgment of the practical understanding?" *Dr Clarke's fifth reply.*

[1] Palmer, in his answer to Priestley, has the following passage: "Though he (Priestley) allows to mankind the 'power of doing whatever they will or please,' he yet makes that will or pleasure subject to some fixed law of nature, something foreign to itself,

still control all his actions, and he is no nearer any originating power within himself, independent of constraint, than he was before. The limits therefore of his so-called liberty must be of the most perfect indifference to him, for they simply mark the point at which he changes one inexorable master in the form of external nature, for another equally severe in the form of human nature. In short, it is in a high degree absurd to say, that the man does what *he wills*, if this act of willing be absolutely determined by laws entirely beyond the control of the man himself.

A person sitting quietly in his house cannot rise from his chair and walk *through* the mountain, because he is prevented by physical laws. But, according to the above theory, just as little can he walk *over* the mountain; for the fact that he has remained sitting is a proof that the laws of human motives are such as to have compelled him to remain in his room. To say that he could have walked out if he had willed it, is nothing more than to say, he could have done so if the laws of human motives were such as to have made him act in such a manner, in short, were otherwise than they actually are; but then we may say with equal reason, he could also walk *through* the mountain, if the physical laws were differently constituted. That he could do it if he willed it, is, therefore, no greater argument for a man's freedom, than if I were to say a prisoner in a dungeon is free,

that is, the influence of motives, by which it is in every instance determined in an invariable manner. So that after all this seeming allowance of liberty to man, he really possesses no other power than that of doing what he is unalterably determined, or in other words, irresistibly impelled to do." *Observations in defence of the Liberty of Man, &c.* by John Palmer. London, 1779, p. 4.

because he could walk out, if the laws of nature were such that his prison-walls would yield to a touch. In either case the man's conduct has absolute limits imposed on it by laws which he has not made himself, and consequently in either case he is not free. The only difference between the two cases consists in the greater knowledge we possess of the laws of physical nature than of those of human motives. We are thus able to define the former with far more precision than the latter, and to say, the man certainly cannot walk *through* the mountain, but we only know by the result whether he can walk *over* it. If however he sit quietly in his room, it is because the laws of motives so decree; for on the Necessarian hypothesis, the laws of external nature are not more imperious or powerful in forbidding his action to overstep the limits they impose, than the laws of human nature in dictating the course it is to take within them.

It has not been my object in the foregoing remarks to attack Necessarianism on its own ground, but merely to repel its encroachments on that of its opponents. Like every other system, it must stand or fall on its own merits, and not take credit to itself for a position to which it has no sort of claim. I object, therefore, to Locke, Collins, and Priestley, that they have all adopted a language which appears to imply a belief in some sort of liberty, whereas in fact they deny all liberty whatever. If a man's actions are confined to certain limits by the laws of matter, and then within these limits absolutely determined by the so-called laws of his moral nature, (in the making of which he has had no more concern than in the determination of the laws of matter,) how can we say that the man, or his will, does anything at all in the whole business? The man's body or mind may be the subject-matter of the laws, in the same manner as a cannon-ball is the subject-matter of the laws of motion. But, upon the hypothesis of Priestley, it would not be more absurd to speak of the flight of the cannon-ball as its own action, than of any human volition as the act of the man.

Directly we make the whole of human conduct depend upon laws, man ceases to act in any other sense than that in which the expression may be used of a machine[1]. For let us consider in what sense a machine is said *to act*. A watch considered *purely objectively*, is nothing more than a quantity of matter in a certain form, and has *in itself* no more meaning than a pebble. All the parts of both pebble and watch follow certain fixed laws of nature, and by their gravity, elasticity, electricity[2], and other properties,

[1] Clarke, in his answer to Collins, puts this Necessarian liberty in its right light in the following passage: "I observe that the author endeavours to impose upon his readers a false definition of liberty. 'I contend,' says he, 'for liberty, as it signifies a power in man to do as he wills or pleases.' And this he elsewhere styles a valuable liberty. Now, in this definition, besides the forementioned ambiguity of the words, *wills or pleases*, it ought carefully to be remarked that the word *do* has no signification. For his meaning is not that the man acts or does anything. But the liberty or power in man to do as he wills or pleases, is with him exactly and only the same as the liberty or power in a balance would be to move as it wills or pleases, supposing the balance endued with such a sensation or intelligence as enabled it to perceive which way the weights turned it, and to approve the motion, so as to fancy that it moved itself, when, indeed, it was only moved by the weights."

[2] The reader will observe, that I purposely mention properties which have no immediate connexion with the mechanical action of the watch, as I wish to call attention to the fact, that the effect of the weight of the watch, or of its electricity, is just as much one of its effects as the rotation of the hands, although, it is the latter alone to which the maker attaches peculiar importance.

act upon the surrounding objects, which, in their turn, re-act upon them. Each may be said, in a certain sense, to act; for each produces certain definite effects. What then is the difference between them? The watch produces, though quite unconsciously and involuntarily, among others one effect which is the especial object of the man who constructs it. The idea of the watch, or its unity, is in short purely subjective, *i.e.* not in the watch itself, but in the mind of the inventor. On the other hand, the pebble, lying on the sea-shore, is no machine relatively to man, as he has not placed it there for any particular end. But as soon as we regard the pebble as created and placed in a certain portion of space by the Deity for a particular end, and in order to produce by its gravity and other qualities precisely the effect which it does produce, it also becomes one of God's machines; the idea or unity which makes it so, being in the Divine Mind. A machine therefore is not an objective idea, but merely an arrangement of substances, which blindly following the laws of nature produce an effect desired by some thinking subject, but not by the machine itself. And the idea of the *action* of a machine, implies nothing more than that certain of its effects are combined in the mind of another being, under the conception of an *aim* or *end*.

Now, as I have already observed, directly the whole of man's volitions are determined by laws *not made by himself*, but imposed upon him from without, his actions cease to be his in any other sense than the rotation of the hands is the action of the watch. There may be a unity and an idea at the bottom of them, but this is not objectively in the man, but only in the thinking subject who made his moral and emotional nature, and determined the fixed laws of motives that absolutely control it; in other words, in his Creator.

But Priestley would perhaps have objected, that the laws of motives act upon the *mind* of man, and that consequently his actions are at least not a blind product of these laws, as he knows both what he wills, and why he wills it. But this argument will not avail him, for in reality the man cannot be said to will the act himself. He may think or reason over his motives for any length of time, but still, according to Priestley's own theory, each of these thoughts, and reasonings, and deliberations, is a volition determined for him by fixed necessary laws, not made by the man, but imposed on him from without. It is impossible therefore ever to arrive at any ultimate unity in the mind of the man himself, from which the unity of his actions may proceed; but on the contrary, we are always obliged to have recourse to the unity imposed on them by that thinking subject which made the man what he is, and determined the laws which govern his motives. In other words, the man is a mere machine, though he may claim the Almighty as his inventor.

If the reader has followed the above reasoning, he will at once perceive that Necessarianism, by subjecting the whole will to the dominion of causal law, has absolutely denied all liberty whatever. It follows from this, that any formula for Libertarianism must at least contain the unqualified contradiction of Necessarianism; and we may therefore assume the following, contradictory of the Necessarian formula, as at least a part of the formula required:—

Every human soul contains a principle of action not dependent on the law of causality.

This definition is a mere negative determination of the will, as it states nothing more than that it is not dependent on the law of causality, but does not add what the will is in itself. It might therefore at first sight appear desirable to base our formula on the considerations in the commencement of this chapter, and define the will as an Unconditioned Cause. This proposition is however in reality no less negative than the former; and I think it will not be difficult to shew the insufficiency of any positive definition, and indeed that none but a negative one is admissible.

Every positive formula pretending to give an analytical definition of a simple notion is necessarily unsound. It may be analytical in form, but it cannot be so in matter; for as the notion is simple and contains no parts, it cannot be divided, and will therefore either be excluded from the predicate—in which case the proposition is false—or else be contained in it in its entirety, and then there is no analysis. In the latter case the proposition is essentially one of identity, though perhaps its nature may be disguised by the language employed. If, for instance, we were to define the reason as the faculty of drawing conclusions, every mind endowed with reason will at once comprehend to what faculty we refer. But the conception of an act of reason is already contained in the word conclusion, and consequently the definition is no analysis, as the whole of the conception to be defined is already contained in the predicate.

Now as all Libertarianism starts from the hypothesis that the will is a simple faculty of the soul, it follows from the above observations that any positive definition of it is impossible. It is on the same principle that such a definition of liberty as that given by Reid is totally inadmissible. "By the liberty of a moral agent," says Reid, "I understand a power over the determinations of his own will." Now the conception of a power involves that of its possible exercise; but the exercise of a power is itself an act of the will, and, if the will be free, a free act, or an act with liberty. According then to the principles of Libertarianism, the power over the determinations of the will is a conception already containing the very liberty which it is intended to define, *i. e.* the whole subject is contained in the predicate, and the definition has not brought us one step nearer to an understanding of the subject defined. And indeed, generally speaking, any definition of the will through liberty, or of liberty through the will, is necessarily unsound; for, from the Libertarian point of view, the conceptions of the will and of liberty are inseparable, and consequently they are merely conceptions of the same faculty in different relations. In short, the will is the faculty itself,—the liberty is the faculty considered with relation to the sphere of its activity; and neither can a faculty be conceived independently of the conception of a sphere of activity, nor a sphere of activity independently of the conception of a faculty.

It will appear at once from the above considerations that there is a fatal objection to any positive Libertarian formula as the basis of an argument with the Necessarians. The latter deny the existence of all will and all liberty in any sense in which the Libertarian wishes to assert them. It is useless therefore to adopt any proposition as a starting-point for the argument, which, by the use either of these or of cognate terms, makes a direct appeal to the very faculty denied. A similar objection does not hold against the Necessarian formula, inasmuch as the predicate, causality, is a conception whose reality is acknowledged by both parties. That there are things which have a nature and come under the dominion of causal law, is a fact admitted by all; and the only question is, whether the will be one of them. By taking the issue therefore on the latter question, the main controversy is reduced to a single point; whereas to establish any positive Libertarian formula it would first be necessary to prove the reality of the predicate in general (the conception of liberty), and then that it is contained in the conception of the will. Of course, whatever formula be adopted as a starting-point, the controversy must ultimately resolve itself into an appeal to the disputed faculty; for it is only on the assumption that his opponent possesses such faculty that the Libertarian could ever attempt to convince him of the fact. But an argument founded on the nature of causality has the character of a friendly parley on a comparatively neutral ground, rather than that of a direct onset, and is therefore far less offensive to the Necessarian opinions than an open challenge to the acknowledgment of liberty in any form[1]. In short, if the Liber-

[1] If the Libertarians and their opponents would only agree as to the conception of the liberty which the former assert and the latter deny, a very fair argument in its favour may be based on the mere fact of the controversy, as it is impossible to argue about the existence of a conception without having it. The argument is well expressed by William Windle, in the following passage, but

tarian cannot attack his adversary in front by a direct appeal to his consciousness of liberty, he must endeavour to find some more assailable point on his flank, and one not previously occupied by the

his conception of liberty is very faulty, as I shall presently proceed to shew.

"By human liberty," says Windle, "is meant a power to act or not to act as the mind directs. And that man has such a power, may be demonstrated from the following propositions :—

"First, that we have an idea of such a power. And

"Secondly, that the idea of that power is a simple idea.

"That we have an idea of such a power must be granted; or else it will follow that it would be as impossible to reason or discourse about it, as for a blind man to reason about colours, or of the modes of perception, which other beings may have by a sixth sense, of which he has no manner of conception or idea at all.

"That it is a simple idea is evident from hence, that when any one endeavours to explain it, it is no otherwise than by mentioning the concomitant circumstances of the idea, and not by definition; for a definition being a recital of the several simple ideas that coincide to make up the composition of a complete one, it is impossible to define what hath no composition at all, and consequently to explain it by any other method than by appealing to what every one experiences or feels within himself when he acts.'

"It follows therefore, if we have an idea of that power, and if that idea is a simple one, that we must be possessed of the power which constitutes liberty or freedom, because otherwise we never could have had the idea of the power; it being as impossible for any one to have the idea of a power of which he was never actually possessed, as for a blind man to have that of colours which he never saw, or for one that is deaf to have that of sounds, which he never heard." *An Inquiry into the Immateriality of thinking substances, human liberty, and the original of motion.* By William Windle, A. B., London, 1738, p. 92.

The above argument appears to me to be perfectly sound, but the definition of liberty with which it commences is extremely faulty. Windle makes liberty to consist in the power to carry out the directions of the mind, and thus places it subsequent to such directions. This however is nothing more than that sham liberty for which the Necessarians contend, and would be perfectly consistent with an absolute system of laws of human nature, determining what the mind shall direct. In short, such liberty refers to nothing more than the amount of power physical or mental which the man may possess to carry out his intentions, and has no concern whatever with the origin of such intentions, which is the only real question at issue.

contested opinions. Now the Necessarian formula declares causality to extend to the whole human soul. Let then the Libertarian choose this as the point at issue, and without introducing such terms as *will* or *liberty*—which, by the very conditions of the controversy, can never be employed in the same sense by both parties—assert simply that *the human soul contains an element independent of causality.*

Now there are two distinct methods which may be adopted in the investigation of the truth of these formulas, as indeed of all other propositions. The first is the direct method, in which we examine the nature of the conception contained in the predicate, and having clearly ascertained its limits, inquire whether the subject comes within them. The second is the indirect, in which we endeavour to bring to a clear consciousness the contradiction which would arise if we place the subject entirely without the predicate,—in other words, if we deny the correctness of the proposition under examination. If we would employ the former method, we must analyse our predicate, which consists of the subjection to the law of cause and effect, and determine what are the conditions of this subjection, and then observe if these conditions are fulfilled by the whole human soul, or if it contains any principle which is not in accordance with them. If, on the other hand, we would employ the second, we should have to shew that upon the supposition of the whole soul not being subject to causality, numerous difficulties and contradictions would arise, *e. g.* that then it would be impossible to arrive at any knowledge of human nature, or form any conjecture as to what would be the conduct of a man under certain circumstances,—

in short, that all human actions would be the mere sport of chance. The advocates of both sides of the question have generally preferred the second method, especially the Libertarians, who have always placed their chief strength upon the impossibility of reconciling Necessarianism with man's moral responsibility. When they have attempted the positive and direct method to establish their doctrine, they have generally started from a positive enunciation of Libertarianism, and by making a simple appeal to our consciousness have laid themselves open to the objections stated above. As a proof of this assertion, I would observe that while much has been written on the nature of the law of cause and effect and the grounds of our belief in it, these subjects have been for the most part only cursorily touched upon in English controversial works on the will. And yet if the simple question of the freedom of the will depend upon the question, in how far it answers the conditions requisite for bringing any object under the dominion of causality, it is evident that the determination of these conditions must precede every direct solution of the problem. The preference which has been too exclusively given to the indirect method is easily accounted for, as, whichever side we may embrace, it is much easier to point out the difficulties arising from the theory of our opponents than to defend our own.

I am, however, far from wishing to deny the advantages which must often attend the indirect method. Still, I think it ought not so entirely to have taken the place of the direct method, as has been the case in treatises on this subject. The whole problem may be briefly stated thus: God having, by his free and unconditioned causal act, imposed a conditioned causality on nature, does the will of man answer the conditions, and therefore come under the rule of such causality, or does it not? To answer this question, it is perfectly clear that we must first arrive at a distinct conception of conditioned causality itself and the grounds of our belief in it. This will accordingly constitute the next subject of our investigation.

CHAPTER II.

The Conception of Causality.

IT appeared at the conclusion of the preceding chapter, that if issue be joined on the Necessarian formula, an investigation into the nature of conditioned causality is absolutely indispensable to the direct solution of the problem. This subject resolves itself into two principal questions, namely,—What is the nature of the conception of causality[1]? and,—What are the grounds of our belief in it? The first of them will occupy our attention in the present chapter.

Dr Brown, in his Inquiry into the Relation of Cause and Effect, restricted his notion of causality to the single fact, that the same phenomena as causes are invariably followed under similar circumstances by the same phenomena as effects, and argued from this that our notion of power is nothing more than the belief in such invariable sequence, and not anything in the objects themselves. "It is," he says, "this mere relation of uniform antecedence, so important and so universally believed, which appears to me to constitute *all* that can be philosophically meant in the words *power* or *causation*, to whatever objects, material or spiritual, the words may be applied." (p. 11.) * * * * "We give the name of *cause* to the object which we believe to be the invariable antecedent of a particular change; we give the name of

[1] In the following pages, where the word "causality" is employed without qualification, conditioned causality is always to be understood.

effect reciprocally to that invariable consequent; and the relation itself, when considered abstractly, we denominate *power* in the object that is the invariable antecedent,—*susceptibility* in the object that exhibits, in its change, the invariable consequent." (p. 12.)

* * * * "A cause, therefore, in the fullest definition which it philosophically admits, may be said to be that which immediately precedes any change, and which, existing at any time in similar circumstances, has been always, and will be always, immediately followed by a similar change. Priority in the sequence observed, and invariableness of antecedence in the past and future sequences supposed, are the elements, and the only elements, combined in the notion of a cause." (p. 13.) * * * *

"When a spark falls upon gunpowder, and kindles in into explosion, every one ascribes to the spark the power of kindling the inflammable mass. But when such a power is ascribed, let any one ask himself, what it is which he means to denote by that term, and without contenting himself with a few phrases that signify nothing, reflect before he give his answer; and he will find that he means nothing more than this very simple belief,—that in all similar circumstances the explosion of gunpowder will be the immediate and uniform consequence of the application of a spark." (p. 27.)

According to this, causality would only come into play by fits and starts, whenever, and only whenever, the favourable circumstances for any particular change might occur. It would thus assume a merely historical form, and refer to isolated events alone, scattered through all past and future time, but not forming a continuous whole. During the periods intervening between two explosions of gunpowder, there would be nothing in the objective world corresponding to the law by virtue of which the explosions take place. All that would remain would be a mere intellectual act, remembering that such explosions had taken place before, and believing that they would take place in future, whenever the peculiar circumstances should again arise.

The writer of an interesting article in *Blackwood's Magazine* (The Metaphysician, No. II. July, 1836, p. 124) has opposed this doctrine of Brown's. Referring to the passage last quoted, he says, "Let us then apply the test by which Dr Brown proposes that the truth of his views shall be tried. Let us ask ourselves what we mean, when we say that the spark has power to kindle the gunpowder, that the powder is susceptible of being kindled by the spark? Do we mean only that whenever they come together this will happen? Do we merely predict this simple and certain futurity?

"We do not fear to say, that when we speak of a power in one substance to produce a change in another, and of a susceptibility of such change in that other, we express more than our belief that the change has taken and will take place. There is more in our mind than a conviction of the past, and a foresight of the future. There is, besides this, the conception included of a fixed constitution of their nature, which determines the event; a constitution which, while it lasts, makes the event a necessary consequence of the situation in which the objects are placed. We should say then that there are included in these terms 'power' and 'susceptibility of change,' two ideas which are not expressed in Dr Brown's analysis—one of necessity, and the other of a constitution of things in which that necessity is established. That these two ideas are not expressed in the terms of Dr Brown's analysis, is seen by quoting again his words, 'he will find that he means nothing more than that in all similar circumstances the explosion of gunpowder will be the immediate and uniform consequence of the application of a spark.'"

* * * * * * *

"When it is said by any one that a spark has the power to kindle a train of gunpowder, what more does he mean, than that in the spark and in the powder there is some hidden adaptation to produce that effect, which he cannot see; but which, if he could discern, as possibly higher intelligences may discern, the ultimate constitution of bodies, he might see the two to be necessarily connected?" (p. 129.)

Now I entirely agree with the above criticism to the extent, that the objects of nature have a certain fixed constitution, and that our conception of power is something more than that of mere invariable succession. I cannot however find in any part of the essay a clear definition of the sense in which the writer uses the terms "constitution" and "adaptation," upon which indeed the whole question turns. Might not Brown reply in some such language as the following?

Suppose I grant this constitution of the objects of nature, what after all does it mean? We can only understand by it that if our senses were absolutely perfect, the objects would produce certain effects upon them, *i. e.* would produce certain phenomena, which we should find invariably succeeded under certain circumstances by certain other phenomena; and thus we should merely increase the length of the chain by filling up links now imperceptible to sense, but should still have arrived at nothing further than the principle of invariable succession. I will grant, for instance, that gunpowder contains something in its constitution which adapts it for explosion on contact with a spark. But if I attempt to conceive what this something is, I can only represent it to myself as some quality or qualities which are possible objects of experience, that is to say, which might be perceived by a sense sufficiently fine for the purpose. I may thus suppose a series of such hidden qualities capable of producing sensible phenomena, and imagine that when the spark is applied they follow each other in succession according to some law, until the last visible effect is produced. Still I have not got beyond the mere succession of phenomena; and all that this supposition of an inward constitution amounts to, will be the filling up the interval between the perceptible phenomena with a series of intermediate links, consisting of possible phenomena, which however we are not able with our present powers to make direct objects of sense.

But the same writer supposes that if we could discern the ultimate constitution of bodies, we might see the necessary connexion between cause and effect. Now this opinion appears to me to be based on an incorrect conception of the nature of necessity as applied to this subject. We believe that all causes produce their effects, whatever they may be, necessarily, but we can never see the necessary connexion between any particular effect and its cause, as we only discover the particular connexion at all by experience, and could easily have conceived its being otherwise. We believe that a spark explodes gunpowder, and that a body falls to the ground *necessarily;* but we can never attain the least glimpse of this necessity by intuition. However far we carry our investigation of nature, we never get beyond the purely empirical, or approximate in the least degree to an intuition of this necessity, in which we believe only from a general principle of thought. Hence if we conceive our senses perfected till they are able to perceive all the most latent processes in the objects of nature, we have no ground for believing that we should perceive the necessity of them, any more than we do at present. It follows from this, that to base our conception of the constitution of any substance upon our belief of the possibility that the *necessary* connexion of its particular properties might be an object of intuition to other beings, is to base it upon our conception of the possibility of a new faculty, differing in kind from, and offering no analogy to, any of the mental faculties with which we are acquainted. I am far from denying the possibility of such a faculty in beings differently constituted from ourselves, but it clearly cannot be made the foundation of an instinctive and universal law of human thought[1].

[1] If I might be allowed to anticipate the results of a later page, I might perhaps make this objection somewhat clearer. No form of necessity can be discovered in the object alone, as we can never learn from any object that another object may not present itself, upsetting the supposed necessity. Hence necessity can only be found in the subject, and indeed in a law of thought, declaring, that only in so far as objects conform to it, can the subject admit them as objects at all. That two phenomena therefore should appear necessarily connected, they must be capable of subsumption under some subjective form of receptivity, whether sensuous or intellectual, as otherwise they cannot be subject to the same law. Acids, for instance, turn vegetable blues red. But as man possesses

Now I believe that Brown fell into his fallacious theory of power from neglecting the principle of the continuity of causality. This continuity again is deduced from two important considerations, which he appears to have entirely overlooked,—first, that causality extends to phenomena contemporaneous in space, as well as successive in time; secondly, that in our investigation of nature, we are not concerned with the concrete phenomena themselves, but only with the abstract conceptions under which we subsume them. I shall now proceed, first, to establish the theory of contemporaneous causality; secondly, to seek a formula or formulas for causality generally, (in the course of which investigation I shall have occasion to demonstrate that the causal relation of phenomena can only be recognised under abstract conceptions); thirdly, to shew the bearing of the principles evolved upon the doctrine of Brown; and lastly, to determine the sphere of causality as far as this is possible from its conception alone.

The phenomena of the universe stand in certain determinate relations not merely to their antecedents in time, but also to contemporaneous phenomena in space. If two equal weights be suspended by a cord over a pulley, and both be in a state of perfect rest, no one would hesitate to say that each weight is the

no form of receptivity (in the present example no sense) common alike to taste and sight, it is not the mere perfection of the senses which can ever enable him to see a necessary connexion between these phenomena, but on the contrary, an absolutely new faculty would be indispensable for the intuition of such necessity.

The reader will perceive from this, that it is not my intention to deny that *à posteriori* knowledge may subsequently become *à priori*, but merely to assert that this is impossible where the whole cognition does not fall within the same form of intuition, as is the case with a large proportion of our empirical knowledge. But this is a wide subject, which I can only glance at here.

cause of the suspension of the other, though the phenomena are perfectly contemporaneous. In the same manner, wherever any bodies are in a state of equilibrium, they may be said to be respectively the causes of the particular position of each other. Neither is this remark applicable to a mechanical equilibrium alone. If the electricity in any body is neither increasing nor decreasing, the cause is to be found in the circumstance that the surrounding objects contain precisely the same proportion of electricity, and are therefore in a state of electrical equilibrium with it. Popular language is quite in conformity with this view. A weight resting upon a spring is said to be the cause of its tension, and a tree is said to be the cause of the shade beneath it, though in both these cases the causes and their effects are contemporaneous.

But perhaps it may be objected that in the abovementioned instances the objects were considered as quiescent, whereas in reality all nature is in a state of never-ceasing though often imperceptible change. This is undoubtedly true; but because phenomena may always be viewed under the relation of succession in time to their antecedents, it by no means follows that there is not also a reciprocal causality between contemporaneous phenomena. The velocity and direction of the earth's motion at any one moment is the antecedent partially determining its position in the next. But this latter is also determined by the earth's contemporaneous action and re-action on other bodies. The attraction of gravitation is not an influence acting by starts, as if there were first so much gravitation as cause, and then such a degree of curvature in the earth's orbit as effect, but on the contrary, a steady unvarying force, by which the earth and all the other planetary bodies are kept in their precise course.

It appears from the foregoing remarks on contemporaneous causality, that Nature does not present us with a number of distinct and isolated series of phenomena, each to be considered merely in its succession in time, but rather with an organic complex of phenomena in space, which must therefore be considered in their collateral and contemporaneous relations. In short, causality has two dimensions; one corresponding to space, and the other to time. The collected phenomena of the universe considered in space, are kept at every moment in their peculiar relative states by their reciprocal action on each other. The whole of these phenomena considered in time are determining in each moment the nature of the phenomena that are to succeed them in the next.

If these remarks are correct, the most general conception of causality will contain nothing more than the determination of one phenomenon as effect by another as cause, without regard to the priority of the latter in time.

Kant, in his *Criticism of the Pure Reason,* has restricted his definition of the conception of causality to successive phenomena in time. He has however advocated the doctrine of contemporaneous causality under the name of "commerce," which he explains to mean the reciprocal influence which bodies exercise upon each other. Now in his investigation of this category of commerce, he has employed the terms "cause," "effect," and "causality." The following is a literal translation of the passage to which I refer:—

"That alone which is the cause of another thing, or

its determinations, determines the place in time of that other thing. Every substance therefore (as it can only be a consequence in respect of its determinations) must contain within itself the causality of certain determinations in the other, and at the same time the effects of the causality of the other, *i.e.* they must stand in dynamical commerce (immediate or mediate) if their contemporaneousness in any possible experience is to be cognised."

Now if this conception of the commerce of substances can only be explained by the conception of causality, it is quite clear that this commerce is not an ultimate conception or law of thinking, but only a particular instance of the higher conception of causality. It appears therefore highly illogical to restrict causality to the succession of phenomena, when we are afterwards obliged to employ the same conception in our definition of the relation between phenomena which are contemporaneous.

Kant himself appears to have entertained some misgivings on this subject, for in his second edition he substituted another explanation of the category of commerce, in which the expressions, *causality, cause,* and *effect,* are entirely avoided. That this was a mere change of language however, and not of matter, will appear from the substituted passage, of which the following is a part :—" Now the relation of substances, in which one contains determinations, whose ground is contained in the other, is the relation of *influence,* and if, reciprocally, the latter contains the ground of determinations in the other, it is the relation of commerce, or reciprocal action." Here we have the expressions, "ground of determinations," and "reciprocal action," instead of "causality," and "cause and effect;" but the meaning intended to be conveyed is evidently the same in both cases. Kant may possibly have had some deeper motive for this apparently illogical analysis, but I cannot help suspecting it was the wish to preserve the symmetry of the categories at all cost. And I must here remind the reader that I am far from denying the difference between successive and contemporaneous causality. I merely contend that they are different developments of a higher law of causality in general, according to which phenomena determine phenomena, both contemporaneous and successive.

Before we can arrive at any formula for the doctrine of causality, it is necessary to distinguish between two of the senses in which the word cause may be employed. This is the more necessary, because the only form of causality which either is or can be applied to any practical purpose by the human mind, is that in which causes and effects are arranged under abstract conceptions, while in popular language we are accustomed to express ourselves as if concrete causes and effects were the sole object of our thoughts. The billiard-player, for instance, will not hesitate to assert that his cue is the cause of the motion of the ball, nor the astronomer that the moon is the cause of the tides. How far such language is correct or the reverse, will appear more clearly from the following investigation.

When we speak of a phenomenon as an effect, we may either mean the actual object of sense exactly as it is in the outward world, and including all its parts, whether they appear essential or non-essential, or we may understand by it those particular parts of it, and their relation among themselves, which constitute the peculiar subject of consideration for the time. If we use the word in the former concrete sense, and make no distinction of parts, we must consider the whole complex of phenomena which determined all these parts of the effect, as its cause; and as we have no ground for a distinction between the parts of the cause, (and therefore none for an abstraction,) it will be concrete also. If, on the other hand, we use the word in the latter and abstract sense, to signify phenomena falling into a certain relation to each other, the cause will be found in that other relation of phenomena, which invariably precedes or accompanies it, and will therefore also be abstract. But this distinction will become clearer by an example.

Supposing, for instance, we say that the falling of the wind has produced a shower of rain. Now we may either contemplate the shower of rain exactly as it fell, every drop of a particular size, falling in a particular direction and with a particular velocity, and consider this precise shower as the effect in question, or we may consider as such the shower of rain under its general conception, of a quantity of water falling to the earth in drops, without considering all those details which may be unessential to the purpose in hand. Taking then the word effect in the latter abstract sense,—that is, taking the conception of a shower and not the actual concrete shower in the precise form in which it appeared in nature,—we should say the cause was to be found in the wind and its cessation, employing these terms, however, to represent a class of phenomena, which, according to a law discovered by experience, are found to be succeeded by a class of phenomena termed a shower.

This is evident from the consideration, that if the phenomenon of the falling of the wind had been slightly different from what it actually was in nature, it would still have been considered as the same cause, inasmuch as the shower, though also slightly different, would have come under the same abstract conception under which we view the effect. But if we mean by the effect the actual concrete shower exactly as it occurred, then we shall find that all the preceding phenomena which influenced the shower in any way, were the cause of the shower, as all of them contributed towards making it precisely the shower that it was.

Now if we seek for a formula of causality expressing the actual state of things as they are in nature, it is clear that we must look for it in some expression of the relationship between concrete causes and their effects. But if, on the other hand, we seek for a formula which shall be available for the extension of human knowledge and the determination of the course of nature, abstract causes and their effects can alone help us on our way. To prove this, I will submit the two following arguments for the reader's consideration.

In the first place, the concrete cause is inexhaustible.

Every atom in the universe is acting on every other atom, and reciprocally acted on by the same. Annihilate ten grains of the moon's substance and you will not only diminish the influence of its attraction on the sea, and thus affect the tides, but you will alter its attraction of all the bodies in the solar system, and every atom in them. A fly crawling on the dome of St Paul's alters the centre of gravity of the earth with every step he takes. The electrical telegraph renders the instantaneous action and reaction of distant particles of matter an actual object of vision; and such telegraphs are in constant operation through the whole of nature, only we unfortunately do not understand the dials, and cannot therefore read the messages they might otherwise convey to us. And in the same manner there is not an object in any part of the world which does not, through the laws of gravity, electricity, and other mysterious agents of nature, affect the course, number, weight, temperature, or direction of the drops of a shower of rain. That the shower, therefore, has been precisely such a shower, and no other than it has been, is the effect of a cause coextensive with the universe.

We have all of us laughed at the philosophy of the old man who told Master More, that Tenterden steeple was the cause of Goodwin sands. But directly we consider the actual concrete Goodwin sands as the effect, and ask for the actual concrete thing that was the cause of them, most assuredly was Tenterden steeple a part of it. After the steeple had been built, every wind that blew against it met with a new object of resistance, and was slightly altered in its course. It thus affected other currents of wind, produced a different effect on the waves of the sea, which rolling with greater or less violence, or in a somewhat different direction, deposited certain grains of sand otherwise than would have been the case had there been no steeple at Tenterden. A sand-bank might have arisen just the same, but it would not have been the identical sand-bank which did arise; and directly we allow any change in the phenomenon to be unessential, we have then left the phenomenon itself, and are discoursing only on an abstract conception, as that alone can be equally applicable to both cases. Hence we see that the concrete cause of every phenomenon is the complex of all the phenomena of the universe that preceded it, and therefore that it is inexhaustible to human observation.

The second reason why the study of abstract causes can alone lead us to a knowledge of nature, arises from the dissimilarity of all phenomena considered in the concrete.

It is impossible to give an absolute proof that two entirely similar phenomena have never taken place since the creation, but it is easy to shew that the probabilities against it are as infinity to one. Millions of boys have walked by the sea-shore and cast millions of stones into the sea, and each of them has in its flight described a parabola; and yet as the number of such possible parabolas is infinite while the number of stones actually cast is finite, the chance that no two of the curves so described are of exactly the same form, is also infinite. In the same manner we may predicate of all the forests of America with their billions of trees, that they never produced two leaves exactly alike in all their parts, and of all the waves of the Atlantic, that no two bubbles floating on their surface have ever been exactly similar.

It is true there is a possibility of two similar phenomena, but it only appears at the limit; that is to say, the chance in its favour is infinitely small, and may therefore be neglected.

Considered then purely objectively, and merely as phenomenon, the outward world presents a vast organic whole, undergoing a succession of change, no two parts of which, either in time or space, exactly coincide with each other. From this purely objective point of view it is absurd to use the language sometimes employed, and to say that the same (meaning, precisely similar) phenomena as effects succeed the same phenomena as causes, inasmuch as there never are any *same* phenomena at all. Neither, on the other hand, is the succession of cause and effect very nearly the same at all times, in short, an approximation to perfect law. The natural philosopher cannot always measure the exact results of natural laws, but he never entertains a doubt that these laws are carried out in the external world with absolute and mathematical precision, and that not a single grain of sand lies a hundredth of an inch from the spot where such laws must inevitably have placed it. As then the phenomena in the different cases are dissimilar, while the laws they observe are absolutely the same, it follows that it is not the phenomena themselves, but the abstract conceptions of the relations between the phenomena, which can alone constitute the subject-matter of the laws.

Let us take as an instance the curve described by a projectile. The actual line of flight of two stones will never be precisely the same, so that the two curves would coincide if placed together. But the mathematician has discovered that whenever a body is projected into the air, whatever be the angle of its direction or the velocity of its motion, it will describe a curve possessing certain properties, and he accordingly states it as a law of nature, that projectiles describe a parabola.

Now we may readily see by this instance that the law does not consist of mere sensible phenomena alone, but of their relation to each other. The mind knits up a certain number of phenomena into one conception, and considering this as a cause, observes that it is invariably succeeded by another set of phenomena, which also admit of being similarly brought under one conception, and called an effect. Impulsion in a certain direction by some force, attraction in another direction by gravitation, are the partial abstract conceptions in the above instance united in the conception of the cause; the flight through the air in a curved line, every point of which is equally distant from a certain imaginary fixed point and an imaginary straight line, are the representations united in the conception of the effect.

It follows from this, that phenomena cannot be compared as mere objects of sense, and classed under the category of cause and effect, by the observation of the fact of their contemporaneousness or succession alone, but that they require an additional act of the understanding, in short an act of abstraction, by means of which we discover some relation of their parts, and thus frame a law for such connexion. Instead therefore of saying that the same or similar phenomena as antecedents are invariably succeeded by the same or similar phenomena as consequents, it would be more correct to say, that phenomena falling under a certain relation as causes are invariably accompanied or succeeded by phenomena falling under a certain other relation as effects.

The above remarks are not at all intended to invalidate the position that what we perceive objectively in each particular case is the mere succession or contemporaneousness of the phenomena. It is only when we view these phenomena under the relation of cause and effect, when, in short, we wish to extend the application of our experience and determine the law, that we find we cannot deal with the concrete phenomena, but are obliged to seek for some conceptions in our understanding under which respectively to subsume them.

This twofold signification of the words cause and effect, will give accordingly a twofold definition of causality, the one concrete and objective, the other abstract and subjective. The former has reference to the whole law of nature, and is valid of the entire objective phenomenon, without any of its parts being disregarded as unessential. It may be stated as follows:—*Every phenomenon is determined by the complex of all other phenomena antecedent to or contemporaneous with it.* The latter or subjective law of causality refers only to the laws discovered by the understanding, and concerns abstract ideas under which the phenomena may be arranged. It may be stated thus:—*Phenomena falling under certain relations are determined by phenomena falling under certain other relations respectively according to a law.*

Now of these two formulas, the former simply supplies the principle which lies at the foundation of the latter, but does not itself admit of any immediate application, as it refers to the complex of all the properties of nature, which we are of course never able to exhaust. It has no concern with the several laws of nature, as law presumes abstraction and classification, whereas it only considers the whole course of nature in the concrete as one indivisible unity. The second formula, on the other hand, is the one which mankind is constantly applying in the observation of nature; but it has one great disadvantage, inasmuch as it can never lead to absolute certainty. Whenever certain phenomena falling under the abstract conception A, have been followed, in all the cases that have come under our observation, by phenomena falling under the conception B, we state it as a law of nature, that if A is, B is. But we are liable at any moment to find an exceptional case upsetting the law, and making further observations necessary. In the first cases from which we established the law, each of the phenomena may perhaps have had some property, making them also correspond to conception A', and this last quality may have been wanting in the exceptional case. We then amend our law, and say, if A' is, B is; but we are still never secure from stumbling upon fresh exceptional cases, making additional amendments necessary.

Each formula then has its imperfection, as the former, though perfectly correct in itself, is totally unavailable; the latter, referring to partial laws of nature, is always applicable, but enables us to arrive at only an approximation to truth. To sum up in few words, the first is the formula of the theoretical principle, the second that of its practical application.

Now as I have already observed, the principal fallacy in Brown's theory of power, consists in his entirely ignoring, in the first place, all causality between contemporaneous phenomena, and in the second, the important fact that phenomena must be arranged under abstract conceptions, before the causal relation between them can be an object of human inquiry. He thus placed every phenomenon in a state of complete isolation. A spark is observed to explode gunpowder. He accordingly assumes that a spark always has exploded, and always will explode gunpowder, and asserts that this statement of fact respecting certain isolated events, scattered through the past and the future, is our whole conception of the power of the spark to produce such an effect. But by means of abstraction, we discover that phenomena differing widely in many respects, but similar in others, may be comprised under the same law, and that the above example of an explosion is isolated neither as regards the spark nor the powder. A red-hot poker or a flame will explode the powder as well as the spark, thus shewing that the quality of heat which is common to them all is the cause of the phenomenon in question. A spark, on the other hand, will not only produce the decomposition of powder, but also of other substances with which it may come in immediate contact, though often in a far less perceptible degree. Its power therefore of exploding gunpowder is not an entirely new phenomenon, isolated in time, but simply the continuation of the decomposing power of the spark under circumstances which render the effects of this power more immediately palpable to sense. This extension of the sphere of a law may often be carried still further by continuing the process of abstraction. As we rise from lower laws to higher and more comprehensive ones, we often abstract from the conception of change, and thus arrive at laws which not only determine the relations of phenomena as successive to each other in time, but also include those which are contemporaneous in space. The same law is thus made to comprise the rule according to which one phenomenon determines another contemporaneous with, or successive to it, just as the circumstances may require. Innumerable instances will probably at once suggest themselves to the reader's mind. A body at rest, and acted on by no force, will continue at rest. A body in motion, and acted on by no force, will continue in uniform motion. Now both these phenomena may again be brought under the higher law of the *vis inertiæ*, according to which, bodies whether in rest or motion, when unacted on by any force, will continue in their respective states. Again, the motion of the magnet determines the motion of the steel that is attracted by it. The repose of the magnet determines the repose of the steel; and both are simply two instances of the same law, according to which the position of the magnet considered generally determines that of the steel. To take a still more simple instance, the same law of gravity, according to which a body falls with a certain momentum, also determines the degree of downward pressure it exerts when in a state of rest. This gravitation is therefore a continuous power, acting just as strongly in the reciprocal and contemporaneous pressure between the body and the earth it rests upon, as between the earth and the same body when falling through the air.

It will appear from these considerations that our notion of the powers of natural objects is not that they may produce peculiar effects intermittently, and only as peculiar circumstances arise, but that they are something continuous, never inoperative, but always determining other phenomena, either to remain in their then state, or to undergo a certain change. If I say there is a certain latent property in gunpowder which makes it susceptible of explosion, I say nothing more than that there is some phenomenon which gunpowder when not exploding would present to a sense sufficiently fine, and which might be brought under the same law as the phenomenon of its explosion. It is undoubtedly true that a spark has the power to explode gunpowder only on certain occasions, viz. when it is brought in contact with it. But we think of this power as objective in nature under a higher and more general law in connexion with the phenomenon of its heat, and conceive the spark as igniting or decomposing the objects in its immediate vicinity, whether it consists of an imperceptibly small portion of air, or the magazine of a man of war. To speak therefore of the power of a spark to explode powder as a particular and isolated power producing an isolated event, is to impose an arbitrary and unphilosophical limitation upon our language, which we do not adopt in our thought; for we cannot even think of this quality in a spark, without its immediately suggesting the conception of its power to produce sensible heat, which experience teaches us to associate as the abstract cause with the phenomenon in question.

If these views are correct, the constitution of a body is the complex of its powers which have a continuous existence in time, and produce various results according to the various relations in which they may stand with the powers of other bodies. They are only cognisable by the human mind in as far as they can be brought under certain relations of thought, *i. e.* under those abstract conceptions which are suggested by comparing phenomena with one another. But though conceived under abstract conceptions these powers are by no means ideal, but have as real a ground in nature as the bodies themselves. For it must always be borne in mind, that it is precisely by means of abstraction that various effects are attributed to the same power, and thus its continuity and permanence rendered conceivable. Without this continuity power dwindles down into a mere notion, as in the theory of Brown, possessing no objective ground, merely starting into a galvanic life upon particular occasions, and again relapsing into nonentity till the same circumstances occur again.

The inexhaustibility of the relations of phenomena among each other, and the infinite diversity of nature, would therefore render all observation of it an absolute impossibility, if it were not for the mental process of abstraction, by means of which we recognise the same principle in different forms. But abstraction is the selection by the mind of those partial phenomena which admit of being subsumed under one principle. Now it is clearly impossible that this uniting principle should originate in the objects, for another principle would always be necessary in the subject, in order to recognise the unity of the principle in the objects. The principle therefore originates in the subject; and as this is valid of all our observation of phenomena, it follows that the sphere of the application and validity of causality is limited by subjective principles of thought, and cannot be predicated of those things with which the subject has no concern, *i. e.* of things which are not objects for it at all.

That the subject cannot predicate it of itself, except in so far as it becomes an object, also follows from the considerations, first, that unless it were an object it could contain no distinctive parts to be united in a law; and secondly, that another subject would always be wanting to contain the unity or principle of the law for the combination of such parts. Hence it follows from the nature of causality, as explained above, that, *though it arises in the subject, it can only be predicated of objects.*

This then is the result of our analysis of the conception of causality; and we might rest satisfied here if it were not that we have throughout assumed the necessity and validity of this conception, and simply endeavoured to explain what it is. Our next object must be to shew the manner in which we arrive at this conception at all, and why we are obliged to assume it in our observation of nature.

CHAPTER III.

On the Grounds of our Belief in Causality.

SECT. I.—*The Belief in Causality not based on Experience.*

IN the last chapter I have endeavoured to shew what causality is. In the present I propose to investigate the grounds of our belief in it. The problem resolves itself into two parts. First, where are we to look for the grounds of this belief? Secondly, what are they?

Now whenever the first of these questions is proposed to an unsophisticated understanding, we may be tolerably sure of receiving the answer, that the ground of our belief in causality is to be found in experience. The answer seems plausible enough, and may be very satisfactory to those who deny the possibility of all *à priori* knowledge whatever. It contains, nevertheless, a logical fallacy, which I shall now endeavour to expose.

To attempt to deduce our belief in causality from our experience of objects is to reason in a circle, for experience itself rests upon causality. If we do not assume causality, if in short we do not assume that nature follows fixed laws, her phenomena become a mere meaningless play of the senses, and nothing that we observe to-day can be regarded as a ground of belief as to what will happen to-morrow. If I find that to-day the event *B* has repeatedly followed the event *A*, I shall certainly (as my mind is now constituted) expect to find the same succession to-morrow; but the extent of this expectation is the measure of the probability assumed by my mind that *B* is determined by *A*, according to some natural law. Causality, therefore, as an historical fact, may have been true yesterday, and the same causes may have been followed by the same effects from sunrise to sunset. But unless I assume the unchangeableness of the laws of nature, in short this very causality itself, the truth of the doctrine yesterday, considered as a mere generalisation of yesterday's facts, is no reason for its truth to-day. Hence it is evident, that to make causality rest upon experience, when all experience must itself rest upon causality, is a glaring circle which metaphysical subtlety may attempt to conceal, but can never hope to defend with success.

Hume was the first philosopher who placed this argument in a clear light. In his *Inquiry concerning the Human Understanding*, and in the section entitled *Sceptical Doubts concerning the Operations of the Understanding*, when speaking of the inference that certain sensible qualities and secret powers will be conjoined in the future, from the fact that we have found them conjoined in the past, he proceeds as follows: "To say it (this inference) is experimental, is begging the question. For all inferences from experience suppose, as their foundation, that the future will resemble the past, and that similar powers will be conjoined with similar sensible qualities. If there be any suspicion that the course of nature may change, and that the past may be no rule for the future, all experience becomes useless, and can give rise to no inference or conclusion. It is impossible therefore that any arguments from experience can prove this resemblance of the past to the future, since all these arguments are founded on the supposition of that resemblance. Let the course of things be allowed hitherto ever so regular, that alone, without some new argument or inference, proves not that for the future it will continue so[1]."

As then experience presupposes causality, we must evidently seek for some other principle, if we would establish the latter on a sound foundation. In the first place, causality contains the conception of absolute universality. We do not say "some phenomena are now and then determined by others," but we predicate this of all phenomena, and at all times. For if there were exceptional cases, as they would be exceptional to empirically determined law in general, and not to any law in particular, they would follow no law at all, and would be absolutely indeterminable. It would follow from this, that we could never distinguish whether any particular case were an exception or not, so that the whole law would become unsound, from the impossibility of knowing what secret flaws might lurk in it unseen. In short, it would cease to be a law at all. Now where there is absolute universality, there must also be necessity; for where there is no necessity, there may be exceptional cases, the possibility of which is inconsistent with the conception of universality. Necessity is therefore an essential element in the conception of causality.

This principle affords an immediate clue to the problem before us; but the manner in which it does so, will become more intelligible by an illustration. There are, for instance, manufacturing processes, which, when conducted with the greatest skill and accuracy, do not always produce precisely similar results. But the manufacturer never for an instant

[1] Hume's *Inquiry concerning Human Understanding*, Sect. IV.

supposes that there is no cause for such variations, but always attributes them either to a slight difference in the quantity or quality of the ingredients he employs, to the mode of procedure, or to some other minute circumstance which has escaped his attention. Thus the absolute invariability of the laws of the external world is assumed as axiomatic in all cases, even in those lying beyond the reach of the powers of human observation.

Now there are two things to be considered here, first, the unknown object which the imagination conceives as a cause, in order to explain the variation in the phenomena, but of which by the hypothesis it has no actual experience; secondly, the subject which conceives it. This object is quite unknown, and cannot, therefore, supply us with the conviction that it also comes under the law of causality. Hence the subject alone remains, in which we can seek for this idea; and we are, therefore, obliged to conclude that the subject is conscious of a law of its own action, that, whatever object may be proposed to it can only be perceived under the condition of causality.

The same argument may be put in a slightly different form. If we endeavour to derive this relation of cause and effect from objects alone, we can never know that some new objects may not be presented to us at a future time in which it does not hold good; and we are, therefore, compelled to renounce the idea of necessity as one of its essential elements. But this is contrary to our hypothesis, and we are therefore obliged to seek for it in the subject. An illustration will perhaps make this still more evident. If a series of objects are passing before me, I can never know what will be the colour of the next that presents itself. But if I apply a green glass to my eye I can then anticipate that, whatever the natural colour of the object may be, it will appear with a green tinge. In this case the glass represents the mind, and the green tinge the peculiar condition of its activity, namely, the conception of causality through which alone the objects are viewed.

The same principle lies at the bottom of all these arguments, and I have merely repeated it in various forms, for the sake of greater perspicuity, and because accidental circumstances may make each of them respectively more forcible than the others to the minds of different individuals.

It is in the thinking subject then that we must search for the origin of our conception of causality; but in doing so we must beware lest we regard this subject simply as an object of experience, and thus fall into the very error which it has been our chief object to avoid. Experience is no less based upon causality, when applied to the phenomena of the mind, than when applied to those of matter; and, consequently, it will equally be reasoning in a circle, whether we derive such causality empirically from the one species of objects or from the other. This was the fallacy that Hume fell into, in his attempted solution of the difficulties he had himself raised. He was most unquestionably right in rejecting our empirical knowledge of outward objects, as the ground of our belief in the causal connexion, and in seeking for this ground in the subject. But, unfortunately, he did not see that his arguments were equally valid against all empirical foundation for this belief, and, consequently, in total disregard of his own principles, hc ascribed this latter to custom or habit. When speaking of the principle which leads us to draw inferences respecting the future from our observation of the past, he says, "This principle is custom or habit. For, wherever the repetition of any particular act or operation produces a propensity to renew the same act or operation, without being impelled by any reasoning or process of the understanding, we always say that this propensity is the effect of custom. By employing that word, we pretend not to have given the ultimate reason for such a propensity. We only point out a principle of human nature which is universally acknowledged, and which is well known by its effects[1]."

Hume states this doctrine so modestly, that he almost seems to give up the question altogether. In so far, however, as he considers it as a solution at all, it is evidently open to the criticism of his former section, as we can only arrive at a knowledge of this custom by our empirical observation of the past. Brown has shewn the futility of Hume's solution in the following passage. He says, "Why should the future resemble the past? At every stage of observation this question may be equally put, and at every stage it is equally unanswerable. If we can give any reason for our belief of the similarity, we do not need custom to convince us of it; and if we cannot give any reason for it, it is surely vain to appeal to custom, which is only a portion of that very past concerning which there is no difficulty whatever, and not a portion of that unexisting future in the believed similarity of which is to be found the only difficulty that perplexes us[2]."

[1] Hume's *Inquiry concerning Human Understanding*, Sect. V.
[2] Brown, *On the Relation of Cause and Effect*, Part IV. § 3.

It is not only in the subject then that we must look for the ground of causality, but in some *à priori* principle in the subject, or one entirely independent of all empirical foundation. Unfortunately, however, for the progress of metaphysical science in England, the very possibility of *à priori* conceptions has been disputed, and that by a writer who, whatever his merits may be in the department of logic and metaphysics, undoubtedly takes very high rank in that of political economy[1]. This circumstance, as also the importance of the subject to the solution of the main question under consideration, render it necessary that I should examine the nature of *à priori* knowledge somewhat more fully; and I shall, therefore, devote the following section to its investigation.

Sect. II.—*The Nature of* à priori *Knowledge.*

I propose to treat the question which this subject involves in the following order. In the first place I shall explain the meaning of the expression; in the second, I shall endeavour to shew that we really possess such knowledge, and to refute some of Mr Mill's arguments against it; and in the third, I shall investigate its peculiar characteristics.

It is of course quite indisputable, that in a certain sense any knowledge whatever may be termed experience, inasmuch as the possession of it has been one of the incidents of our lives—one of the mental phenomena which we have experienced. The language may be somewhat unusual, but not the most zealous defender of *à priori* knowledge would

[1] John Stuart Mill.

consider that there was any impropriety in the statement,—that in the whole course of his mathematical *experience*, meaning thereby his mathematical studies, he had never met with such and such a proof of a given problem. In short, until conceptions have been in our consciousness and thus formed a part of our experience, they are not our conceptions at all.

To speak therefore of conceptions *à priori* to experience in the above sense of the word, is an absurdity, as it is equivalent to making the conceptions *à priori* to themselves. A little consideration however of the operations of the understanding will shew that this expression may be employed in a somewhat different sense, and one which is not open to the above objection.

For an intellectual act it is manifestly necessary that the intelligence should answer certain conditions. This is already assumed, in the employment of a particular word, "intelligence," to signify a being capable of an intellectual act, *i.e.* answering the conditions necessary for such act. Were not certain conditions indispensable, any being whatever might be an intelligence; and an inanimate object might understand the differential calculus as well as a mathematician. Independently therefore of the intelligible nature of the object, the subject that understands it must possess a certain nature, either a mere receptivity or a mode of activity by which the intellectual act becomes possible. Thus much will be granted by the opponents of the doctrine of *à priori* conceptions as well as its advocates. They possess, however, another ground in common. Both parties will allow, at least as a matter of fact, that the intellect possesses the power of concentrating its attention upon one or another part or relation of the object presented to it, and thus of distinguishing between various parts of the whole intellectual act,—in other words, that the intellect is endowed with a faculty of abstraction. It is impossible, for instance, to picture to the imagination a colour without extension. But in the intellect we are able to distinguish between these conceptions, and to speak and think of various colours without regarding the conception of extension.

These two positions then, are, as I believe, allowed by all: First, that the intellect has a nature by virtue of which it is intellect, and not something else; secondly, that the intellect has a power of abstraction, or a faculty of distinguishing between various parts of an object, even though it cannot separate them in the imagination. Now the *à priori* philosophers do nothing more than bring these two principles, which are separately recognised by their opponents, into immediate relation to each other, by extending the operation of abstraction to the conditions of the intellect itself. They assert that the understanding, by its power of abstraction, is not only able to distinguish between different parts of the object presented to it, but that it is also able to distinguish between that part of the act which is dependent on the object, *i.e.* which is supplied by the senses and is called the matter, and that which depends on the nature of the subject, which in short is supplied by the conditions of the intellect, and is called the form.

The real meaning of the expression *à priori to experience* will have become obvious from the above observations. In employing it, I do not intend to assert that a conception, as a complete act of thought, has existed in the mind prior to the cognition of an object, but rather that a certain law of the understanding has existed prior to such cognition, and has predetermined its form; and further, that when such cognition takes place, the mind is able to distinguish that part of it which is absolutely determined by the conditions of its own activity, (or perhaps more correctly, which is one of the conditions themselves,) from that other part which is dependent solely on the nature of the object. The former is then declared to be *à priori* to experience, because the understanding has recognised it as a law limiting the possible sphere of its own activity, whatever objects may be proposed to it, and consequently as independent of such objects. This, however, is not in any way irreconcileable with the fact, that our consciousness of the law only arises when the objects of experience are presented to the senses. Thus the mind and all its hidden wealth of *à priori* conceptions may be compared to a cabinet containing many drawers and secret places stored with precious things, and presented to every human soul on its entrance into the world. The cabinet and all its contents are the legitimate property of the soul from the first moment of its existence; but only after patient search does it find the hidden springs which reveal those secret places, and make it conscious of its wealth.

I shall next endeavour to shew by means of an example that the understanding really does possess the power of distinguishing the subjective from the objective elements in one of its own acts. The corner of a house or the stem of a poplar seen against the sky suggest the conception of a straight line. On further examination I perceive many inequalities in the outline of these objects, and accordingly pronounce them to be not exactly straight. I then turn to other objects in art or nature which appear to be bounded by lines still straighter than the house or poplar; but minute examination always leads to the same result; and at last I conclude that there is no such thing as a perfectly straight line in the whole external universe. Now in this case I evidently possess a conception, that of perfect straightness, which has been suggested by external objects, but is nowhere realised by them. There is, therefore, a certain something in the conception which cannot have been derived from the objects, for none of them possess it. Where then am I to seek it? The answer is self-evident, for the subject alone remains. The objects, by their approximate conformity to certain relations of thought, have stimulated the intellect to the consideration of a certain relation of points, and have thus rendered it capable of constructing a line according to this relation by its own activity, and comparing the objects with the conception thus produced. In this case, the conception is the product of the imagination when describing a line determined by the law, that each successive point is absolutely determined by any two of the preceding. To express the same thing somewhat differently: if I draw a line in my imagination, I find, on determining each successive point, that there is only one bearing precisely the same relation to any two of the preceding points determined by the same law. And it must be particularly observed, that I find this to be the case in my imagination, in short, in my intuition of space, without which no such laws could have any significance for me whatever.

Now in the above example, if I were to deny that the straight line is constructed according to a law furnished by the pure intuition of space, and maintained that the conception was derived entirely from the observation of visible lines, I could never conclude that there is in nature no such thing as a perfectly straight line; for I could never have obtained from all the lines in the world, a conception of a greater degree of perfection than that presented by the actual phenomena themselves. Again, if my understanding presented me with no mental law by which to construct a standard of perfect straightness, there would be no reason for my choosing even the straightest of observed lines, as a standard for those less straight rather than the reverse. Without a common intellectual standard more perfect than either, there would be as much reason for my condemning the straighter line as the less perfect, on account of its differing from that which is less straight, as for condemning the latter as less perfect, on the ground of its differing from the former. Directly, therefore, I pass judgment on a sensible straight line, with reference to its apparent straightness, I have recognised an ideal standard as a distinct element in the cognition, and by a process of abstraction, have separated the mere image, as a product of the senses, from the *à priori* conception, which is supplied by the pure activity of the understanding, and determined by its conditions. This argument has been so extremely well put by that fine old philosopher, Ralph Cudworth, that I cannot support my argument better, than by quoting the following passage.

"If there were material lines, triangles, pyramids, perfectly and mechanically exact, yet that which made them such, and thereby to differ from other irregular lines, imperfect triangles and cubes, could be nothing else but a conformity to an antecedent intellectual idea in the mind, as the rule and exemplar of them; for otherwise an irregular line and an imperfect triangle, pyramid, cube, are as perfectly that that they are, as the other is; only they are not agreeable to those anticipated and preconceived ideas of regular lines and figures actively exerted in the mind or intellect, which the mind naturally formeth to itself, and delighteth to exercise itself upon them, as the proper object of art and science, which the other irregular figures are not. Wherefore, whenever a man looking upon material objects, judges of the figures of them, and says this is a straight line, this is a perfect triangle, that a perfect circle, but those are neither perfect triangles nor circles, it is plain, that here are two several ideas of these lines and figures; the one outwardly impressed from those individual material objects from without upon the sense of the beholder; the other actively exerted from his inward mind or intellect. Which latter busy anticipation of it is the rule, pattern, and exemplar, whereby he judges of those sensible ideas or phantasms. For otherwise, if there were no inward anticipations or mental ideas, the spectator would not judge at all, but only suffer; and every irregular and imperfect triangle being as perfectly that which it is, as the most perfect triangle, the mind now having no inward pattern of its own before it, to distinguish and put a difference, would not say one of them was more imperfect than another; but only comparing them

6—2

with one another, would say, that this individual figure was not perfectly like to that; upon which account the perfect triangle would be as imperfectly the imperfect triangle, as the imperfect was the perfect[1]."

From conceptions *à priori*, our next step must be to judgments *à priori*, the simplest of which, perhaps, are those offered by the axioms of geometry. That two straight lines cannot enclose a space, is such a judgment, and follows directly from the *à priori* conception, by which we construct a straight line in the imagination. For by the rule for the construction of a straight line, all its points are absolutely determinable by any two of them. If, therefore, two straight lines pass first through the point A, and then meet in the point B, the two points A and B determine all the other points for each line absolutely in the same way, or in other words, the lines coincide, and are really the same line.

Mr Mill has endeavoured to invalidate the entire theory of *à priori* knowledge, and explains the above axiom as the simple result of experience. After stating some of the arguments of his opponents, he proceeds: "To these arguments, which I trust I cannot be accused of understating, a satisfactory answer will, I conceive, be found, if we advert to one of the characteristic properties of geometrical forms—their capacity of being painted in the imagination with a distinctness equal to reality: in other words, the exact resemblance of our ideas of form to the sensations which suggest them. This, in the first place, enables us to make (at least with a little prac-

[1] Cudworth, *On Eternal and Immutable Morality*, Book IV. chap. iii. § 9.

tice,) mental pictures of all possible combinations of lines and angles, which resemble the realities quite as well as any which we could make upon paper; and, in the next place, makes those pictures just as fit subjects of geometrical experimentation as the realities themselves; inasmuch as pictures, if sufficiently accurate, exhibit of course all the properties which would be manifested by the realities at one given instant, and on simple inspection: and, in geometry, we are concerned only with such properties, and not with that which pictures could not exhibit, the mutual action of bodies one upon another. The foundations of geometry would therefore be laid in direct experience, even if the experiments (which in this case consist merely in attentive contemplation) were practised solely upon what we call our ideas, that is, upon the diagrams in our minds, and not upon outward objects[1]."

If Mr Mill had employed the word *painted* in the above passage, to signify that the geometrical forms can be *constructed* in the imagination with a distinctness equal to reality, he would have virtually admitted, though under another name, that very *à priori* nature of the conceptions which he is attempting to disprove. The rest of the passage, however, as well as the context generally, exclude this interpretation; and I believe that, in perfect consistency with the rest of his theory, he has employed the expression to signify, that the geometrical forms are copied from the objects of sense. In this case I would submit, first, that geometrical forms cannot be so painted with a distinctness equal to reality, or in other words, that our *ideas* of form do not bear an *exact* resemblance to the sensations which suggest

[1] Mill's *System of Logic.* 2nd Ed. Vol. I. p. 309.

them; and secondly, that if our ideas of form did not admit of a far greater degree of accuracy and precision than the suggesting sensations, they would be of no avail to the mathematician. To establish these points, it will be necessary to distinguish between two very different ways in which the conception of a figure may be produced in the imagination.

If I contemplate an irregular line,—such, for instance, as the outline of a country in a map,—and then shut my eyes, I may reproduce in my imagination a picture of a line bearing a great resemblance to it. While regarding the line itself I may form a judgment of the proportionate distance of several of its irregularities which may be an approximation to the truth. If I afterwards attempt to form such a judgment from the picture in my imagination, I shall find a much greater difficulty, and the result will in all probability be far less correct. This is not owing to any defect in the judgment, but because I find it impossible to reproduce the line in question with perfect accuracy. The imagination therefore, as far as the mere sensible picture in the sensorium is concerned, is far less trustworthy than the senses themselves. If I make a similar experiment with a straight line, the result is the same; for if I contemplate a sensible line which appears to me to be perfectly straight, and then, closing my eyes, endeavour to form a picture of it in my imagination, I am at once aware of the difficulty of fixing its parts, and that the line so pictured may have many small irregularities. I must, however, remind the reader that I am speaking here only of the sensible image in my sensorium—that faint picture of a line which I imagine myself to see—just in the same manner as I recall the image of a flower, a human face, or any other external object,—and I believe that no one will venture to claim for such a picture even as great a degree of perfection as can be attained by drawing a straight line upon a sheet of paper.

Now, in the case of the irregular line, I find that my imagination has no other means of reproducing it than that afforded by the recollection of the sensible impression, and I must therefore content myself with the imperfect picture obtained in this manner. With the straight line, however, I find a far more powerful faculty at my disposal, and therefore instinctively reject the less accurate process. Instead of having recourse to my memory, by means of which I can only reproduce a mere visible picture of what I have seen, I *construct* a line in my imagination, according to a definite rule supplied by the understanding; and directly I am conscious that any point diverges to the right or the left, *i. e.* assumes a position not absolutely determined by any two of the preceding points, I reject it, and correct my image accordingly. That this rule is supplied by the understanding and not by experience, is at once evident from the fact, that I employ it as a standard for experience itself, and reject all lines as not straight which do not conform to it.

Perhaps this distinction between the mere sensible picture of a figure in the imagination, and its construction by the understanding according to a rule, may be made still clearer by another example. The mathematician can easily combine four circular arcs in such a manner as to present a considerable resemblance to an ellipse. A person unacquainted with mathematics would in all probability at once pronounce the figure to be an oval, and, in endeavouring to reproduce the picture of it in his imagination, would not be able to make any distinction between such a figure and a real ellipse. In reality, however, the figures are absolutely and essentially different from each other, and no part of a figure so constructed as above mentioned, could be made to coincide with any part of a real ellipse. The mathematician, on the other hand, who is acquainted with the difference between the figures, constructs the ellipse in his imagination according to a law; and the picture thus produced will be far more accurate than in the former case. But even the mathematician will attain but an approximation to the ellipse, as far as the mere picture in his imagination is concerned, and the instant he considers it as an object of mathematical reasoning, he is obliged to have recourse to the theoretical rule for its construction. Instead, therefore, of conceding to Mr Mill that mathematical forms have the capacity of being *painted* with a distinctness equal to reality, I should say that they can be so *constructed.* In short, if Mr Mill employs the word *painted* in the same sense in which I have used the word *constructed,* he has really admitted the *à priori* nature of these forms, as all construction presumes some previous rule or plan according to which the construction takes place. In so far as he employs it to signify the mere copying of an object in the sensorium from recollection, I maintain that such painting is absolutely incapable of being made the subject of mathematical reasoning.

Should the reader feel any hesitation in admitting this last position, I would ask him, How he would commence the deduction of a single property of the parabola from the mere picture of one, apart from any rule for its construction? Perhaps it might be answered, that if a tolerably accurate drawing of a parabola were offered for examination, the mathematician, after a number of experiments, might find out some one of its properties by actual measurement, and from this might deduce the others. In replying to this objection, I will waive the consideration that such a sensible picture is necessarily imperfect, and therefore the property in question and deductions from it only approximately true, and come at once to the principal point, namely, that deductions so arrived at would be valid only of the actual figure measured, and any others constructed according to the discovered property; but without introducing this element of construction, the mathematician could claim no universality for his deduction, and would therefore have to determine the above-mentioned property by actual measurement in each individual figure.

At another place, when speaking of the advocates of *à priori* knowledge, Mr Mill says, "They cannot, however, but allow that the truth of the axiom, Two straight lines cannot enclose a space, even if evident, independently of experience, is also evident from experience. Whether the axiom *needs* confirmation or not, it *receives* confirmation in almost every instant of our lives; since we cannot look at any two straight lines which intersect one another, without seeing that from that point they continue to diverge more and more[1]. Experimental proof crowds in upon us in such endless profusion, and without one instance in which there can be even a suspicion of an exception to the rule, that we should soon have a stronger

[1] Mill's *Logic*, Vol. II. p. 306.

ground for believing the axiom, even as an experimental truth, than we have for almost any of the general truths which we confessedly learn from the evidence of our senses. Independently of *à priori* evidence, we should certainly believe it with an intensity of conviction far greater than we accord to any ordinary physical truth: and this too at a time of life much earlier than that from which we date almost any part of our acquired knowledge, and much too early to admit of our retaining any recollection of the history of our intellectual operations at that period. Where then is the necessity for assuming that our recognition of these truths has a different origin from the rest of our knowledge, when its existence is perfectly accounted for by supposing its origin to be the same[1]?"

[1] Professor Ulrici, in an Article on "The so-called Inductive Logic," after quoting the above passage from Mill, continues, "We must at the very outset dispute both these positions. The truth of the axiom in question is by no means evident from experience; for experience shews us only that two straight lines in all cases that occur, do not enclose a space, but not, that they *cannot* enclose one. This impossibility *can* never be made evident from mere experience, as that which does not occur in experience, or rather, which has not yet occurred, is by no means impossible on that account. Neither is it by any means indifferent whether the axiom need confirmation from experience or not, but rather, if it did not need such confirmation, it would be indifferent whether it received it or not. Even, if we see that two lines cutting each other diverge more and more from the point of intersection, we by no means *see* that they *cannot* enclose a space. At the most are we able to *conclude* this from such seeing, or rather from our internal intuition; but the certainty and truth of this conclusion, just because it is a mere conclusion, evidently rest, *not* on experience, but on the nature of our thought and the immanent necessity of thought, which fact contradicts Mill's assertion."

Sogleich diese ersten beiden Sätze müssen wir bestreiten. Die Wahrheit des in Rede stehenden Axioms ist keineswegs—"gemäss der Erfahrung" evident. Denn die Erfahrung zeigt uns nur, dass zwei gerade Linien in allen vorkommenden Fällen keinen Raum einschliessen, nicht aber, dass sie ihn nicht einschliessen *können.*

This extract appears to me to contain at least three fatal errors. The assumption at the outset is manifestly incorrect, as no *à priori* philosopher could concede "that the truth of the axiom, two straight lines cannot enclose a space, even if evident, independently of experience, is also evident from experience." For, in the first place, the whole question refers to lines absolutely, not approximately straight; and it is beyond the powers of sense to determine which lines do, and which do not, entirely conform to our conception of straightness. In the second place, for the reasons already given, the conception of absolute straightness must be derived from the understanding, or rather from our pure conception of space, if, according to a very generally admitted fact, no objects entirely correspond to it; and even supposing the senses did present us with straight lines as well as irregular ones, we should still require some intellectual conception for arranging the former under a particular category by themselves. For argument's sake however, and in order to explain the third objection, I will waive these points, and suppose not only that

Diese Unmöglichkeit *kann* nie aus der blossen Erfahrung erhellen, da, was in der Erfahrung nicht vorkommt oder vielmehr bisher nicht vorgekommen ist, darum noch keineswegs unmöglich ist. Ebenso ist es keineswegs "einerlei," ob das Axiom der Bestätigung durch die Erfahrung bedarf oder nicht: vielmehr, wenn es dieser Bestätigung nicht bedürfte, so wäre es einerlei, ob es sie durch die Erfahrung erhält oder nicht. Wenn wir auch sehen, dass zwei sich schneidende Linien vom Durchschnittspunkt an immer mehr divergiren, so *sehen* wir damit doch keineswegs, dass sie keinen Raum einschliessen *können*. Wir können diess höchstens aus jenem 'Sehen' oder vielmehr aus der innern Anschauung *folgern;* aber die Gewissheit und Wahrheit dieser Folgerung würde, weil sie eben eine blosse Folgerung ist, offenbar *nicht* auf der Erfahrung, sondern auf der Natur unseres Denkens, auf jener immanentem Denknothwendigkeit beruhen, was der Behauptung, Mill's widerspricht. *Zeitschrift für Philosophie*, Vol. XXI. pp. 174—5.

straight lines are presented us by external objects, but that experience could decide certain lines intersecting each other to be absolutely straight.

In a particular given case, these lines may diverge at a sensible angle, and the mere pictures formed in our imagination from our observation of the sensible lines, may lead us to the conclusion, that these individual lines intersecting at this perceptible angle can never meet again. This however is no proof from experience, that two other straight lines *cannot,* but only that these particular lines *do not* enclose a space. For as long as we keep within the province of sense, whether applied to an outward object or a picture in the imagination, such object cannot by any possibility be evidence of the truth of a universal proposition, inasmuch as an intellectual conception is requisite, as a principle for the extension of the predicate from the particular to the universal. On the assumption however that our senses are sufficiently perfect, a single object may be accepted as evidence of the falsity of such universal; for if the proposition does not hold good in any single instance, it cannot be universally true. Now in the case of the proposition before us, although we could never establish it through sense alone, by a single instance, or any number of instances, it is possible to conceive an object which should appear to disprove it, the error arising from the imperfection of sense.

For let us suppose, that two visible lines of a mile in length, which taken separately appear to be absolutely straight, when brought together are found to coincide at their extremities, and yet to enclose a space the eighth of an inch in breadth. Now in this case, our senses would not be capable of detecting the imperfection in either line. If we shut our eyes and attempt to form a mere sensible picture of such lines, we are not able to arrive at even so great a degree of accuracy, as that presented by the lines themselves; and thus lines declared to be straight by our unassisted sense, would be found first slightly to diverge, and then to approach each other; and yet we should not for an instant surrender our axiom. On what principle then should we maintain it? Clearly this: In addition to the imperfect picture of the straight line which we merely paint in our imagination, we are conscious of a rule for its construction, which is not limited by the imperfection of the senses, and which declares that every point which is not determined by any two other points in a straight line, must lie out of it. In this manner we decide against the straightness of the lines, from the fact that they enclose a space, and conclude the existence of inaccuracies which our senses are unable to discover, because the lines do not harmonise with our previous conceptions. So far therefore from deriving our axiom from the observation of such lines, we should rest our judgment respecting them on the predetermined truth of the axiom.

Mr Mill's reasoning appears to me to violate a very sound and simple principle enunciated by Aristotle rather more than two thousand years ago. In the first book of the Later Analytics, ch. 31, we find a passage which may be freely translated as follows. "Neither is it possible to know through sense. For even if sense refers to the quality of a thing, and not to some particular individual, yet the act of perceiving by sense, can only be exercised with reference to some particular thing determined in space and time. But it is impossible to perceive by sense the universal and that which is inherent in all; for it is neither a particular thing nor at a particular time, for if it were so, it would not be universal. Since, therefore, demonstrations are of universals, and it is impossible to perceive universals by sense, it is clear, that knowing is not attained by sensation. But it is manifest that, even if it were possible to perceive by sense that the angles of a triangle are equal to two right angles, we should still seek for a demonstration, and should not know it, as some say. For perception is necessarily only of individuals, but knowledge is by the cognition of the universal[1]."

The soundness of this principle is self-evident; but the empirical philosophers would ignore it altogether. They appear to forget that as the axiom is absolutely universal, it can only be based on the observation of a visible angle, by assuming that what is true of such visible angle is equally true of an angle too small to be an object of sense; and this assumption again is only justifiable by the consciousness that all absolutely straight lines must be constructed on the same pattern according to a certain rule not limited by the power of the senses, and

[1] Οὐδὲ δι' αἰσθήσεως ἔστιν ἐπίστασθαι. Εἰ γὰρ καὶ ἔστιν ἡ αἴσθησις τοῦ τοιοῦδε καὶ μὴ τοῦδέ τινος, ἀλλ' αἰσθάνεσθαί γε ἀναγκαῖον τόδε τί καὶ ποῦ καὶ νῦν. Τὸ δὲ καθόλου καὶ ἐπὶ πᾶσιν ἀδύνατον αἰσθάνεσθαι· οὐ γὰρ τόδε οὐδὲ νῦν· οὐ γὰρ ἂν ἦν καθόλου· τὸ γὰρ ἀεὶ καὶ πανταχοῦ καθόλου φαμὲν εἶναι. Ἐπεὶ οὖν αἱ μὲν ἀποδείξεις καθόλου, ταῦτα δ' οὐκ ἔστιν αἰσθάνεσθαι, φανερὸν ὅτι οὐδ' ἐπίστασθαι δι' αἰσθήσεως ἔστιν. Ἀλλὰ δῆλον ὅτι καὶ εἰ ἦν αἰσθάνεσθαι τὸ τρίγωνον ὅτι δυσὶν ὀρθαῖς ἴσας ἔχει τὰς γωνίας, ἐζητοῦμεν ἂν ἀπόδειξιν καὶ οὐχ ὥσπερ φασί τινες ἠπιστάμεθα· αἰσθάνεσθαι μὲν γὰρ ἀνάγκη καθ' ἕκαστον, ἡ δ' ἐπιστήμη τῷ τὸ καθόλου γνωρίζειν ἐστίν. *Post. Anal.* Lib. I. cap. 31.

Cudworth quoted this passage (*Eternal and Immutable Morality*, p. 230.) but as cap. 25, instead of 31. The text, moreover, of his edition must have been very faulty, as he omits a whole line in the commencement of the chapter.

so far from being in any way dependent on possible experience, on the contrary, determining for such experience what lines are straight, and what are not.

The question now arises: What is the peculiar characteristic of *à priori* conceptions by which we are able to distinguish them from conceptions *à posteriori?* Or, in other words, what is the principle of that act of abstraction by which we can separate the form from the matter in our cognition of an object? To answer this question it will be necessary to refer shortly to the nature of empirical knowledge in general.

We possess no formula or process of thinking by which we can so regulate our observation of natural bodies as to exhaust their properties, and be able to say that we are thoroughly acquainted with all the phenomena they are capable of exhibiting. Many centuries had elapsed before mankind were aware of the existence of such an agency as galvanism. Many centuries hence mankind may perhaps discover some new agency equally extraordinary. Such discoveries may be repeated at intervals for millions of years, and we shall never be able to place any fixed limit to them, and assert, that now we have completed the entire circle of possible experience. The vast field of the undiscovered thus assumes the form of an infinite series; but the activity of these undiscovered powers is not limited by our ignorance; and, although we have never made them the object of individual perceptions, yet are they not on this account a less important element in the production of natural phenomena. Hence arises the impossibility of predicating absolute certainty of any empirical law; for we can never know that some essential circumstance has not been overlooked from our ignorance of its existence. The law may appear to have held good for centuries, and yet the exceptional case, arising from the absence of the circumstance in question may still occur on some future occasion, and shew that it is really no law, inasmuch as it does not possess universal validity. Thus the observation of individual phenomena,—that is, of the particular in space and time,—is the foundation of whatever approximation to certainty we may attain in our empirical knowledge, and the impossibility of exhausting these particulars is the reason that this certainty can never become absolute.

Now in the case of a geometrical axiom, we can attain such absolute certainty, for although the field of the undiscovered in mathematical truth is also infinite, yet each mathematical conception is accompanied by the consciousness of its absolute independence of all individual sensible phenomena. No new discovery, therefore, can ever upset, or even modify it. When I reflect on the axiom, that two straight lines cannot enclose a space, I am not only sure of its truth here, and now, but I find the conception accompanied in my consciousness with the conviction, that it is equally true in the most distant fixed star, and will be equally true a million ages hence: no new galvanism can touch it. It is, in short, absolutely independent of all particulars in space and time, and sets contingencies at defiance.

This remark is equally applicable to the whole province of *à priori* reasoning. The solution of a problem may be separated from the first axioms upon which it is based by a wide interval embracing so many intermediate steps, that no human mind is able to unite them all in one immediate intuition, and thus intuitise the truth of the result. But during the whole process of the reasoning, each step has been accompanied by the consciousness of its entire independence of the particulars in space and time, and thus the condition of its *à priori* character is still preserved.

Dependence on particularity in time and space is thus shewn to be the touchstone which divides our empirical from our *à priori* conceptions. In order therefore to distinguish them, it is not necessary to refer historically to the manner in which they first entered our minds. Every time I consider the above-mentioned axiom, it is equally accompanied by the test which determines its *à priori* character, viz. independence of all particular phenomena in space and time.

But perhaps it may be urged, that when we are working any mathematical problem, we are not accustomed to examine each step in our reasoning, by endeavouring to conceive it under widely different circumstances of time and space, and thus testing its independence of them. This is perfectly true; but the act of abstraction by which we *do* test this independence is performed by virtue of an analogous law of thought, which I call the law of *intellectual differentiation.* I shall have occasion to examine this law and its other applications more fully at a future page, and shall therefore only hint at its nature now.

By repeated observations of the phenomena of nature, we are enabled to arrive at an empirical law respecting them; and although we may have omitted in our observations some essential circumstance, we are at any rate justified in considering the law as an approximation to truth, and adopting it accordingly. Directly however we step beyond the particular circumstances of our observation, and attempt to apply the law to a different set of circumstances, however little they may vary from the former, we feel that we cannot proceed with the same degree of certainty; in other words, we feel that the law is dependent on, or a function of, the particulars in space and time. Now in the case of *à priori* conceptions, if we first conceive an axiom as true in one set of circumstances, and then vary the circumstances by a mere infinitesimal change, we are conscious that no change takes place in the axiom. To express this in mathematical language we should say, that if we differentiate the axiom relatively to the particularities in space and time, the differential coefficient always $= 0$, and we are thus justified in assuming that the axiom is no function of these particularities. Now it is precisely because the change in the particulars need only be infinitesimal, that we are not obliged to try our axiom under widely different circumstances, but are able by the law of our consciousness, which I have termed intellectual differentiation, to recognise its independence of these circumstances, and consequently its *à priori* character, at the limit.

I have spoken above of the particularity of space and time, but in reality, the former is only a particular case of the latter. For if I endeavour to separate any portion of space and particularise it, I can only do so by means of some of its relations to phenomena. Now as these are ever changing, or at least susceptible of change, for all we know to the contrary, I can only particularise them by a reference to a particular time, which is thus found to be the ultimate foundation of all particularity whatever. This will become more evident by an example. Supposing I were to specify some particular portion of space by its relative position to the planet Jupiter, I must also specify a particular time, as Jupiter is itself always in motion. To take a still stronger case, supposing I would determine the point in question, by referring it to a fixed star. This reference still obtains the whole of its value from some particular empirical observations, which have of course been made at a particular time, and have proved the star to be a fixed one. The particular in space therefore, is in all cases determined by the particular in time, or in other words, by the particular phenomena, either physical or mental, which become the objects of our consciousness.

Now whenever the necessary act of abstraction has been completed, and that part of a cognition which is independent of particulars in time and space, has been separated from that which is so dependent, we claim for the former the rank of *à priori* knowledge. That all judgments of this class are accompanied with absolute certainty, is a fact which admits of a very simple explanation. For as they must have an origin somewhere, and as this origin by the hypothesis is not to be found in objects, it must be sought in the subject, and,—as the subject supplies only the form but not the matter of judgments,—in the formal laws, either of our pure intuitions of space and time, or of our thought in general. These *à priori* judgments, therefore, are nothing more than the enunciation of the laws, either of our pure intuition, or of our understanding. But neither our intuition nor our understanding can contradict themselves, and we cannot therefore either intuitise or think the contradictories of their laws. Hence it follows, that the contradictories of these laws are absolutely inconceivable, and the judgments enunciating the laws must be attended with absolute certainty.

The consciousness of the necessity of a judgment, or the impossibility of conceiving its falsity, has been very generally adopted as the criterion of its *à priori* character. This position however is open to one very great objection, inasmuch as the certainty is not always immediate. It is, for instance, the wonderful and almost mysterious nature of our pure intuition of space, that by far the majority of its properties, though capable of expression in a single judgment, cannot be brought into a single intuition, but have to be deduced by *à priori* reasoning from a number of axioms, or such *à priori* intuitions as are the results of single intuitions. The contradictory therefore of such a mediate proposition does not contradict any single intuition, and is thus quite conceivable to him who has not previously gone through all the intermediate steps, and intuitised the necessity both of each individually, and of their logical connexion in the understanding. Supposing, for instance, a mathematician were to tell a person unacquainted with geometry, that when two lines intersect each other in any point within a circle, the rectangle contained by the segments of the one, will never be equal to the rectangle contained by the segments of the other, except when the lines intersect each other similarly, the person thus deceived, might easily be made to understand the terms of the proposition, and yet have no difficulty in conceiving its truth. He would, however, not only conceive what is not true, but what to the mind of the mathematician is simply inconceivable. We cannot therefore predicate at once of the results of mathematics, that their contradictories are inconceivable, but only that they are truths the contradictories of which may be made inconceivable to those who comprehend the necessary processes for that purpose.

It will readily appear from this, that the certainty we feel in the truth of an *à priori* proposition, is not always equal in degree to that we feel in a merely empirical truth, but it is different in character. If I work out a long mathematical calculation, I may perhaps have arrived at a perfectly correct result, and yet I may feel much more sure that the sun will rise to-morrow, than that my sheets of symbols do not contain a single error. In this manner we see, that I may have deduced a correct and indisputable *à priori* truth, I may fully understand the resulting formula, and yet feel less confidence in it, than even in an empirical discovery, provided it has received the confirmation of numerous experiments. There is however a very striking difference in the nature of the certainty I attach to the two cases. For though my confidence in my problem may not be very great, I entertain no doubt whatever, that its relation to truth is susceptible of absolute demonstration to a human intelligence, and that its correctness or the contrary may be rendered utterly inconceivable. This holds good of no empirically ascertained fact whatever.

If the views advocated in this section are correct, certainty cannot be made the distinguishing characteristic of *à priori* truth, for two reasons. In the first place, all *à priori* cognition is the result of an act of abstraction by which we separate the form of a cognition from its matter; and, as in the case of any other mental operation, we can never have any absolute guarantee that this act has been correctly performed where it has been attempted, or that it is impossible in other cases where no attempt has been made. In the second place, there are *à priori* judgments which cannot be brought under a single intuition, and consequently their contradictories are perfectly conceivable to those who have not gone through the successive steps necessary to establish them. It follows therefore, that the field of *à priori* cognitions is not necessarily exhausted, and may receive still further additions through the successful application of the operation of abstraction. As an instance of such progress, I may adduce the fact that not many years have elapsed since the laws of motion were universally considered to be of empirical origin; Dr Whewell however has advocated the opinion that they are *à priori*, and I am inclined to believe he is right.

The following is a general summary of the results arrived at in the foregoing section. Our conceptions, and the propositions we form by their combination, are either derived from the repeated observation of phenomena; or they are intuitions embraced as certain on their first appearance in the consciousness; or else they are derived from combinations of the latter by processes of reasoning, the correctness of which is of an equally axiomatic character. The first class are said to be empirical, or *à posteriori*, on account of their being subsequent to, and dependent on, experience, and embrace all our knowledge of natural phenomena. The second class are *à priori* on account of their enunciating the formal laws of our thought and intuition, and thus being prior to and independent of, any particular experience,—as, for instance, the axioms of geometry. The third class are also *à priori,* as they are deduced by *à priori* reasoning from *à priori* premises, and include, among other things, the results of the processes of pure mathematics.

The first class of truths admit of a degree of probability so great, that it falls short of absolute certainty by a quantity almost inappreciable. That the sun will rise to-morrow, or that if I throw a stone into the air, it will fall to the ground, are propositions of this character. So far as all moral conviction is concerned they are certain; but they are not absolutely so, because not only are their contradictories conceivable, but *we can conceive no form of reasoning by which they can be shewn to be absolutely inconceivable.*

The second class admit of absolute certainty. They stand or fall with the human intellect itself. No greater degree of certainty is conceivable than that attached to the proposition, that two straight lines cannot enclose a space. Its contradictory is absolutely inconceivable.

The third class differ from the second class, inasmuch as their falsity contradicts no single intuition, and is therefore perfectly conceivable even to persons who have a clear conception of the terms of the proposition. But they are, nevertheless, susceptible of absolute demonstration, as they can be deduced from axioms by *à priori* reasoning.

The distinction between *à priori* and *à posteriori* knowledge was well known in the philosophy of the Academy, though it received a somewhat different and fanciful explanation. For Plato, finding it impossible to base our mathematical intuitions on experience alone, attributed them to our recollection of knowledge acquired in a former state of existence, and thus, under the name of Anamnesis, really laid the foundation of the modern theory of intuitions and judgments *à priori.*

Before leaving this subject I would observe that *à priori* judgments are of incalculable value for the extension and consolidation of human knowledge, as they always carry with them the conviction of their universal validity and absolute necessity. The observation of a phenomenon, unaccompanied by an act of abstraction distinguishing between the purely subjective and objective elements, yields us knowledge of that particular object alone. If we endeavour to extend this knowledge by making the observation the ground of an universal judgment, we do so at the risk of finding our hypothesis contradicted by a subsequent observation. Where, however, the observation is accompanied by an act of the understanding claiming a certain part of the whole act as one of the conditions of its own activity, we obtain a result as permanent and universal as the activity of the understanding itself. We are then able to say, without a moment's hesitation or misgiving, that whatever fresh object may be presented to us, this *à priori* judgment remains unassailable as a law of human thought or intuition.

SECT. III.—*Causality an* à priori *Conception.*

In the first section of this chapter I have shewn that the ground of Causality is to be found neither in our experience of external objects, nor in any empirical observation of mental phenomena, inasmuch as all empirical knowledge is founded on causality, and presupposes it. We must therefore seek it in some *à priori* law of thought. It is however evidently not an immediately intuitive axiom, for although we do always think in conformity with this law, we can at least conceive that the Almighty could ordain a phenomenon y to follow a phenomenon x in one case, and yet in precisely similar circumstances ordain that in another case x should be followed by a different phenomenon z. The only alternative remaining is, that the law of causality is one of those laws of thought, the *à priori* character of which can only be made evident by a process of reasoning. I shall now endeavour to develop this process, by giving a short analysis of an act of consciousness in general. I say, *in general*, because our investigation is to be strictly *à priori*, and must therefore abstract from all particular phenomena, and only concern itself with those conceptions which apply to all our acts of consciousness, and their reference to an object in general.

In every act of consciousness there is a reference of diverse parts to some unity. I cannot be conscious of myself, or of any external object, without referring the various parts of my own thoughts in the one case, or of the object in the other, to some one uniting principle, by which the parts are all conjoined as *my* thought, or *my* perception. This will appear at once, if we consider what would be the result of the diversity without the unity, or *vice versâ*. To take the former case, the mere affection of the senses by phenomena would alone never be able to penetrate to our consciousness. Had we sensation, and nothing else, we could be no more conscious of what was going on either within or without us, than a wall is sensible of the sun that warms it. Supposing, for instance, the eye were directed towards a house, so that rays fell upon the retina from every part of it. This alone would not be sufficient to produce the perception of the image of a house, for there would be no principle uniting the parts into a whole,—there would, in short, be no *ego*, who could say, "I see the door, and windows, and *other* parts constituting one building." If twenty men were each to look at a different part of the same house, so that each saw only a small portion of it, between them all, they might see the whole, and yet not all of them together would obtain an image of the house; simply because all the various parts would not be referred to the same conscious unity. Now the twenty retinas constitute a precisely analogous case to one retina consisting of an infinite number of parts, but without any unity to combine the partial sensations. The whole retina might receive impressions from all the various parts of the object; but the reference to the unity of consciousness is necessary to combine the sensations in the different parts of the retina, before an image of the whole can be obtained; and this reference to a consciousness, separate from sensation, is itself something more than sensation.

Now supposing we superadd to the sensation this first unity, or the unity of the intuition in space, so that the house is not only presented to the sense as complete in all its parts, but also as forming one image. This unity of the phenomena in space certainly brings us one step nearer to an act of conscious perception; but another important element would still be wanting before we could complete it, namely, the unity of consciousness of successive representations in time. Wherever we are, or whatever we are doing, in no two successive instants of time are our senses affected in an exactly similar manner. External phenomena are always passing before us in an uninterrupted succession, like the objects presented in a moving panorama; and although the changes may follow each other with greater or less rapidity, yet the motion never wholly ceases. Now the merely positive affection of the senses by these phenomena, even though united in one intuition in space, would alone never be sufficient to enable us to carry on the slightest intellectual act respecting them. For supposing each momentary object produced its effect, gave place to its successor, and then passed away from our minds as completely as if it had never existed, we could not unite any two of these momentary sensations in any form of conception, as this requires a recollection of the past, as well as a perception of the present. All the phenomena passing before us might be in rapid change and motion, but it could not be perceived by us; as the perception of motion, or indeed of any change whatever, requires the conception of the phenomenon having been in a different state or position in the preceding instant. In order therefore to think, or to refer our sensations to some unity of consciousness, we must possess a faculty of memory, which is only possible by the unity of time, or a faculty of conjoining the different parts of time in one intuition.

But memory alone would not suffice to enable us to refer objects to our consciousness. We could combine the conception of the past sensation with the sensation actually present; but before we can refer them to our unity of consciousness, we must be conscious of this unity as a permanent being, different from the mere changing phenomena, and susceptible of such reference. Without this, the combination of the past and present becomes a mere fortuitous concurrence of phenomena, and could have no reference to a conscious subject at all. Now this conception of a permanent being, and one independent of the actually observed phenomena, includes the conception of a possible reference of phenomena in general to our unity of consciousness in future time also. But this conception of phenomena in general, that neither are nor have been, is only possible by the faculty of imagination, which thus appears to be also necessary to a complete act of consciousness.

The above is a short sketch of that mental act by which the polarity between subject and object is developed, under the form of consciousness when referred to the former, and perception when referred to the latter. I must however remind the reader that the various unities are not independent essences, but merely the understanding when viewed under the different phases of its activity. In the foregoing investigation, I started from the object, and analysed successively the conditions it imposed upon the subject. I shall now, in some measure, reverse the

operation, and endeavour to discover what conditions she subject imposes on the object.

In[1] every act of consciousness we are able to fix ourselves as thinking in a particular time. To do

[1] The argument against idealism contained in the text, is simply a popular exposition of Kant's argument in the second edition of the *Criticism of Pure Reason.* The passage, as completed in a note to the Preface, is as follows:

Proposition.

The mere, but empirically determined, consciousness of my own existence proves the existence of objects in space without me.

Proof.

I am conscious of my existence as determined in time. All time-determination presumes some permanent in the perception. But this permanent cannot be an intuition in me. For all grounds of determination of my existence which can be met with in me are representations, and require as such a permanent distinct from themselves, with reference to which, in respect of the changes in the same, determination can be made; consequently, a permanent with reference to which my existence in the time in which they change can be determined. (The peculiarity of the German construction of the last sentence, makes a strictly verbal translation impossible). Thus is the perception of this permanent only possible through a thing out of me, and not through the mere representation of a thing out of me. Consequently, the determination of my existence in time is only possible through the existence of real things which I perceive out of me. Now the consciousness in time is necessarily connected with the consciousness of the possibility of this time-determination; therefore, it is also necessarily connected with the existence of the things out of me, as the conditions of the time-determination; *i. e.* the consciousness of my own existence is at the same time an immediate consciousness of the existence of other things out of me.

Lehrsatz.

Das blosse, aber empirisch bestimmte, Bewusstseyn meines eigenen Daseyns beweist das Daseyn der Gegenstände im Raum ausser mir.

Beweis.

Ich bin mir meines Daseyns als in der Zeit bestimmt bewusst. Alle Zeitbestimmung setzt etwas Beharrliches in der Wahrnehmung voraus. Dieses Beharrliche aber kann nicht eine Anschauung in mir seyn. Denn alle Bestimmungsgründe meines Daseyns, die in mir angetroffen werden können, sind Vorstellungen, und bedürfen, als solche, selbst ein von ihnen unterschiedenes Beharr-

this we must distinguish a past moment from the present, or our *then* from our *now.* But as pure time is perfectly homogeneous, this is only possible by means of change; for were there absolutely no change, the past moment would be indistinguishable from, and absolutely merge in, the present. Now change requires at least three things, viz. two states, and a permanent subject in which they take place, *e.g.* this paper (the permanent) was white, (the first state,) and is now black, (the second state). But it is no change if I say, there was a sheet of white paper, and now there is a sheet of black, as the two states of white and black are not, in this case, referred to any one thing.

Where then are we to seek the permanent? There is most unquestionably a permanent *in* me, for this is contained in my unity of time. As explained above, I could not unite my representations of different times and their contents, without containing in myself some permanent independent of time, for it would not be *my* present, which is constantly flowing into *my* past, unless I were conscious of a permanent

liches, worauf in Beziehung der Wechsel derselben, mithin mein Daseyn in der Zeit, darin sie wechseln, bestimmt werden könne. Also ist die Wahrnehmung dieses Beharrlichen nur durch ein Ding ausser mir und nicht durch die blosse Vorstellung eines Dinges ausser mir möglich. Folglich ist die Bestimmung meines Daseyns in der Zeit nur durch die Existenz wirklicher Dinge, die ich ausser mir wahrnehme, möglich. Nun ist das Bewusstseyn in der Zeit mit dem Bewusstseyn der Möglichkeit dieser Zeitbestimmung nothwendig verbunden: also ist es auch mit der Existenz der Dinge ausser mir, als Bedingungen der Zeitbestimmung, nothwendig verbunden; d. i. das Bewusstseyn meines eigenen Daseyns ist zugleich ein unmittelbares Bewusstseyn des Daseyns anderer Dinge ausser mir. Kant's *Kritik der reinen Vernunft.* Rosenkranz's Ed. Leipzig. 1838. Supplement XXI. p. 773, completed in note Sup. II. p. 685.

unity combining them both, and constituting my identity.

But is this permanent *in* me sufficient, or must I also assume one *out of* me? Let us first try the idealistic theory, and assume that there is nothing out of me, but that the only permanent is something in me. Now on this supposition, the two states assumed above to distinguish between the past and present, are nothing more than two states of my mind, and the permanent in which they take place, is the mind itself. But when I recall my past state to unite it in one consciousness with my present, it becomes the present also; for just so far as I recall the past, does it become the present. I could not, on this hypothesis, recall the past state with the consciousness that it was a past state, by referring it to a past time, because I could only distinguish this past time by a past state of consciousness, no other objects being given me as a reference for the determination of past time; and just so far as I recall this past state of consciousness, does it become a present one. And here it must be particularly observed, that I do not say that I *cannot* recall a past state of the mind as such, and distinguish it from the present, but merely that I could not do so, if there were nothing else to mark the difference between my *then* and my *now*, beyond these different states of the subject. We see then that if there were no permanent out of me, I could not distinguish my past from my present. But I can do so, and must therefore assume the existence of such a permanent.

The same argument may be put rather differently. I can recall my past state of mind, as a past state, and divested of that full force of present reality which would make it my present state. What I recall, therefore, is only a part of the past state, a recollection of some of the feelings without the consciousness of their present existence. Now, if the only distinguishing mark of the past time were the subjective state of my mind, this partial representation of the past time would not be correct, as it would represent a different state to that intended to be recalled. But if the past time can be determined objectively by some other particulars out of me, and independent of my state of mind, the mere partial representation of my past state, in which the conviction of present reality is wanting, is still sufficient, as the particular past time is definitely determined by a reference to external objects.

Hence we see, that as long as we look for the permanent in our thinking subject alone, the past merges in the present, and becomes indistinguishable from it. Our *then* is lost in our *now*, and we are unable to fix ourselves in time[1].

We are thus reduced to the only remaining alternative, of assuming a permanent out of, and

[1] The idealism of Berkeley admits of another very simple refutation. Berkeley denies of the objects of sense, a certain conception, namely, externality. But to be able to deny a conception of anything we must first have the conception. Now where does he obtain the conception of externality? It must either be an *à priori* conception, or else derived empirically. On the former supposition, that is, if space be a subjective form of intuition, in denying externality, he simply denies this form of intuition of those very objects which we can alone intuitise in this form; which is absurd. If on the other hand the conception of externality be empirical, idealism involves the yet greater absurdity of denying a conception of the very objects from which it has been empirically derived.

Berkeley is generally considered as the earliest English Idealist, but incorrectly. See Appendix (B) on this subject.

independent of, ourselves, and hence arises the necessity of the assumption of an external world.

Having now discussed the nature of the permanent, the next subjects for consideration are the two states, and their relation to this permanent and to each other. Now although we are obliged to assume this permanent, we can only recognise and particularise it by means of its state. In more popular language, though I find myself obliged to assume the existence of an external world in order to distinguish between the events of yesterday and to-day, yet I can only recognise, and distinguish between the particular objects in the world by the phenomena they present to me. This in some measure determines the relation of the phenomena to the *thought* object. The full nature of this relation, however, is a mystery from which we can never hope, while in this world at least, to raise the veil. With regard to their relation to each other, there are two cases for our consideration. Either the second state is not determined by the first, or it is so determined. Let us assume the first hypothesis, and examine the results to which it will lead us. A permanent is given me which is only recognisable by some external phenomenon, or affection which it produces on the senses; but this phenomenon does not determine that which immediately succeeds it. Now upon this hypothesis, that which I hold in my hand, and which this minute seems to be a pen, and to have the qualities of such, may in the next produce the phenomenon of a walking-stick, in the third of a crossbow. But there is no reason why it should present the same phenomenon for as long a period as a single minute, or indeed for any two succeeding instants of time. For after the object in question has represented a pen for one instant, as there is no law to determine its next form, the number of possible phenomena, any one of which it may represent in the succeeding instant, is infinite; and consequently the chances are as infinity to one that it does *not* represent a pen. It must also be observed that not only would the second phenomenon be different, but totally different from the first, as from their independence of each other all continuity is broken off. This infinitely rapid and never-ceasing change would render it impossible to identify the permanent out of me, as *this* pen, or *this* walking-stick; for the absence of all connexion between the phenomena would prevent the possibility of our recognising the same permanent under such different forms. All objects would thus vanish from the world, and nothing be left us but a perfectly unintelligible play of phenomena, utterly destitute of order or arrangement, a mere chaos of sensation, in which nothing could be grasped or fixed, either by intellect or sense.

But directly we lose sight of the permanent, we lose sight with it of the change, which has been shewn to be necessary to enable us to fix ourselves in time. It follows therefore that our last hypothesis is incorrect, and that the second phenomenon or state of the permanent, cannot be independent of the first, but must be determined by it.

In the foregoing example I have developed the *à priori* grounds of our conception of causality, but only in reference to the objects of the external sense. In order however to determine the whole sphere of the conception, we must examine the principle of the argument in its most general form. We shall then find that it admits of a far more extended application than the above, and that it is equally valid of the objects of the internal sense, as also of all those faculties, affections, and desires, which have any objective reference whatever.

Let a, a', a'' &c. represent an object in general, either of a perception of the external or internal sense, or of any natural desire, in successive instants of time.

Let x, x', x'' &c. represent the corresponding faculty or desire in the successive instants respectively.

Let y, y', y'', represent the corresponding perceptions or feelings respectively.

Then $y = ax$, $y' = a'x'$, and so on of the rest; *i. e.* the perception or feeling is the product of the faculty or desire and its respective object.

Now if y is to be susceptible of recognition by the human mind in any form of consciousness, its successive values y, y', y'', &c. must evidently be continuous, as it is only by the continuity that its identity as the same feeling or perception is possible. But if either a' or x' or both of them are absolutely arbitrary and independent of a and x respectively, $a'x'$ or y' assumes a value perfectly independent of ax or y; and thus by the breach in the continuity in the values of y, the cognition of y generally in successive instants is rendered impossible. Hence it follows that a' and x' are determined respectively by a and x.

Should the reader have any difficulty in understanding the problem in its symbolical form, perhaps the following explanation may make it clearer.

Whatever may be the relations in which our consciousness stands towards an object, whether as perception of object or practical instinctive desire of it, they must have a certain duration, for without it there can be no consciousness. The relation of the second moment must therefore be capable of being subsumed under the same conception with the relation of the first moment, in order to be in any way identified with it; and consequently these successive relations, be they perceptions or feelings, must themselves stand in some definite relation to each other. Now if either of the factors in the second relation (either subject or object) be arbitrary, and therefore independent of the corresponding factor in the first, the second relation itself will necessarily be arbitrary also. But it has been shewn that this is not the case, and consequently each factor in the second relation is dependent on and determined by the corresponding factor in the first.

This is the most general statement of the argument. It leads to the conclusion that the same principle extends to every part of our thought and feeling in which there is an objective element. I have already considered it in its application to an external phenomenon, and shall therefore take the next example from an object of the internal sense.

Let us suppose I am thinking of some past scene I have witnessed,—a funeral, for instance, which I see in my imagination slowly winding along towards a country churchyard. Now it is clear that the object must have a certain duration in my mind in order to be recognised in my consciousness. If, however, the thought of the second instant were absolutely independent of the thought of the first, there would be no unity between them, and therefore no possibility of connecting them in any one image. Were my imagination free from all law, the funeral of one instant might be a wedding in the second, nor could I be aware of the change. For a knowledge of the change implies a consciousness of both the thoughts, and consequently a continuation of the image of the first moment into the second. It follows, therefore, that the consciousness of the image through the succeeding instants requires that the second thought should be conditioned by the first; in other words, that the operations of our inward sense should be subject to law. I will take one more example of this principle from another side of our nature, that of our animal desires.

I am conscious of the sensation of hunger. Now the fact of this consciousness proves its continuance through successive instants, exactly as in the former examples. Precisely in the same manner must the sensation in the second instant bear some definite relation to that in the first; for if the continuity were broken, and the nature of the second feeling fortuitous, there would be no points in common between the successive sensations, and therefore no conception under which I could subsume them and call them by the same name of hunger. Now this sensation is the product of a certain natural instinctive impulse, on the one hand, towards a certain object—food, on the other; and if we allow the second state either of the impulse or the object to be arbitrary and independent of the first, their product, or the resulting sensation, will be arbitrary also. But we have seen that it is not, and we are consequently justified in concluding that not only the objects of our perceptions and the faculties perceiving them, but that our animal desires, are also subject to laws of nature, as otherwise they could never become the objects of our consciousness.

Perhaps it may be objected to the above argument, that I have assumed an absolute subjection to law, where a partial one would have been sufficient to establish the identity of the object of the perception or desire. Thus hunger, for instance, may arise in a certain state of the body, and yet not be entirely determined in its degree or in the direction of its desire by absolute laws. To this I would reply, that upon the above hypothesis, the fortuitous element must either pervade the whole desire, in which case it would destroy all law whatever and leave the above argument untouched, or else it must be separable from the element that is subject to law. In the latter case hunger would be divisible into two elements, a, absolutely subject to law, and x, absolutely fortuitous. Now on this supposition, x is open to the reasoning above pursued, for the x of the second moment would be quite independent of, and undetermined by, the x of the first. In this case x and x' could not be brought into any one conception, or made an object of the consciousness, and would therefore be for us the same as nonexisting. Hence it follows that such an x cannot by any possibility form a part of any such desire; and the same reasoning is equally valid of every object of which we can take any cognisance whatever.

The general result of the preceding investigation may be stated as follows: The grounds of the conception of successive causality are to be found in the necessity of a unity in the perceptions or feelings of successive instants, in order that they may be subsumed under one conception, and referred to the same object.

But to return to the consideration of the external world, the question now arises, whether the law, by which each phenomenon determines its successor in time, is sufficient in itself to enable us to take cognisance of external objects. A line of argument precisely analogous to that just employed, and requiring merely the substitution of space for time, will oblige us to answer this question in the negative. For if the phenomenon in one infinitesimal portion of space were absolutely independent of that in the adjoining portion, and the whole external world were thus broken up into an infinite number of independent and incongruous infinitesimal atoms, we could never subsume any number of them under one conception, or combine them in a unity of thought, and should seek in vain for an object among a mere chaos of mathematical points of sensation.

Perhaps it may be urged that the unity of space would alone be sufficient for such a combination. But this unity in itself is a mere empty form of our intuition, and only unites the parts of space until an object in space be given it. Now if we would think of an object in space in general, it can only be as having some qualities, (though we may not determine what,) in other words, as coming under some general conception common to its various parts; for if it had no qualities it would dissolve at once into empty space. But this general conception, under which the parts are to be subsumed, is incompatible with the mutual independence of infinite points of sensation above alluded to, and involves, therefore, a reciprocal determination of such parts among themselves.

It follows at once from these considerations, that the conception of contemporaneous causality is also necessary to our conception of an object in space, and is therefore one of the necessary conditions with which the external world must conform in order to become an object of our consciousness.

Now contemporaneous causality is the reciprocal determination in space of any two phenomena in a particular instant of time. If, therefore, *a* and *b* be two such phenomena, *a* must not only determine *b*, but also the particular time which it occupies, and similarly *b* must determine the particular time occupied by *a*, for otherwise there would be no contemporaneity. It follows from this, that the mere general form of the conception of an object in space, by presuming the reciprocal causality between its parts, presumes moreover the determination of every object in a particular time.

This principle, which is thus established *à priori* on the ground of its necessity to the conception of objects in space in general, leads to very important and extensive results. Let *a*, *b*, *c*, *d*, and *e* represent the partial contemporaneous phenomena of the *whole* universe. Any one of them, *b* for instance, is, by the condition of the conception of an object in space, fixed in time, that is to say, there is something by which its existence in that particular time is determined; and the first question is, by what? We cannot get rid of this question by referring to *b*'s antecedent, or other events in the same series, as the whole series may be pushed forwards or backwards in time without affecting it. We must therefore look for something determining that particular time, and the only possible answer will refer us to some other contemporaneous phenomenon *c*. Thus, *b* is now that *c* is, and in the same manner *c* is now that *b* is, *i. e.*

b fixes the time of c's existence, just as c does that of b. But if we want to fix the time of the collective phenomenon $b+c$, we must refer it to d, and similarly if of $b+c+d$ we must refer it to e, and of $b+c+d+e$ to a. We might therefore have said, in the first instance, that any phenomenon a is fixed in time by the collective phenomena of the rest of the universe, and reciprocally, the phenomena of the rest of the universe by the phenomenon a. But that phenomenon which determines another is its cause. We find therefore that this reciprocal causality extends to all the contemporaneous phenomena of the universe, and that they mutually determine the particular times of each other's existences.

I must here particularly guard the reader against attempting to introduce abstract conceptions of the cause and effect, or imagining that I am speaking of such causality as can be reduced to the form of a law. I am here speaking of the entire phenomenon exactly as it takes place, without regarding any one part of it as more essential than any other. The felling of a tree in New Zealand may not produce any effect on the weather at the Baltic that man will ever be able to perceive, make the object of an observation, or bring under a law. But yet the weather will not present absolutely the same phenomena in all its parts as if the tree had not been felled. Some effect on the electric currents which permeate the world with an incalculable velocity, or on the direction in which gravitation acts, will have caused each drop of rain to fall a billionth of an inch more north or south than it would have done had no such tree been felled.

But perhaps it may be objected that the theory

may be true as a physical fact, but that it cannot be deduced *à priori* as one of the conditions imposed by the laws of thought upon its objects. As I consider this problem to be one of the most abstract of those which I have as yet had to treat, I shall make another endeavour to place the subject in a clearer light, by investigating the principle of reciprocal determination in space, which is really contained in that of time.

The general conception of an object in space has been shewn to involve the conception of its determination in a particular time. But if the particular object *a* is determined in a particular time, it is quite clear that *a* must itself be absolutely determined in other respects, as otherwise we should have nothing more than the determination of the existence of some object or other in the particular time, and not that of *a* in particular. Hence it follows that *a* is also determined in space, and that the conception of an object in space involves not merely the conception of its determination in a particular time, but also in a particular space. Now if I endeavour to determine the particular space occupied by an object *b*, I find that this is only possible by contemplating its position relatively to some other object, *c*, and that there must be some definite distance between their parts, which though perhaps in a state of change, can only be so in conformity with the law of continuity, and is determinable at any particular moment. It is *c* therefore which gives me a starting-point, (in mathematical language, an origin of co-ordinates) from which to determine the particularity in space of *b*. It must be *c* therefore which *actually* determines this particularity in space for *b*, for there is nothing else upon which this determination in a particular space required for b can be based.

If, however, it should be urged that another object d determines b, that e determines $b + d$, and so on, we need only repeat these successive determinations till we have exhausted all the other contemporaneous phenomena of the universe (just as at a former page, when speaking of the reciprocal determination in time), and arrive at last at the conclusion, that $a+b+d+e+$ &c. are determined in space by c, and that c is reciprocally determined by $a+b+d+e+$ &c.

And to bring our deduction to its conclusion, not only does an object a determine another object b in space and time, but also with respect to its nature. Indeed, the latter is virtually included in the former, just as the determination in space follows from that in time. For were it otherwise, a would only determine some object in general in the particular space and time, but not the particular object b; as this particularity, apart from its determinations in space and time, can only be determined by its particular nature.

That the above deduction of universal reciprocal causality should not meet with immediate assent is far from improbable, but I believe the difficulty of its reception will arise entirely from the unconscious substitution of abstract causality for concrete, with which alone we are here concerned. I do not for an instant assert that we can reduce this mutual dependence of contemporaneous phenomena under laws, but simply that its existence is demonstrable.

In the above deduction of the conceptions of substance and causality, the strictly *à priori* character of the argument has been preserved throughout. For although empirical matter has been occasionally introduced by way of illustration, yet has this been only in the same manner as the geometrician represents his problem by a sensible diagram, that is to say, the particular object has only been employed as the representation of an object in general. In each step of the argument we regarded only the nature of an act of consciousness in general, quite independent of all particular objects; and as all phenomena must conform to the laws of such consciousness, (for otherwise we could not be conscious of them) we were able to assume with absolute certainty that no possible phenomena in time or space could affect the correctness of our conclusions.

The general result of the analysis may be stated as follows: An act of consciousness is only possible on the assumption that the objects of such act are subject to the law of causality. No attempt has been made to prove the truth of the law in itself, and I much doubt if such a proof lie within the sphere of the human intellect. Still less are we able to determine *à priori* the particular laws of nature, and thus anticipate the results of experience. But our consciousness has been constructed on such a pattern as to enable us to assert that whatever is not subject to causality can never become its object, or, in other words, to predicate causality of all the objects of possible experience; and as this conclusion is based on the nature of an act of consciousness in general, and is quite independent of all particular phenomena in space and time, it is strictly *à priori*.

We found, in the first place, that we conceive an act of consciousness as taking place in a certain time;

that the particularity of this time can only be determined by the objects in it; that to prevent the absorption of the past in the present, (by the distinction between which, particular times are alone possible,) we must have objects external to our thinking subject; and lastly, that the latter would be absolutely incognisable by a human mind, if there were no law binding their parts in space and time into one whole. All this has been shewn to follow simply from the nature of an act of consciousness in general, and to be quite independent of any repeated observations of particular objects either sensible or intellectual. The deduction is accordingly strictly *à priori, i.e.* independent of all particular experience.

Berkeley, in his Idealism, and Hume, in his theory of causality, committed the same fatal error at the very commencement of their investigations. They first *assumed* conscious thought, and then searched for the grounds of our belief in an external world, and the law of causality. As they looked in the wrong place, the search was unsuccessful, and they consequently denied the existence of its object. Berkeley, the more consistent of the two, accordingly gave up the external world, while Hume endeavoured to explain our instinctive belief in the relation of cause and effect, on the ground, not of reason, but of the mere habit of association. Their error consisted in not seeing that these two conceptions, Substance and Causality, stand at the very portals of our conscious thought, as the conditions under which alone we are allowed to enter. It is not that we think first, and then find reasons for our belief, but in the very first act of thinking we have already accepted these two conceptions as the inexorable conditions under which human thought is alone conceivable. If I may be allowed to illustrate so severe a subject by a simile, I would say that the external world is the landmark by which we determine the position of our consciousness as it floats on the ocean of time. The law of causality, on the other hand, is the strong bond of cohesion between all the parts of the external world, which prevents it from becoming a mere shifting sandbank, for ever evading the mariner's calculations.

The conception of causality appears then to be in so far subjective, as that our knowledge of it is derived from the subject alone. This however does not prevent us from predicating it of objects of possible experience, but only shews that when we do so, it is not by virtue of our knowledge of the objects themselves, but because the subject imposes causality on them as the only condition under which they can become objects for it at all. As then the conception of causality originates in the subject, and is only transferred to other things in consequence of their becoming its objects, it follows that we cannot predicate it where this relation of subject and object never arises, *i. e.* we cannot predicate it of things in themselves.

In the last chapter I analysed the conception of causality itself without regard to its origin, and found that it could only be applied to abstract ideas, and therefore required the assistance of subjective principles of thought upon which such abstractions should be based. This led me to the conclusion, that causality being only applicable through the subject could only be predicated of objects, or such things as stand in a certain relation to the subject. But one thing was still wanting for the solidity of the reasoning, namely, some firm ground for the conception of causality itself. Now to shew why nature has continued, or will continue, her uniform course, is a problem lying entirely beyond the reach of our logical faculties, as it would demand a perfect knowledge of the Almighty's universal plan. We may form hypotheses, and probable ones too, on moral grounds, but we can do no more. To shew however that such regularity in the course of nature is a necessary condition of human thought, lies quite within the reach of our faculties, as it requires nothing more than the contemplation of the faculties themselves. This then is the ground we had to seek; and I have endeavoured to supply it by proving that the conception of causality is so intimately bound up with the very heart-strings of all our conscious thought, that if we assume thought at all, we assume causality with it.

It follows therefore that causality is not only subjective in the form of its application through abstract ideas, but subjective also in its origin, and consequently that it is not predicable of things in themselves, but only of objects of possible experience, that is to say, of such things alone as the subject can represent to itself as objects.

CHAPTER IV.

Liberty a Self-determination of the Subject.

SECT. I.—*Determination of the Spheres of Law and Liberty as the Elements of Human Action.*

IN a former chapter I endeavoured to prove, that the whole question between Necessarians and Libertarians turns upon the relation which the will bears to nature, and I expressed the conflicting opinions on this subject in two propositions, of which the one includes the whole human soul within the limits of causality, while the other excludes from them a part of it. In order to decide between these contradictory formulas, it was necessary to determine the sphere of causality, and I have accordingly attempted in the last two chapters to deduce the conditions of its validity, partly from the nature of the conception itself, and partly from the grounds of our belief in it. I shall now proceed to combine these results, by considering the following question: Does the whole soul answer the conditions of causality?

Now it appears from the foregoing analysis, that the condition which anything must answer in order to come within the sphere of causality, is simply that of its being an object for us. The above question, therefore, resolves itself into the following: Is the whole soul an object for us?

At first we might be inclined to answer, that the soul must be such an object, in as far as we can know anything about it or its existence. Upon reflection, however, we find that there is a certain something in us of which we can never be conscious as an object, as we can never present it to ourselves in any one conception whatever. We are conscious of it, simply as an active unity combining objects, but not itself belonging to them, and the name we give it, is 'the I' or 'the Ego,' in short, the principle of our individual personality.

If I examine all the representations in my mind, whether belonging to the inward or the outward sense, I find no one among them which I can separate from the rest, and place before me as my *ego.* The outward objects surrounding me affect my senses in various ways, but no single affection or any combination of them, is what I mean when I speak of myself. This is equally true of the objects of my imagination, whether they be abstract conceptions or any other possible states of the mind. My thoughts may be wandering over the scenes of the past, conjecturing the contingencies of the future, contemplating external nature, or concentrated on my own being, but I seek in vain for any one conception, which I can place as an object before my mind, and say, Here is *my I;* this object is my individual personality.

But if my ego does not consist of any one of my representations, just as little is it composed of any aggregate of them. The affections of my outward and my inward sense can never be summed up by any process of mental addition into my personality, but on the contrary, are themselves only bound together into one whole by that uniting principle, to which they are all referred as to a common centre, and from which they all derive their life and mutual significance. I am never conscious therefore of this principle as a single object, or as an aggregate of objects, but simply as an incessant activity, always eluding my attempts to envisage it, or give it form in any the most figurative sense of the word, yet ever necessary to those unities of space and time which have been shewn to be the indispensable conditions to any act of consciousness whatever. The only answer then to be given to the above question is, that the whole soul is not an object for us, as it contains a principle which we can never objectivise, and which therefore is not entirely subject to the law of causality.

Let not the reader imagine, that in the above remarks I have thrown the slightest veil of idealism around the central principle, as if I had asserted that there was an activity without an actor. All I have said amounts to this,—that we know nothing of the actor except through his activity, and that neither the one nor the other can ever be made an object, or in any way envisaged either to the outward or the inward sense. For in every act of consciousness there is an activity on the one side (the subject), and a limitation to such activity on the other (the object) ; and the consciousness of the act is generated simultaneously with that of the limitation. But this observation will receive some additional light from the investigation into the relation of the will to the intellect contained in a later chapter.

The foregoing analysis has not only led to the irresistible conclusion, that the soul contains a central principle exempt from the law of conditioned causality, but it has enabled us to predicate this exemption of the very principle to which the universal language and consciousness of mankind assign the attribute of liberty. For if we were to ask any unsophisticated person, who or what it is that had been the agent in his voluntary action, the answer would be, that he had willed it *himself*, and not that his mind or any other faculty had been the originating actor. He might perhaps add, that his reason or his understanding had enabled him to see the policy of the action, but the action itself will always be attributed to the ultimate principle of his personality. Thus, the negative argument for liberty, which is based on the impossibility of predicating conditioned causality of the whole soul, and the positive argument arising from the consciousness of an unconditioned activity, merge in the same fact: the existence of a unity, of which we are conscious as neither sensation, intuition, nor conception, but only as the activity of the subject of consciousness itself[1].

There is however another conclusion to be derived from the same analysis, and one which is a no less important element in the determination of human conduct. The *ego* has been found to be free, because it is not objective. But whatever is objective in us, must according to the conditions of causality fall under its laws. This places all our thoughts and impulses under strict law, in as far as we can give them an objective form, in short, in as far as they possess that species of opacity to our mental vision, or resistance to our faculties generally, by which we recognise any form of existence external to the pure act of the ego.

[1] "The will is the last thing in the soul, and the ultimate resolution of all others." Cudworth's *Letters to his Stepfather, Dr. Stoughton.* See Appendix (B.)

Now here we have two principles occupying between them the whole field of human thought and impulse. On the one hand there is liberty, the seat of which is confined to the subject, or the ego; on the other we have law, reigning over the entire objective side of our spiritual nature. The problem therefore now before us is, to determine with the greatest attainable accuracy, the position of the frontier that separates these two powers, and (if I may be allowed the figure) the international law which regulates their mutual relations.

In the first place, whatever may be the scope of the liberty of the subject, it is not free to decide between action or inaction, for the former is imposed on it as the first condition of its very existence. I may be conscious of some power in the choice of my thoughts, and the actions that result from them, but I am conscious of no such power to annihilate or suspend the operation of the mind entirely. This, therefore, is clearly not the province of liberty.

Secondly, if I must act, and yet enjoy a certain liberty, this can only consist in the determination of the nature of the action.

Now, if we grant the subject considered as will the power of immediate choice between two actions, we must also grant it the power of comprehending the difference between them, and thus make the will an intellectual faculty; for, although we should assign to the understanding the task of determining between the merits of two objects, and say that the intellectual part of the operation having been performed by the understanding, the will had no other function than that of choosing between them, this act of choice is still an impossibility without the intellectual power of distinguishing between the objects of the choice proposed,—in short, without the power of appreciating the results of the understanding, which is itself an intellectual function, and therefore part of the understanding.

The above conclusion will not be in any way affected, if, instead of adopting the usual philosophical language, and speaking of the will and understanding as if they were distinct entities, we regard them—as what, in fact, they really are—*modi operandi* of the same being—the conscious subject; for the question will then assume the form, Do I choose between objects by virtue of an immediate act of my will? To this I must give essentially the same answer as before, and say, that as I cannot take any cognisance of the difference between two objects except by virtue of an act of the understanding, and as an act of choice implies a distinguishing between two objects, I cannot possibly choose by virtue of the will, unless it be an intellectual faculty. It makes no difference, therefore, whether I speak of the functions of my will and understanding, or of the actions which I perform by virtue of these faculties. In both cases the position remains equally incontestable, that choice implies a perception of difference, and that a perception of difference is an intellectual act, and refers to objects. Let us assume, then, for argument's sake, that the will is an intellectual faculty, comprehending the differences between objects, and choosing accordingly. Now, on this supposition two cases arise for our consideration. In the first place, let the will recognise the difference between objects, and employ its conception of such difference merely as a means of identifying its choice in the consciousness, but without being in any way influenced by a feeling of preference. This form of will, if conceivable, is a purely arbitrary will, the *Willkür* of the Germans, and its freedom is the freedom of absolute indifference. By its fundamental conception, that of absolute independence of all motive, it can stand in no relation whatever either to moral responsibility or any other principle. But, as Hegel has observed[1], the conception of the freedom of an arbitrary will contains a contradiction; for just by the will's independence of all motive, does it become dependent on pure chance, and thus lose all its freedom in the very moment that it appears to have attained it in the highest perfection. The freedom of absolute indifference, therefore, is in the first place inconceivable, and if conceivable, would be absolutely devoid of all moral value or significance. Schelling has also said most truly of the same subject, that "if liberty can only be saved with the utter fortuitousness of the actions, it cannot be saved at all[2]."

Secondly, let us suppose that instead of merely recognising the difference between objects intellectually, the will also arranges them under the conception of ends or objects, the attainment of which is desired for the gratification of some sentiment, passion, or other affection of human nature. Now, these ends, in so far as they are objects of the particular passions

[1] In der Willkür ist das enthalten, dass der Inhalt nicht durch die Natur meines Willens bestimmt ist der Meinige zu seyn, sondern durch *Zufälligkeit:* ich bin also ebenso abhängig von diesem Inhalt, und diess ist der Widerspruch der in der Willkür liegt. Hegel's *Philosophie des Rechtes.* In the collected works, Vol. VIII. p. 52.

[2] Wenn Freyheit nicht anders, als mit der gänzlichen Zufälligkeit der Handlungen, zu retten ist, so ist sie überhaupt nicht zu retten. Schelling's *Philosophische Schriften*, p. 464.

or sentiments in question, must, by virtue of the universal condition of the possibility of objects, stand towards them under relations of strict causality, and be absolutely determined. The proof of this proposition has been given at a former page, and is not therefore repeated here. The second hypothesis resolves itself again into two cases; either the objects whose nature, as ends, is absolutely determined, are the sole element determining the choice of the will; or else the will, though partially influenced by such objects (for otherwise they would not be ends at all), possesses an independent power of decision beyond their control. The former alternative is strict Necessarianism, as it concedes to the will no determinants except such as are again themselves strictly determined by causal laws. The second alternative is that adopted by Reid and some other Libertarians, but is merely a liberty of indifference. For if we assume the sum of the motives to the action *A* to be greater than the sum of the motives to the action *B*, and yet that the will, by virtue of its liberty, chooses the latter, it is clear that the act of the will, adding the supplementary energy in favour of *B*, is absolutely arbitrary and unmotived. A liberty, therefore, consisting in a faculty of supplying the deficiency of a weaker motive, can have no more moral significance or value than any other form of a liberty of indifference, as it is absolutely independent of all grounds, and must be purely fortuitous.

It appears from the above considerations that if we place the sole activity of the will in a faculty of comprehending the differences of objects and choosing between them, we either find ourselves in the grasp of a rigid Necessarianism or in the bottomless abyss of a liberty of indifference; but in neither case do we meet with any form of liberty possessing value for reasonable beings, or having the slightest connexion with moral responsibility.

But if the province of liberty does not consist in an immediate choice between objects founded on an intellectual appreciation of their difference, where are we to seek it? One alternative alone remains. We must seek it in a *mediate* choice effected through the self-determination of the subject.

Upon this hypothesis the subject, by virtue of its liberty, has a certain power of determining its own *status* or condition. It does not, however, exercise this power by any act objectivising to itself two possible states, and then choosing between them; for such an hypothesis would simply involve a repetition of the former difficulties, by making the will an intellectual faculty. This will become still clearer from the consideration that an act of choice contains a negative element, and therefore an act of the imagination; for there must be at least two objects, neither of which exists, but of which the one is accepted, the other rejected. In an act of subjective determination, on the other hand, there is but one positive element,—the adoption of the accepted state. Neither is this effected by placing the latter before the mind as a goal to be arrived at, but simply by an impulse from within, which by the first condition of its nature can never be objectivised, and therefore like the ego itself, of which it is the time-moment (*i. e.* of which it mediates the determination in time), can never become a conception. The other possible states are not rejected in it, for they are not objectivised either, and therefore do not come into competition with it.

Now the subject by its power of determining in some measure its own state, is able to change one of the principal elements in every action. Objects which excite one set of feelings and motives in the subject in one state, excite a different one in the subject in another state,—and that, without the least violation of their allegiance to the law of causality. The subject, therefore, while it is quite unable to choose directly with perfect freedom between objects, determines such choice in some measure indirectly by the determination of its own state, upon which the feelings and impulses which the objects excite and which are subjected to the understanding for its contemplation and choice, very materially depend. The principle of the self-determination of the subject, and the nature of the changes it produces, will be considered at a future page.

The result at which we have arrived may be stated as follows. Every action, in as far as it is a pure act of the will, and cannot be objectivised, consists in a modification of the empirical character of the actor through the determination of the subject, and is thus the exponent of the individual personality for the moment in which it takes place;—and up to this point it is free. In so far, however, as it is an object of the senses either external or internal, it follows according to laws of human nature from the character so determined as above, and like the latter, therefore, is the product of law and liberty combined.

But, perhaps, it may be objected to the above theory, that it is inconsistent with the facts of our consciousness, inasmuch as we often present to our minds two objects, and choose between them with as strong a conviction of the freedom of our choice as we ever possess. To this I would reply, that the above remarks concerning the subjectivity of the will are expressly limited to the province of pure liberty alone. Directly I introduce another element, and contemplate the combined results of liberty on the one hand and the laws of human passions and affections on the other, I have left the field of pure liberty and have entered the province of the objective, which belongs to causality. But this does not in any way interfere with my consciousness of the liberty as one of the essential parts of the action.

Suppose, for instance, I present to my mind two actions, and, after deliberately weighing their respective advantages, decide in favour of one of them with a feeling that my decision has been the result of a free choice. Now here we have both liberty and law. The liberty of which I am thus conscious is the result of the subjective determination of my soul, by which I have given it a certain posture, and made certain objective grounds of action exercise a greater or less degree of influence than they would have done had I assumed for it a different posture. But, directly I consider this subjective status as determined (in mathematical language, as a constant instead of a variable), all the rest of the mental operation by which motives are balanced against each other belongs to the objective side of my mind, and falls under the dominion of law. In reality however this subjective status is never a constant, but always dependent on our self-determination, and thus this substratum of liberty is felt to influence the results of our choice, even though such results are objective, and consequently obedient to the laws of human nature.

It will be seen at once from the above explanation, that I do not deny either our power of choosing between objects, or the liberty of the choice. I merely assert that the subjective determination of the subject is logically prior to the object, and that the province of liberty extends to the former alone.

The relation between the pure liberty in the self-determination of the subject, and the objective act in which other elements are involved, presents a striking analogy to the relation between pure intuitions *à priori*, and the mere empirical sensations by means of which alone we are able to give them an objective form. I cannot, for instance, objectivise the conception of a straight line without the aid of sense, but I am not on that account the less conscious of the purely *à priori* rule for its construction, which is supplied by the formal laws of thought. In the same manner I can never present, even to my imagination, any act of pure liberty, inasmuch as the matter of every positive act of freedom is an object of the external or internal sense, and introduces, therefore, an element of law limiting the liberty. But this circumstance by no means interferes with the consciousness of the subject of its own liberty in determining the purely subjective element of the act. In short, just as *à priori* laws of thought are the form, but sensible experience is the matter of our cognition of objects in space, so may we consider liberty as the form, and impulses, desires, or motives, generally, as the matter or objective element in the determinants of human action. In neither case can the form be represented in the consciousness apart from the matter in any concrete example; but in both cases is the form separable from the matter by an act of abstraction.

Perhaps it may be objected to the above theory, that by introducing the uncertain element of liberty in co-operation with the laws of human nature, the latter become absolutely nugatory, upon the same principle which makes it impossible to determine the value of an algebraical expression containing an unknown and ineliminable quantity. It must, however, be remembered that in the case before us the pure will, though a variable and independent of law, is still known to the subject in each individual case, as it is the action of the subject itself. In the laws of nature on the other hand, were there any element not subject to law, its very presence would be unknown, and, therefore, it would be incognisable as well as variable. Let us assume, for instance, an element in nature not subject to law, but exercising on some particular occasion such an influence as to make silver gradually assume the properties of gold. This would render all observations of the metal impossible, as we should not be able to recognise even the identity of the object through these unknown changes. If however we attribute to the subject the power of so far changing its own status, that one set of feelings gradually lose their power and make way for another, this would by no means destroy for us the strict conformity of the feelings to law, as we should be immediately conscious of the inward change which had produced a corresponding change in the mental phenomena.

There is another source of the consciousness of liberty, independent of the individual acts of self-determination by which the subject may change its state on any isolated occasion. Every man has at a particular moment of time a certain character. Let us for an instant neglect the element of liberty, or consider it a constant. This character then, in conformity with the laws of human feelings, will dictate a certain course of conduct. If the latter be evil, the result will be to deprave the character; if good, to raise and ennoble it. The present argument does not require that we should determine the manner or degree in which the character is affected by the actions, but the fact that it is so in some measure will be allowed by all. The character, therefore, at a future moment is found to depend on the preceding actions. Now let us introduce freedom again in the subject. The self-determination of the subject has, in conjunction with the former character, also contributed to determine the actions, and consequently the second state of the character. What, therefore, in the first action was pure subjective liberty, has by its influence on the succeeding action become objectivised, and assumed in the second state the form of character.

Here, then, we find that to the consciousness of liberty at any individual moment, we must also add that arising from the experience of past time, in as far as previous acts of liberty have now become crystallised into character. The constant absorption of the former into the latter thus produces a feeling of liberty in the latter itself, independently of the actual self-determination of the subject on any particular occasion.

I have, hitherto, spoken of the acts of the will, the resulting actions, and their effects on the character as finite quantities succeeding each other in time. In the actual process however they are simultaneous; but if considered as successive, with reference to their logical dependence, they must be reduced to infinitesimals. For the least conceivable thought passing through my mind has a corresponding influence on my character, and thus on one of the conditions which are to determine the thought that succeeds it.

The whole of this subject may, perhaps, be made somewhat clearer by an illustration taken from the conception of motion in space.

When mathematicians have to deal with infinitesimal quantities, they have recourse to the following method. They first take finite quantities bearing the same relations among themselves as the infinitesimals which they wish to investigate, and having discovered some formula expressing the law of their relation quite independently of their magnitude, they make these quantities vanish or $= 0$, and observe the effect on the formula, which in its new state will represent the law for the infinitesimals. I shall adopt a similar process for investigating the relation between the infinitesimal acts of the will, their effects on the character, and the nature of the resulting conduct.

An action may be symbolised generally by motion in space, the difference in the direction of the latter corresponding to a difference in the quality of the former. Now at any particular moment my action is subjected to certain limitations, from the position I occupy in the outward world on the one hand, and, in the inward world, that of my character, on the other. This position may be represented by a point *A*, and the whole of the laws limiting its motion by the plane P, in which A is situated. By virtue of its freedom, my action is able to move from A in any direction in this plane ; by virtue of law, it is unable to move out of it.

I will now suppose a small act of the will (W) to take place, by which it moves to another point A_1 situated in P, the direction AA_1, or, in mathematical language, the angle it forms with the axes of co-ordinates, constituting the moral quality of the act. Let us call this angle θ. Now let a second plane P_1 pass through A_1 slightly inclined to the original plane P, and determined in its position partly by that of P, and partly by θ. To express this mathematically, we should say, the coefficients of the equation to P_1 are functions involving θ, and C, (where C represents the coefficients of the equation to P), which being interpreted, is equivalent to saying, that the second state of the character is determined by the preceding state, and the preceding act conjointly. W now proceeds by a second act of will in the second plane P_1 from A_1 to a fresh point A_2, and with a direction θ_1. A third plane P_2 is then supposed to pass through A_2, similarly determined in position by θ_1 and C_1, or the coefficients of P_1. From A_2, W proceeds in P_2 to A_3 and determines a fourth plane P_3; and the process may be considered as continued to any indefinite length. In this manner, W may advance to any distant point A_n, and will always have been limited in its action during the various parts of its progress by an indefinite number of planes P, P_1, P_2, &c. successively. Let us now suppose the number of planes between the first point A and the last A_n to become infinitely great, and the length of each individual act in each plane to become infinitely small. The result will be a line, every part of which is partly determined by these tangential planes representing law, and partly by the individual angles θ, θ_1, θ_2, &c. representing liberty, each plane, moreover, being partly determined by the preceding act of liberty, inasmuch as the coefficients of its equation are functions of θ, θ_1, &c. Let us also consider the axes of co-ordinates, as representing the ultimate principle of morality, and the laws of the outward world, and the motion of W will supply a complete illustration of the mutual relations of law and liberty, considered as the elements of human conduct.

In the above illustration, I have spoken of the act of the will as its motion from the original point A to the second point A_1. This however involved a slight inaccuracy, inasmuch as AA_1 represents not merely the act of the will, but such act as limited by the plane P, or the laws of character and external nature, and is therefore the symbolisation of that objective act, which is the result of law and liberty combined. No inconvenience arose from my starting at once with the entire objective act, instead of considering the mere subjective determination apart from the province of law; and I adopted this plan in the first sketch of my illustration, in order to give it greater simplicity. If, however, we would exhibit the elements of the action separately, and the nature of their mutual relationship, we must consider what is the proper expression for the pure act of liberty. Now it has appeared in the foregoing analysis, that liberty consists in that act of self-determination by which the subject assumes a new posture. This is evidently equivalent in the illustration to a slight alteration in the position of P, and is expressed by the change from P to P_1. But although this change is the pure act of the will, yet as the latter is restricted in its power of self-determination within certain limits imposed by the last state of the character, C, or the coefficients of the equation to P, will enter the functions of w (the pure act of the will), which supply C_1 or the coefficients of P_1.

The manner in which AA_1 is determined, follows at once from the consideration of the nature of the planes P, and P_1; for by the hypothesis the action must lie somewhere in P, and its direction in this plane must also be determined by the act of the will. The latter, however, consists precisely in the production of a new plane, in which (by the conditions of a plane of character generally) the act must also lie. It follows from this, that the objective act, taking place precisely at the moment of transition from P to P_1, lies in both planes at once, *i.e.* AA_1 is determined by the intersection of the new plane P_1, with the original plane of character P.

The new plane P_1 is of precisely the same general nature as P, and the only difference between them arises from their different relations to a particular act of w. Thus P_1 is the result of liberty when considered with reference to the past act of w, but represents strict law when considered with reference to the act of w that succeeds it. In the same manner P has represented law alone, because it has been considered with reference only to the acts that succeed it. When however we inquire into its origin, we must refer it to a previous act of liberty. In other words, the self-determination of the subject is a free act, but after it has once taken place, the overt action must be in strict conformity with it.

There are two points in which the first and second forms of the illustration differ from each other. The first is the order in which θ and C_1 (the coefficients of P_1) have been made dependent on w. For in the first instance, I wished to give the illustration the greatest attainable simplicity, and therefore omitting all consideration of the manner in which AA_1 is determined by the intersection of the planes P and P_1, hastened at once to the objective act AA_1, and having made θ (or the direction of AA_1) a function of w, afterwards made C_1 a function of θ. In the second form I have restored the natural order and made C_1, or the coefficients of P_1, functions of w, and θ determinable by eliminating between the equations to P and P_1. This difference in the order of the dependence of θ and C_1 on w was unessential. The second point of difference, however, arose from a positive inaccuracy in the first form, as θ the overt act was made a function of w alone, instead of w and C.

In the first form therefore, we had

$$\theta = F(w), \quad \text{and} \quad C_1 = f(\theta, C),$$

and in the second,

$$C_1 = \phi(C, w), \text{ and } \theta = \psi(C, C_1).$$

As the quantity w enters the coefficients of each plane P, P_1, &c. and as it has a fresh and independent value in each equation, it might at first be supposed, that no such continuity between the position of the succeeding planes P, P_1, &c. would be preserved as to allow their successive intersections, representing the line of conduct to produce a curve or other line that should preserve any sort of harmony between its parts. It must however be remembered, that the coefficients of P_1 are determined principally by the coefficients of P, and that each single value of w is infinitesimally small, as compared with the whole coefficient, which is the result of all the values of w through a man's previous life. For the character at any moment is the result of a long course of conduct, and offers a considerable resistance to any single act of self-determination. I may, for instance, slightly raise or deprave my character by the direction of my thoughts during the next five minutes; but still an entire revolution in it cannot be effected quite so speedily, and nearly the same rules which regulate my conduct now, will also be valid for its determination to-morrow.

The mathematical illustration must not for an instant be understood as an attempt to base a theory of human liberty on the conception of space. Such an attempt would be absurd, as man's practical nature and the conception of space stand in no direct relations to each other. But certain intuitions have been employed by way of analogy to give a distinct form to the matter of the argument which has been derived from other sources. The real foundation of the scheme proposed consists partly of the original argument for freedom from the nature of conditioned causality, and partly of the empirical matter introduced as it was required in the course of the analysis, —as, for instance, the position that conduct influences character, and every thought, whether good or evil, affects the starting-point of the thought that succeeds it.

The great advantages, in point of precision and perspicuity presented by the analytical form, are a sufficient reason for its adoption wherever the nature of the argument will permit. It enables the student to include in a single glance all the essential elements of the problem before him, as also their mutual relations, and by securing the absence of all foreign matter to prevent any unnecessary complication.

In the present instance it appeared to be peculiarly in place, as the sole object of the investigation has been to shew the possibility of conceiving such mutual relations of dependence between various functions as should exactly correspond to the actual conditions presented by the conceptions of causality and liberty. I have felt, moreover, the less hesitation in employing it, as the merest elementary knowledge of the first principles of analytical geometry is sufficient for the comprehension of the foregoing illustration.

The argument, divested of its mathematical dress, amounts to this. At any instant of time my action is restricted to certain limits by the laws of nature, (human nature included) ; but within them it has free scope by virtue of its liberty. This latter is exercised in a certain act of self-determination of the subject (upon which, as will appear afterwards, its relation to the principle of moral law depends), and the line of action corresponding to the intersection of the two consecutive subjective states, *i. e.* the possible action which is common to the two immediately successive postures of character, is the result.

Let us take an example. The murderer is in the presence of his victim, but he still entertains some feelings of compunction, and has not yet arrived at that culminating point of depravity which is necessary to the act. The plane limiting his immediate possible action, and determined partly by the external circumstances of his position, and partly by the internal circumstances of his character, is a very bad one; but still the act of murder does not fall within it, and he cannot by a single act of will carry out his devilish conception. The various directions which his act may take in this plane correspond to the variety of thoughts still possible to one standing on his moral level. He may encourage the slight gleam of good feeling on the one side, or raise up visions of gain or gratified revenge, on the other. By an act of self-determination he assumes a second plane of character slightly inferior to the first. The objective act resulting from it must, in the moment of transition, be one of the various possible acts conformable to the first posture of character (*i. e.* it must lie in the first plane); but it is one of the worst of such acts, having been so determined by the vicious direction in which the second more degraded plane of character has intersected it. In other words, the precise thought which alone is common to the prior character and the second assumed state, is the thought which is actually chosen. This second state of character, being more depraved than the first, offers a still worse choice for the second thought. A second self-determination of the character producing a third state still more vicious than the second, also determines the second thought, which is perhaps worse than any that was even possible in the first state. The self-determinations thus continue to succeed each other, each being a function of the will and the previous character[1], and each pair determining, by their intersection, the resulting objective act; and, in the

[1] The self-determination of the subject is a pure act of the will alone, but the self-determination of the *character* is such act in its objective results, arising from the state of the subject and the laws of human nature.

case supposed, each act worse than the last. Finally, the last state but one contains the murder, not perhaps as a point, but subtending a large angle of possible action. The last state follows; the common thought contains the murderous volition, and the fatal act is completed.

An objection may possibly be raised to the foregoing theory, which would be serious if it could be maintained, and therefore requires a short notice. It may perhaps be urged that we are not conscious of infinitesimal changes of character, as the result of infinitesimal acts of self-determination, or that we exercise such acts at all; and consequently that the whole theory is not based on the only solid foundation, the facts of our consciousness. To this I would reply, that the law of continuity is a fundamental law of our conception of time, and that by this law, if we find certain reciprocal relations to exist between two quantities in the smallest changes of which we can become conscious, we assume the absolute reciprocity of these relations; that is, their objective contemporaneousness. To apply this to space, for instance; if I pass my hand through the space of a foot in the period of a second, I am not conscious of its having passed through a million spaces, the millionth of a foot in length in a corresponding million portions of time, each approximately the millionth of a second in duration; but I am not the less sure of the fact. Now, as far as we are able to analyse our consciousness, we are conscious in the first place of a moral freedom by which we can raise or depress our moral tone, and thus affect the moral elevation of our conduct; and in the second place, that the moral elevation of our conduct also acts reciprocally upon our moral tone. The consciousness of moral responsibility in any of its time relations,—such, for instance, as remorse and repentance, includes the former; the experience of every day assures us of the latter. The reciprocity therefore in the relations of action and character *is* a fact of the consciousness, as far as the fineness of our consciousness of our moral changes in time will permit us to carry the analysis; and we are therefore justified in applying the law of continuity, and assuming the absoluteness of such reciprocity, or the objective contemporaneousness of the relations; and this is all that has been assumed in the above exposition.

Here then we have a complete symbolization of the two elements of every action—law and liberty, as also of the resulting action itself. The first plane represents the law; the transition to the second plane, effected by a self-determination of the subject, represents the liberty, and the intersection of these planes represents the action or the direction of the motion in the plane of law, determined by the act of liberty.

In the investigation of this doctrine under its various relations, it is of the utmost importance to observe the distinction between the pure act of the will in the self-determination of the subject and the objective action resulting from this act and the previous character. The latter may frequently be foretold,—the former, never. For the character is the product of all the previous acts of the will and the circumstances in which it has been placed, and is by far the most weighty element in the determination of each particular action. The will, on the other hand, adds that single momentary act of liberty which completes the condition necessary for the absolute determination of such action and its performance. Now the preponderance of character may possibly enable us to foretell approximately what a man's conduct will be under any given circumstances, and frequently with a high degree of probability; but the small completing act of liberty prevents this probability from ever amounting to absolute certainty.

That the pure act of liberty is absolutely incalculable beforehand, is evident from two considerations, which in reality, however, are only different forms of the same principle. In the first place, this act, being a self-determination of the subject, can never be objectivized; and secondly, any anticipation based on a knowledge of character, presumes the validity of experience for such act, and consequently that it is determined by causal law, (upon which alone experience can be grounded,) and is not entirely independent of law, or a free act of the will. But a tolerably correct conjecture respecting a man's future conduct, may nevertheless be deduced from a knowledge of his character, and the grounds of such conjectures will appear from the following considerations.

If we consider a man's possible actions in any given circumstances in the concrete, and regard every infinitesimal difference in the quantity or degree of any of their objective elements as constituting an essential difference, their number is absolutely infinite. But for simplicity's sake, let us introduce a slight degree of generalization, and thus reduce them to some finite number, each unit of which represents a very low species. We will assume then, that my knowledge of a man's character enables me to predict that his possible conduct or plane of character, comprizes the actions designated by A, B, C, &c... X, Y, Z, where A represents the generalization of a_1, a_2, a_3 *ad* ∞, B of b_1, b_2, &c. *ad* ∞, and so on of the rest. But as the generalization has only been carried on to a very small extent, it is conceivable that A, B, and C... X, may again be brought under some more general conception ϕ, which is still sufficiently defined to be considered as a particular line of conduct. The actions possible then in the given circumstances, are reduced to ϕ, Y, and Z; but of these the genus ϕ includes by far the largest proportion of them, and I accordingly predict, that he will probably choose the action ϕ, though I have not the smallest power of calculating the final act of pure will on which the particular action must ultimately depend.

Perhaps it may be objected to this theory, that it reduces all our conjectures respecting men's future actions to a calculation of probabilities. I grant that it does so, but this is necessarily the case with all anticipations of the future which rest on partial knowledge alone, to whatever subject they may refer. If however the objection should be aimed at the nature of the actions themselves rather than of our knowledge of them, which is merely subjective, and it should be urged, that upon the proposed theory of an incalculable element of liberty, man's conduct becomes the sport of a blind and absolute chance, I cannot concede that such objection has any solid foundation. The doctrine of chances and the calculations based on it, do not for an instant presume that the events they relate to, such as the rotation of a teetotum, or the fall of the dice, are not strictly determined by natural laws. It is not the absence, therefore, of a determining cause, but simply our inability to take any cognizance of it, upon which chance is founded, and it may be roughly defined as an empirically determined ignorance. Now in the case of human actions, the chance arises partly from our inability to obtain a perfect knowledge either of the character of the actor, or the laws of human nature on the one hand, or any knowledge whatever of the complementary act of pure freedom on the other; but notwithstanding our ignorance of them, the character and the act are not on that account the less real causes in themselves.

The pure act of the will has been shewn to be incalculable, and must therefore ever remain a question of chance as explained above, namely, when considered with reference to our ignorance. But this by no means makes it fortuitous in itself. For the absolutely fortuitous is that which is absolutely undetermined, without reference as to whether the ground of a determination be found in itself, or in something external to it. Now this pure act of the will is independent of all objective determination, but is not on that account the less determined, as it determines itself.

This will become still more evident, from the consideration that nothing would be gained by supposing the subject to determine its state after the contemplation of some objective motive. Suppose, for instance, the subject were to realise the conceptions of good and evil, and to be induced by the beauty of goodness to determine its own state in conformity with it. The question would then arise, what makes the subject open to the influences of this conception of the good, if not a determination towards the good already present in its own nature? Such an hypothesis therefore only removes the difficulty one step further, and leaves the position quite untouched, that a self-determination of the subject towards good or towards evil, must precede all moral influence from objects whatever. To the man that has no eyes, the sun shines in vain, and only for the man who is already in some degree subjectively determined towards virtue, can a virtuous action have any significance, or indeed a conception of virtue be possible. I do not of course for an instant deny, that we place motives before our mental vision, and that the conception of heroism stimulates to heroic conduct. I only maintain, that the motives do not constitute the lowest stratum in the formation of human character and conduct, but on the contrary, that they themselves rest upon a primary and still lower stratum, the self-determination of the subject.

SECT. II.—*The principle of the Self-determination of the Subject.*

The general conclusions at which we arrived in the preceding chapter may be summed up in the following propositions. Human actions are the combined result of law and liberty. The law extends to so much of the action as by its objective nature comes under the conditions of causality. Pure liberty only enters infinitesimally in each particular action as the momentary self-determination of the subject. The whole influence of the latter, however, in the choice of conduct is very considerable, inasmuch as the purely subjective element of one instant becomes objectivized into character in the next. For not only does character assist in the determination of conduct, but conduct reciprocally contributes to the determination of character.

The above solution of the problem of liberty would be very incomplete if I were to leave it here; for it would establish nothing more than the mere form of liberty in general, without touching upon the nature of the sphere of its exercise. I accordingly proceed to the consideration of this sphere, or, in other words, the principle of the self-determination of the subject.

As we possess a consciousness of liberty, and liberty consists in the self-determination of the subject, we must be conscious of this self-determination, and therefore of the changes in which it consists. Now every such change involves some form of consciousness in which it takes place, and also some standard or fixed point in such form, by its reference to which the change may be determined. Neither the one nor the other can be objective; for if the consciousness could find anything in the changes that was independent of its own original personal unity, they would cease to be self-determinations of the subject, and from their objective nature would fall under the law of causality. This standard, therefore, must be some principle in the subject itself, of the presence of which we can only be conscious in the form of a purely subjective feeling; and this feeling will also be the form of consciousness in which the changes take place. For as the principle is the sole measure of the changes, and is at the same time only cognizable in any way through the feeling, it follows that modifications of the feeling are the only media by which we can be conscious of the changes, and that the form of consciousness in which they take place can be nothing else than the feeling itself.

Again, this principle must be something permanent, for otherwise it would cease to be a principle, and would offer no certain standard of comparison. That it must be a form of the will itself, also follows at once from the fact that it is a standard of the will and can therefore be compared with it, which would be impossible if it could not be embraced in the same form of consciousness,—that of the will in general. The latter conclusion is merely a particular instance of an axiomatic proposition of universal application, namely: That principle, by its relation to which the particular state of a simple form of consciousness is determined, must be itself a particular state of the same form of consciousness either real or imaginary. Position in space, for example, can be only determined by its relation to position in space; and a self-determination of the subject or pure act of the will can only be determined by its relation to another self-determination of the subject or act of the will.

The general result of the above remarks is this. The self-determinations of the subject or individual acts of the will are gauged by a fixed principle of willing in the consciousness which may be called the absolute will. This principle is something permanent, and cannot therefore be any specific act of the will in time, but must be a principle of willing in general, of which we only become conscious by the changes of feeling generated by the changes of the relation of the subject to the principle itself.

Now the absolute will has been shewn to be a permanent principle. The individual will on the other hand is constantly changing its state by successive acts of self-determination in time. But the consciousness of the absolute or of any other will can only be attained through that of the individual will. The consciousness of the absolute will must, therefore, be the consciousness of the individual will divested of its element of change, divested in short of all that is purely personal in the individual will, and not of universal application and validity. But the very centre of all liberty, and thus of all real will, has been shewn to be precisely the ego,—the personal individuality. To attain, therefore, the full consciousness of the absolute will, the individuality of the individual will must not be considered as destroyed, but simply as merged by a free act of its own, identifying itself with the will absolute and universal.

It is hardly possible to develop this subject without employing language calculated to mislead by its objective tone. It must however be remembered that the province of the pure will is entirely subjective, and consequently that the will must not be thought as proposing to itself any other state as an object to be attained. The consciousness of the absolute will is not, therefore, a consciousness of such will in itself as something separate from the individual will, but, on the contrary, is the consciousness which the latter has of its own act when divesting itself of all that tends by its purely egotistical character to prevent it from assuming an absolute and universal form. Hence it follows that when the individual will approaches the absolute will or standard of willing in general, it does so, not as if it were approaching a goal (which would be equivalent to making the will objective), but by its own subjective determination, liberating itself from all impulse of merely egotistical origin, and thus unconsciously resigning itself to the will universal. I employ the expression—impulse of mere egotistical origin, rather than that of mere personal impulse, because the will universal is not in itself opposed to the individual wills, but only supplies the principle by which they may be brought into harmony with themselves and with each other.

Here then we have arrived at that regulative principle which constitutes the standard for the admeasurement of all self-determinations of the subject, and is therefore the centre of the sphere of liberty. When considered as the absolute will, it supplies the foundation of moral law, and the feeling arising from the consciousness of the relation of the individual will towards this principle, is the sentiment expressed by the verb, *I ought.* This feeling is entirely subjective, for whatever foundation philosophers may adopt for their ethical system, they can never explain the simple feeling of *ought* on any objective grounds. Thus, whether we adopt the system of the Utilitarians, and assert the principle of morality to be the greatest good of the greatest number, or whether we assume the will of God to be such principle, the question still remains, in what consists the obligation on the individual to trouble himself about either the one or the other? It is useless to answer such question by appealing to our consciousness of the *duty* of doing all the good we can, or of the *duty* of obeying the Creator of the Universe, as such appeals are simply an acknowledgment of this feeling of *ought,* (the existence of which is not disputed,) but are no explanation whatever of its origin. In all such cases, therefore, the original question, what is the meaning of the word *ought?*

remains unanswered; or at least, every answer is one in form only, but not in matter, as it is simply an appeal through other modes of expression to the very feeling to be defined. Whatever then may be our objective system of morality, there is but one conclusion possible as to the ground of its obligation upon us, namely, that it is a simple, innate and purely subjective feeling, arising from the relation in our consciousness of our own individual will to another, higher, absolute principle of willing in general.

That this is its real nature, is no less evident from experience. When, for instance, a first attempt is made to awaken the moral sentiment in a young child, and he is told that he is not to say that which is not true, what is the suppressed thought which completes the reasoning, and gives it weight to the child's mind? Clearly, the thought that there is some more comprehensive will than his own which has determined that he is to go beyond the requirements of his merely personal feelings in the determination of his conduct, and that this will is for him an absolute rule. This absolute will, or universal principle of willing, though subjective in itself, gives rise to two objective ideas, of which the one is the relation of the individual to the absolute will in its objective result as a system of ethics,—the other the personification of the absolute will in the idea of God. I shall add a few words on each of them.

It has been shewn in the last section that every act of the will in the field of pure liberty is a self-determination of the subject. If we consider it with reference to the objective action, we must define it as a self-determination of the subject to such a state as by the laws of human nature shall lead to such a particular result. This is equally true of the absolute will. A system of ethics therefore is a system of such rules of conduct as follow necessarily from the laws of human nature when the subject has determined itself in conformity with the absolute will, or will universal. At first sight it might seem impossible to arrive at any definite and positive results from such an abstract principle. The case, however, is by no means so hopeless as it appears; for as the will absolute is a universal principle, it can, in its objective development, lead to no rules of conduct which cannot be made universal also. It must, therefore, be a principle of harmony among individual wills, and prescribe such limits to the action of each, as shall prevent its encroaching on the action of the rest. The test thus obtained for the morality of an action is its capability of being made a rule valid for all men without involving any contradiction. This is in substance the same as Kant's fundamental principle of ethics, the Categorical Imperative;—act so, as if the maxim of thy action should become through thy will a *universal law of nature*[1].

I have only touched upon the principle of morality in as far as it stands in immediate connexion with the nature of the self-determination of the subject. The vast field of moral philosophy, in which all the various complicated applications of this principle are systematically investigated, does not come within the limits of this work, and I shall therefore

[1] Handle so, als ob die Maxime deiner Handlung durch deinen Willen zum allgemeinen Naturgesetze werden sollte. Rosenkrantz' Edition of *Kant's Metaphysik der Sitten*, p. 47.

confine myself to two of the simplest examples by way of illustration.

Thou shalt not steal, is a moral law which may be stated thus: *thou shalt not take that for thy own property, which is the property of another.* The contradictory of this proposition would be: *thou mayest take that for thy own property, which is the property of another.* Now make this a rule universal, and we have: *every man may take that for his own which is the property of another.* But this is a contradiction in terms; for it is the very conception of *property,* that the owner stands in a peculiar relation to its subject matter; and what is every man's property is no man's property, as it is *proper* to no man. Hence the contradictory of the commandment contains a simple contradiction directly it is made a rule universal; and the commandment itself is established as one of the principles for the harmony of individual wills.

Thou shalt not tell a lie, as a rule of morality may be expressed generally: *thou shalt not by thy outward act make another to believe thy thought to be other than it is.* The contradictory made universal is: *every man may by his outward act, make another to believe his thought to be other than it is.* Now, this maxim also contains a contradiction, and is self-destructive. It conveys a permission to do that, which is rendered impossible by the permission itself. Absolute and universal indifference to truth, or the entire mutual independence of the thought and symbol, makes the symbol cease to be a symbol, and the conveyance of thought by its means, an impossibility.

It appears from the foregoing deduction, that the expulsion from the individual will of all elements that are incompatible with its universality, is the process by which it approaches and partially appropriates the will universal. When therefore the subject having become conscious of a certain striving after a theoretical harmony, which I have called the absolute will, endeavours to think a real object to this conception, it finds the first condition to be, that it must be a will whose entire operation is in absolute harmony with itself, and therefore universal in its character. Now such a will is at once presented to it in the unconditioned cause of the Universe, the whole and every part of which have been proved to be possible objects for the consciousness only on the condition of their utter subjection to the law of causality. Hence the conception of the First Cause as an actually existing will, is found to agree in form with the theoretical principle of willing in the human consciousness; and the merely subjectively conceived will universal becomes, when objectivised, the Will of the Universe, (that is to say, the Will of which the Universe is the objective manifestation,) and is personified in the idea of God.

Honesty and truth are in the ethical world what the straight line and circle are in space,—the simplest conceptions in their respective forms of consciousness. The deduction of the one, like the construction of the other, is therefore peculiarly easy. But in the same manner as the intuition of space is sufficient for the construction of the most complicated figures, so is the principle of the subjection of the individual to the universal will, objectivised in the test of universality, sufficient for the description of the whole sphere of human duty. The various feelings, impulses, sentiments and aspirations, with which man is endowed, are

11—2

all so many points of contact between his individual will and the absolute will of the Creator; all so many clues for the interpretation of the Universe, and to bring all these diverse elements into harmony with each other by divesting his individual will of its purely egotistical individuality, thus expanding it to the comprehensive grasp of the Universal,—this is the highest end and aim of his being; this is the God-like office of Reason.

The above deduction of moral law may appear to some too cold and logical, too utterly deficient in anything that could appeal to the feelings, or gratify the æsthetic side of human nature, to be accepted as an explanation of the moral sentiment. To this I would reply, that it is not offered as such. A system of ethics is a particular application of logic, but the moral sentiment which makes ethics possible at all, is a purely subjective feeling. This sentiment is the consciousness of the free act of the individual will, raising itself to the elevation of the absolute will and identifying itself with it. Now, cold and logical as may be the deduction of moral duties, when the sentiment is to receive its objective interpretation, the sentiment itself is the grandest conceivable, because it is the most comprehensive, and the most God-like,—because it is God's own thought as far as man can grasp it. And here, I may remark, how truly man's instincts have led him in the choice of words: for in all languages we find the same expression used to signify the logical faculty of drawing conclusions, and that perception of moral fitness which is also similarly derived through the principle of contradiction from the identification of the individual will, with the Will

Universal; and man is said to be not only a reasoning, but a reasonable being.

Not the self-annihilation however of the individual will is the true form of the sentiment, but rather its expansion, till its objective manifestation comprehends ideally the limits of the Universe within its grasp, and each lives for all. Where a morbid self-seeking, with an irony all the more bitter because unconscious, has confounded these two very different things, the result is monachism, asceticism, or, in its most exaggerated form,—fakirism; all of them contradictions, for as far as self be really annihilated, they are the annihilations of nothing. Self-sacrifice is indeed a noble virtue; it is the negative side of virtue in general, as it is the pruning of the individual will of all those purely egotistical elements which interfere with its identification with the will universal. But every sacrifice must be a sacrifice to something; and the will that contents itself with this first step, and makes no attempt at developing a positive energy in carrying out its own small part in the will universal, has sacrificed to nothing, and deserves no other name than that of practical atheism.

The general result of the foregoing analysis may be stated as follows: the principle of the self-determination of the subject is the sentiment of duty arising from an innate consciousness of the affinity of the individual will to the Will Universal. It is that dim reflection of the Divine Will within the innermost depths of the human soul, by which it is enabled to recognise the Divinity in all that surrounds it. It is no direct positive revelation of a personal God, but it is that which makes such revelation possible by enabling it to comprehend the God-like. It is that which makes man the image of God. The sphere of human liberty lies all around this principle, and consists in that power of self-determination by which man with a greater or a less intensity conforms his own nature to the Divine, and merges all purely egotistical impulse in his inner consciousness of an Universal Will. Through liberty alone does he determine the elevation from which he will view the objective world. It is the ladder which joins Earth and Heaven. If we mount it manfully, regarding it in a spirit of faith and hope as a means to scale the heights of true nobility of soul, it will lead to all that is great and God-like. But to those who regard it with indifference or distrust, as the toilsome though necessary condition of existence, who, like cowardly criminals mount it trembling as though it were nothing but a treadmill for grinding through the drudgery of human life,—to such it will realise their fear and prove a treadmill indeed; for though wearied by the burden of its responsibility, they will never rise by it, but rather leave it at the lowest step.

CHAPTER V.

The Objective Element in Human Action.

IN the preceding pages, the province of liberty has been found in the subject, or unity of consciousness,—that of law in the diverse phenomena, physical or mental which are combined by that unity, and thus become its objects. While speaking therefore of human action with reference to liberty, we had only this unity before us, silently progressing through time like a fine thread,—so fine as to be itself invisible, and yet giving its colour to the whole web of our moral being. Directly however we assume the self-determination of the subject as complete,—in short as a constant,—and would consider its entire development in the objective world of law, we have passed from the unity of the subject to the multifarious which it unites, and which supplies the matter for its practical as well as its intellectual activity. Prior therefore to any immediate investigation of the phenomena presented by human conduct, we should be justified in anticipating that it must branch off in various contemporaneous series, springing respectively from various points in our objective nature, but all deriving whatever liberty they may possess from the original dependence of these starting-points on the self-determination of the subject.

That this anticipation is justified by our actual experience, will readily appear from the simplest example. Suppose for instance, I sit down to my desk, and leaning my head upon my hand, commence writing a letter to a friend. Here we have at once three very distinct but contemporaneous exertions of energy. In the first place, there is the muscular exertion of my left hand supporting my head,—in the second, the motion of the fingers of the right hand in writing,—and in the third, the train of thought forming the sentences that are to follow. I have mentioned these as the most self-evident, but in reality there are many others ; for the upright posture of the body is the result of a faint volition, so habitual as to escape observation. That it is one however is evident from the collapse that immediately takes place in sleep. Other examples of contemporaneous volitions will readily suggest themselves; such for instance, as a person conversing while playing on a musical instrument, or walking while engaged in thought.

But however numerous the series of contemporaneous volitions may be, they by no means stand in precisely similar relations to the unity of consciousness, inasmuch as there is always one which takes precedence of the rest, and is regarded as the representative of our practical life for the time being. The particular action or series of actions in question, appears to proceed from the very centre of our consciousness; and the others only cluster round it at a distance greater or less in proportion as they are connected with this central series. In this respect there is a striking analogy between the consciousness of activity in our volitions, and that in the perceptions of our senses, vision more especially. In whatever direction I turn my eyes, and however many objects I may *see*, there is always a certain single point at which I seem to be more particularly *looking.* If, for instance, I direct my eyes towards a book on the table, I see the whole of the object, but there is a particular point of it which appears to be the very centre of my glance. The intensity moreover of the rest of the sensation, varies in proportion to its proximity to this point. Thus I see the rest of the book with considerable vividness, as the object is a small one; but the other parts of the table and the surrounding furniture are presented to me with an intensity of consciousness, as far as the mere sensation is concerned, ever decreasing as the distance of the objects from the central point increases, till at last, toward the circumference of my field of vision the sensation becomes extremely faint, and ultimately dwindles away into utter vacancy.

Now the field of our volitions in relation to the consciousness, is exactly analogous to the field of vision. There is always a certain central point in them which is more immediately affected by the self-determination of the subject, which appears to be the nearest to it, and is pre-eminently *the* act of the time being. The nature of the other volitions becomes more and more mechanical, and the consciousness accompanying them weaker, in proportion to their distance from the central volition, till at last those at the extreme verge hardly appear to be volitions at all. At the same time, precisely in the same manner as by turning the head, we can look directly at an object which a moment before occupied the extremity of the field of vision, and of which therefore we were hardly conscious, so can we also direct the whole force of our consciousness upon a series of volitions, which previously were almost of an automatical character, and thus render them for the moment a part of our central series. Thus the act of breathing is, under ordinary circumstances, a volition extremely distant from the centre of highest consciousness; but if the attention be directed to it,—as for instance, by the request of a physician that the patient should draw a long breath to enable him to detect the presence of disease,—this otherwise almost mechanical act becomes for the moment the principal act of his will.

This change in the direction of our consciousness, does not of course differ from any other volition, and is simply the peculiar course which our action takes when determined by law and liberty in the manner already explained.

As an instance of the various degrees of proximity to the central act, and the corresponding intensity of consciousness, let us consider the nature of the physical volitions of a man walking along the road. In the first place, let him be a mathematician reflecting on some difficult problem. In this case the central series is the train of thought, and the volitions connected with his locomotion, engage so little of his attention, and are so nearly mechanical, that he is hardly conscious of making them. Secondly, let him be a physician walking at a rapid pace to see a patient in a dangerous illness, and at the same time revolving in his mind the treatment he will probably have to adopt. Here the locomotion stands in immediate connexion with the subject of the man's thoughts, inasmuch as he is purposely walking as fast as he can in the hopes of arriving in time to save life. The consciousness of the volition will therefore be more powerful, and the volitions themselves more energetic, in consequence of their proximity to the central volition. Lastly, let the man be walking for a wager.

In this case the locomotion itself becomes for the time the central volition, and the consciousness of the energy exerted in moving the limbs, attains a maximum of intensity.

The above observations will make the distinction between a simple volition and an act of the will, immediately intelligible. All those actions, or series of actions, which spring from impulses or instincts on the utmost verge of the field of consciousness, are still volitions, provided only that they are in any degree, however slight, dependent on the self-determination of the subject. But by an act of the will we generally understand a *central* volition, and one therefore containing the point of highest consciousness. Those slight motions of the limbs, which are often made without any deliberate object and almost unconsciously, are all volitions, but they must engross the attention before they can be raised to the dignity of acts of the will. That the consciousness of liberty should be far stronger in an act of the will than in a mere volition, is self-evident. For it is clear, that the self-determination of the subject must at any given time have the greatest influence within the sphere of those passions and affections, with which the consciousness is at the time in question the most intensely occupied. Consequently, the act of the will, or the central volition, as it contains the point of highest consciousness, must in its objective side have reference to those feelings in which the influence of the self-determination is the greatest, and where therefore the liberty is the most strongly felt. In a mere volition, on the other hand, the element of law very greatly preponderates. And yet the distinction between such a volition and a purely mechanical movement is clear and decided, as will appear at once from the readiness with which we distinguish a merely thoughtless volition moving the fingers backwards and forwards, from a convulsive and purely involuntary twitching of the same members, arising from some slight morbid affection in the nervous system.

The objective form assumed by the various impulses and passions is that of *ends*, and occupies a large field of the imagination. The vividness with which they present themselves to us is extremely different, and depends on their proximity to the central point of highest consciousness. Thus, one end may embrace the central point itself, and constitute the principal object of a life. Another may lie on the utmost verge of our consciousness, and perhaps refer to nothing more important than the attainment of a little more bodily ease by the change in the position of a limb. The representation of the end in the imagination, whatever may be its vividness, is called the *motive*, on account of its being the intellectual embodiment of the power that moves the will to make the corresponding volition.

Now motives are in so far subject to the higher power of liberty, as they are dependent for their relative intensity upon the position that may be assumed by the subject in its self-determination; but this position once assumed, all the other elements that enter into their composition are objective, and consequently, their reciprocal relations as well as their individual intensity are entirely determined by law. That the subjection to causality is the only condition under which anything can become an object for us, has been sufficiently proved at a former page. I will therefore only remind the reader, that this law has been there shewn to be absolute and universal, and to be equally applicable to every object of thought and feeling.

Before quitting this subject, I will anticipate an objection which may perhaps be raised to the foregoing doctrine of freedom. If such an action as a mere thoughtless moving of the fingers backwards and forwards be recognised as free, and if all freedom ultimately resolve itself into a self-determination of the subject relatively to its moral elevation, it is clear that such movement must be regarded as in some degree possessed of moral significance, and yet, how is it possible to attribute any significance to such an apparently indifferent act? To this I would reply, that as we are conscious of the act as a volition, there has been some motive for it, however indistinct, or however remote from the centre of highest consciousness. The action therefore has its grounds in a province, the whole of which is more or less determined by the moral status of the subject. In any particular case, it may appear too curious to attempt to define the particular moral relations of a very trivial act; but as it *is* the motived act of a moral being, such relations must exist. What appears therefore absolutely indifferent, is not so in reality, but the moral element is so small as to render its isolation in a distinct act of consciousness extremely difficult, if not impossible. We meet with a precisely analogous phenomenon in other forms of consciousness, and draw instinctively an analogous conclusion. If I move my finger through the space of an inch, I am as certain that it moves through a million spaces, each a millionth of an inch in length, as if I had a separate consciousness of each of the million acts constituting the whole movement.

CHAPTER VI.

Critical Consideration of the Three Conceptions of Liberty, as propounded in the doctrines of Necessarianism, Arbitrarianism, and the Self-determination of the Subject in a single Transcendental Act.

IN the preceding chapters I have endeavoured to develop such a scheme of liberty as should fulfil the various conditions of the problem, and satisfy the requirements of our moral nature without encroaching on the province of law. I shall now examine, in their general types, certain other solutions which have been offered of the same problem, and shall state briefly the grounds on which I object to each of them.

As all admit the influence of motives, and the existence of a human nature, on the one hand, and, at least in name, of a liberty, on the other, as the determinants of human conduct, the various solutions must turn upon the reciprocal relations of these elements. In the first place, liberty may be a determinant above, or exterior to, the motives. This is the opinion of Reid and the Prospective Reviewer already quoted, and may be called the Arbitrarian view. Secondly, the liberty may be a determinant in the motives, by constituting one of their factors; and this hypothesis again assumes two distinct forms accordingly as the liberty is regarded as a constant or a variable. The former is the doctrine of Kant and Schelling; the latter is the view adopted in the present treatise. To these theories of liberty must be added, *by courtesy*, the *soi-disant* liberty of the Necessarians. I say, *by courtesy*, for whatever weight may attach to their arguments in favour of an absolute necessity, under no conceivable pretext can it be seriously conceded that they assert any liberty whatever. I shall now proceed to consider these views, commencing with the Necessarian Liberty of Collins, Priestley, Edwards, and others.

It has been shewn, at a former page, that human action, after emerging from the field of pure liberty in the self-determination of the subject, and entering upon that of law, branches out in its objective development into numerous contemporaneous series. These originate in various sources of human energy and passions, and are subject to certain laws limiting the spheres of their operation. The laws of human nature, again, both physical and mental, present for our investigation somewhat similar conditions to the laws of external nature; inasmuch as each actual result is for the most part dependent on a combination of influences; and therefore the individual powers engaged, or the range of their exercise, cannot be directly measured by the concrete effect. The fact, for instance, that all the conditions of my conduct do not allow of my throwing myself out of a window, or performing any similar insane act, is no measure of my physical powers. By means of the imagination, however, the various powers may be isolated, and their limits and general character approximately determined. It is then found, as might be expected, that the sphere of imaginary action, limited by a single conditioning element, is far greater than the real action which is limited by all the conditioning elements in conjunction. In other words, the sphere left open to human action by the laws of each individual form of human energy or passion, when taken separately, is far less restricted than that which results when their reciprocal and limiting action on each other is admitted, as in the case of actual experience. Thus, as far as a man's pride alone is concerned, there may be various courses left open to him; and similarly with regard to his benevolence, his intellectual abilities, or his physical strength. But if we consider all these together, as well as all the other conditioning elements of his action, there will be as many conditions as human conduct has dimensions, and the result will be absolutely determined. Hence it follows that the sum of the spheres of human powers taken separately, is considerably greater than the sphere of their sum.

The above observations are sufficient to expose the utterly illusory nature of the liberty which the Necessarians claim as a part of their system. Starting from the position, that the complex of the laws of human nature entirely determines a man's actions (in which, saving the self-determination of the subject, I fully concur), they conclude that all his conduct is absolutely necessary. Up to this point their argument is at least consistent. But now they observe that the physical laws *alone* do not absolutely restrict a man to a particular action,—that he can, for instance, move his hand to the right or the left as he pleases; and this power they call his liberty. Unfortunately however, by their own theory, what he pleases is entirely settled for him by the laws of human motives, and thus their liberty turns out to be nothing more than a product of the imagination conceiving the laws of man's physical motion abstractedly from all the other conditions that determine his actions, and in short entirely neglecting these conditions. In reality therefore Necessarian liberty is an abstraction having no objective existence; for however easily I may isolate in my imagination the laws regulating my physical activity, and find that they leave a certain sphere of action open, there are always numerous other conditions imposed by other parts of my nature which are no less imperious, and no less real than they; and these other conditions, by intersecting the sphere of possible action at a certain point, determine the result without appeal.

It is hardly necessary to observe, that the Necessarians might with no less reason have created a fresh form of liberty, equally valuable, for every set of laws conditioning human actions, by isolating such laws and neglecting all the others.

The following illustration may serve to give an insight into the nature and value of the Necessarian liberty. Three balls, black, white, and red, are offered for choice. The black ball has a hole in it, and the red ball has a notch in it; complete liberty of choice is granted, as far as the colour is concerned, but there are two other little conditions to be observed. First, no ball may be chosen that has a hole in it; secondly, no ball may be chosen that has a notch in it: but as long as I determine to ignore all other considerations but colour, my liberty of choice will appear unrestricted, as there is no law respecting it.

The next theory of liberty for our consideration is that of Arbitrarianism, or the liberty which consists in unmotived, and therefore fortuitous action.

I am well aware that its advocates would hardly subscribe to this description of it; but I shall endeavour to shew that it is nevertheless essentially correct. The form which the controversy respecting it has generally assumed, is the following question: Is the action absolutely determined by the strongest motive? To avoid all ambiguity in its consideration, it will be necessary, in the first place, to call attention to the two senses in which strength may be predicated of a passion or desire. Thus, a passion is said to be strong; first, if it engross a large portion of the consciousness, and be accompanied by excitement and intensity of feeling; secondly, if it exercise a considerable motive power in determining to action. The two forms of strength are frequently found together, but they are by no means identical, or even necessarily combined. Each is strength, for each is a degree of power to produce a certain effect; but in the one case the effect is the intensity of consciousness, in the other it is action; and it is with passions, feelings, and sentiments, as with individuals,—not always that which makes the greatest commotion is the most efficient in producing a practical result. A starving man, surrounded by his hungry family, may be suffering such torment from the pangs of hunger, that the physical sensation may command a far larger share of his consciousness than his paternal affection; and yet the latter sentiment may be the more powerful of the two, when considered as a motive, and perhaps induce him to divide his last loaf among his wife and children without reserving a morsel for himself. Hence the power of a passion to engross the consciousness must not be considered as an unerring measure of its power to produce action. Or to take another example, let us suppose a man of high moral principle, but of strong animal desire, to resist successfully a powerful temptation to illicit indulgence. His whole frame may quiver with the excess of his passion,—his consciousness may almost seem to be engrossed by it, and wherever he turns the forbidden thoughts beset his path to lure him to his fall. But through all the storm and tumult of his feelings there is one fine thread of consciousness, so fine indeed as to be hardly perceptible, but strong as a cable to enable him to hold his ground. Now in such a case it would not surely be correct to say, that the sense of duty was the weaker motive, because it did not display as much violence in its mode of affecting the consciousness as the passion which it resisted? If a hundred pieces of artillery were discharged against a mountain of granite, there would be no lack of noise on the side of the artillery, but great lack of effect.

Now the present question refers to passions or feelings as motives only,—that is to say, with respect to their motive power, and not to their power of engrossing the consciousness and raising its intensity. Its solution therefore must depend upon the manner in which we answer another question, namely, whether there are any immediate determinants of human actions besides motives?

The Necessarians, as also some Libertarians, deny that there are; the former because they do not recognise any liberty in the determination of volition; the latter because they assert the logical priority of the liberty to the motive, in the belief that the man never acts contrary to the motives, but possesses a power of determining, within certain limits, one of the factors of the motives themselves. But whatever may be the grounds on which they form their opinion, those who admit no ultimate determinants but motives can only answer the present question affirmatively, and assert that the strongest motive determines the action. It must however be observed that this proposition is simply one of identity, and enunciates no philosophical principle, for the resulting action is the only absolute test of the relative strength of the motives which we possess. Hence the proposition, both from the Necessarian point of view, as well as that adopted in this treatise, is devoid of all importance.

But although I reject the proposition in the present form as a valueless truism, it springs from an idea which must be regarded as a very important truth,—namely, that the strongest or prevailing motive is determined by laws of human nature. In this proposition I, of course, regard the subject as a constant.

Some Libertarians adopt a contrary opinion, and assert a power of the will to determine the action not through, but extraneously to, the motives, and in opposition to their net result. This is the view entertained by Reid, as will appear from the following passages:—"How insignificant soever," observes Reid, "in moral estimation, the actions may be which are done without any motive, they are of moment in the question concerning moral liberty. For if there ever was any action of this kind, motives are not the sole causes of human actions. And, if we have the power of acting without a motive, that power, joined to a weaker motive, may counterbalance a stronger[1]." Again, "Contrary motives may very properly be compared to advocates pleading the opposite sides of a cause at the bar. It would be very weak reasoning to say, that such an advocate is the most powerful pleader, because sentence was given on his side. The sentence is in the power of the judge, not of the advocate. It is equally weak reasoning, in proof of necessity, to say, such a motive prevailed, therefore it is the strongest; since the defenders of liberty maintain that the determination was made by the man, and not by the motive[2]."

I have quoted the last passage principally for the purpose of introducing the following note on it by Sir William Hamilton:—"But was the *man* determined by no motive to that determination? Was his specific volition to this or to that without a cause? On the supposition that the sum of influences (motives, dispositions, tendencies) to volition *A*, is equal to 12, and the sum of influences to countervolition *B*, equal to 8,—can we conceive that the determination of volition *A* should not be necessary? We can only conceive the volition *B* to be determined, by supposing that the man *creates* (calls from non-existence into existence) a certain supplement of influences. But this creation as actual, or, in itself, is inconceivable; and even to conceive the possibility of this inconceivable act, we must suppose some cause by which the man is determined to exert it. We thus, *in thought*, never escape determination and necessity. It will be observed, that I do not

[1] Reid, *on the Active Powers*, Essay IV. Chap. IV. In Sir W. Hamilton's Ed. p. 610.

[2] *Ibid.* p. 611.

consider this inability to the *notion*, any disproof of the *fact* of Free Will[1]."

This argument appears to me unimpeachable; and even if such a liberty as that supposed by Reid were conceivable, it would be utterly valueless. Let us suppose for instance a man's motives to commit a sin to be equal in strength to 12, and the strength of his moral feeling acting as countermotive to be equal to 8, but that by his will he supplies a force equal to 5, and resists the temptation. In such a case, there is no moral value to be attached to the supplementary 5 of will, for he has had no motive in adding them. If we say that he has added them from his love of virtue, or for any other reason, we have based them on a motive, and we ought to have estimated the strength of the countermotive at 13 in the first instance.

The unsoundness of Reid's comparison of the will and motives to a judge and counsel is self-evident. When a judge pronounces sentence in favour of the side of a weaker advocate, it is because there are motives in his own mind for doing so; whereas to make the simile complete, we must suppose the judge to determine without any motives besides those already figuratively represented by the counsel. Directly we regard the will as sitting in judgment on the various motives, and deciding in favour of the weaker side *because* it is a better one, we are attributing to the will a *motived* activity outside, or beyond the sum total of the motives, which are supposed to have been exhausted in our comparative estimate of their weight and value.

That mankind instinctively presume a motive for every action, is evident at once from an argument

[1] *Ibid.*

which daily experience has made familiar. What possible motive could I have had for such an action? is the question with which the assertion of innocence is frequently corroborated. The argument derives the whole of its weight from the suppressed major premise, that every action has its motive. Its validity, however, as far as the principle is concerned, is always admitted, though not necessarily its particular application; and this fact is at once conclusive as to the first unprejudiced testimony of the consciousness.

But Reid asserts at another place, that many trifling actions are performed without any motive whatever. He has several passages to this effect, but it is sufficient for the present purpose to cite the following:—"I do many trifling actions," says Reid, "every day, in which, upon the most careful reflection, I am conscious of no motive; and to say that I may be influenced by a motive of which I am not conscious, is, in the first place, an arbitrary supposition without any evidence, and then, it is to say, that I may be convinced by an argument which never entered into my thought[1]."

It would appear from the last sentence, that Reid acknowledges nothing as a motive which does not assume the form of an argument appealing to a man's reason; and if he were justified in thus restricting the sense of the word (motive), I should have no hesitation in agreeing with him. But surely there are innumerable little sensations operating as incitements to action, and therefore entitled to the name of motive, which lie on the extreme verge of our consciousness, and with which arguments and conviction

[1] Reid, *on the Active Powers*, Essay IV. Chap. IV. p. 609.

have nothing whatever to do. While engaged in writing, for instance, I frequently rise from the table and take two or three turns up and down the room, without any deliberate motive, but still not without *a* motive—or feeling moving me to the act. The relief arising from the change of position, the refreshment produced by the slight muscular exertion, and other similar causes, have all operated as motives, and certainly require no unmotived and arbitrary act of the will for their explanation.

The author of the article on *Mesmeric Atheism,* already alluded to, entertains a similar opinion on this subject to that of Reid, as will appear from the following passage:—"The question is, 'Whether when two competing principles of action solicit us, and a volition ensues, the Will, being passive, must yield itself to the stronger irrespective of its worth; or, being active, can determine on the worthier irrespective of its strength?' As the impulses and the will are not accessible to perception,—can be neither seen, heard, nor smelt,—but only experienced in feeling, it is difficult to imagine how, but by subjective reflection, their mutual relations can be ascertained. To discredit this evidence, is no less fatal to the case of the Necessarian, than to that of his opponent. If he would prove that the strongest motive prevails, surely he means, the motive that is most strongly *felt;* and in what way, if not by feeling, is this to be recognised? Declare the feeling delusive, and what measure is there of the relative strength of a number of impulses? You can only appeal to the resulting action, and regard it as a practical indication that the impulse with which it accords was strongest: and so you fall into the vulgar fallacy, of assigning the motive's force as cause of the action, and then pleading the action in proof of the force[1]."

This passage appears to me to contain two fallacies. The Necessarian or Libertarian who asserts the certain victory of the strongest motive, does not understand by it "the motive that is most strongly felt," but the motive that most strongly acts. As I have already pointed out, we may understand by the strength of a passion or a principle, either the measure of its power of engrossing the consciousness and increasing its intensity, or the measure of its power of determining to action; but the strength of a *motive*, which is a passion or principle considered as moving power, can never be anything else than its power of moving, or be measured by anything else than the result. This does not throw any discredit on the evidence of our feeling; for the motive which is most strongly felt, is allowed to be the most strong, not indeed as a motive, but in the particular respect of making itself felt. Strength is only a relative term, as that which is strong to effect one thing is weak to effect another; and in the present instance it appears to me, that the writer has confounded two sorts of strength referring to different objects.

But then, says the Reviewer, if you appeal to the resulting action and regard it as a practical indication that the impulse with which it accords was strongest, you fall into the vulgar fallacy of assigning the motive's force as cause of the action, and then pleading the action in proof of the force. To this I would reply, that such a procedure may make the proposition in question one of identity, in short a truism, but not a fallacy. It would surely be no fallacy to

[1] *Prospective Review*, May, 1851, p. 243.

say, that the greater weight will bring down the scale, and that the bringing down the scale is a proof that it is the greater weight; and yet this proposition is precisely analogous to the case objected to by the Reviewer. In short, the Reviewer appears to confound a proposition of identity with an argument in a circle; but the latter only arises where one of the premises of an argument is pròved by means of the conclusion. If I say that all A is B and all B is A, I have a proposition of identity, but no circle. But if I would establish that a certain C is A because it is B, and then prove the premise that C is B, by means of the conclusion that it is A, I have a circle. Thus there is no fallacy in arguing, that a certain motive must be the strongest, because it has determined the action, and in adding that it has determined the action because it is the strongest. But if I proceed to base my knowledge of the *fact* of its having determined the action on the ground that it is the strongest, I reason in a circle.

In the above observations I must not be understood to deny that there may be certain laws determining the particular motive which is to prove the strongest in respect of other relations. I merely assert that the result is the only absolute criterion by which we can recognise it. Just in the same way as the weight of a body is supposed to be proportional to its density multiplied by its volume; but the only absolute criterion of its weight is the effect it produces on the balance.

It is not very improbable that an objection may be taken to the scheme of liberty advocated in the preceding sections, on the ground of the very argument I have employed against the liberty of indifference, or action absolutely unmotived. I have endeavoured to shew, that a liberty which consists in an unmotived supplementary act, giving a weaker motive the preponderance over a stronger one, if conceivable, would be absolutely worthless, and would have no relation to moral responsibility for the very reason of its being unmotived; and yet I have maintained that the very essence of liberty consists in an unmotived self-determination of the subject. Now on what grounds, will it be asked, can I claim a moral value for the unmotived subjective self-determination, which I deny to an unmotived objective volition?

To answer this question, it will be necessary to recur for an instant to the nature of a motive. Every motive contains two factors, a principle or passion making a certain end desirable, and the anticipation of such end in the imagination, as the result of a certain act. The anticipation may be accompanied with very various degrees of intensity of consciousness, in some cases it may rise to a clear and distinct intellectual conception, in others it may be little more than a dim instinctive feeling; but be this as it may, it serves for the moment as the ground for the determination of the volition. In every action therefore based on a motive, there are two distinct elements,—the volition as the means, and the anticipation of the end lying before it at a distance greater or less according to the circumstances. This anticipation, or the looking forward through the intervening time, is the reason that an action considered in relation to its motive is said to be not performed blindly. Now if we would get rid of the motive, as Reid and some others have done, by denying its existence entirely[1], the action becomes not only blind, but also an absolutely fortuitous occurrence, without either end for the man or reason in the Universe,—a mere inexplicable nonentity, having no relation to moral responsibility or any other principle that could make the liberty of performing it desirable. But let us suppose the motive to be got rid of, not by the supposition of the absolute non-existence of a reason for the act, but by the identification of the act and its own reason, thus making the distance between them to vanish, and with it the anticipation, and the relation of means to an end, which are essential elements in a motive. In this case the act ceases to be motived, inasmuch as there is no anticipation of an end which has served as a rule for its determination. The end, which in the case of the motived action was contemplated in the consciousness, proceeds here *pari passu* with the act, and is not only simultaneous but absolutely identical with it.

Now this is the nature of the self-determination of the subject. It is a purely positive act, placing the will of the individual in obedience to the will universal with a certain degree of intensity; not however from any foreseen reason, but simply for the sake of the act itself. The relation of means and end which is essential to the conception of a motive, is here entirely abrogated by their merging in each other. In the case of any motived action, the man performs it because it is the means to some end, and there is an interval between them. But the unmotived

[1] This of course refers to the supplementary act of will or manifestation of energy, giving the victory to the weaker motive; and this act is, by the hypothesis, unmotived.

self-determination is its own act and end in one, and the man takes up his own moral stand, because that is precisely the moral stand which he does take up, and the act itself is its own explanation. Other acts are lifeless things in themselves, and derive all their value and significance from the motives of their performance. But the self-determination of the subject is no dead fact, first deriving life and meaning from without, but on the contrary, is, in itself and throughout its whole essence, its own motive; for in whatever degree a man is morally *good*, he is so for the sake of the goodness *itself*, and not with any ulterior object. If therefore we were to ask the question, why are you thus self-determined? which would be equivalent to saying, why are you in this degree good? the only possible answer would be, because I *am* thus self-determined, *i. e.* my act of self-determination is not fortuitous or groundless, but it has no motive, because its ground lies within, and not out of itself. In a complete objective act of duty, one therefore involving law as well as liberty, the outward act is motived by its goodness, which corresponds to the moral elevation of him who performs it. But the whole act within the sphere of pure liberty is limited to the determination of the will to be good in such and such a degree; and here this degree, which at the same time constitutes the action, is the sole motive.

This may perhaps become clearer if we consider that the ultimate inner kernel of a man's moral being *must* be independent of motives. For supposing we were to say that the conceptions of the Deity or the Universe, or any other form of religious or moral influence, induced him to take up his stand on the particular moral elevation which he may have obtained, we are still obliged to confess that such influences are not dependent for their power on objective elements exclusively, but that they presume a certain subjective capacity for their reception. Allow therefore to motives as large a field as you will, you must still concede ultimately a certain degree of moral susceptibility, which is entirely unmotived. Now all that is asserted in the present scheme is this: that this ultimate, unmotived, moral elevation in the subject is within certain limits determined by the subject itself, and is thus the true field of pure liberty.

To say that we cannot form a conception of this act of self-determination is no argument against it, but on the contrary a necessary result of its nature. In order to be conceived, it would have to contain some objective element, whereas by the very hypothesis it is purely subjective. But although we cannot conceive it, or place it before us in any form of objective representation, we can be perfectly conscious of its existence, as we are ourselves acting in it, and feel its reality every moment of our lives.

The scheme of liberty advocated in the foregoing pages has so much in common with the doctrine of Kant on the same subject, that it may perhaps at the first glance be considered as identical with it in principle. This opinion however would be very incorrect, as the foregoing scheme is directly opposed to the Kantian doctrine in one of its most important positions. The following extracts from the *Criticism of Pure Reason,* will shew the numerous points in which I have followed the great German Philosopher, as well as the one point on which I have ventured to differ from him.

Possibility of Causality through Liberty, in Conjunction with the General Law of the Necessity of Nature.

"In an object of the senses I name that *Intelligible*, which itself is not phenomenon. If therefore

[1] The passage in the original is as follows:

Möglichkeit der Causalität durch Freyheit, *in vereinigung mit dem allgemeinen Gesetze der* Naturnothwendigkeit.

Ich nenne dasjenige an einem Gegenstande der Sinne, was selbst nicht Erscheinung ist, *intelligibel.* Wenn demnach dasjenige, was in der Sinnenwelt als Erscheinung angesehen werden muss, an sich selbst auch ein Vermögen hat, welches kein Gegenstand der sinnlichen Anschauung ist, wodurch es aber doch die Ursache von Erscheinungen seyn kann, so kann man die—*Causalität* dieses Wesens auf zwei Seiten betrachten, als *intelligibel* nach ihrer *Handlung*, als eines Dinges an sich selbst, und als *sensibel*, nach den *Wirkungen* derselben als einer Erscheinung in der Sinnenwelt. Wir würden uns demnach von dem Vermögen eines solchen Subjects einen empirischen, ingleichen auch einen intellectuellen Begriff seiner Causalität machen, welche bei einer und derselben Wirkung zusammen statt finden. Eine solche doppelte Seite, das Vermögen eines Gegenstandes der Sinne sich zu denken, widerspricht keinem von den Begriffen, die wir uns von Erscheinungen und von einer möglichen Erfahrung zu machen haben. Denn da diesen, weil sie an sich keine Dinge sind, ein transcendentaler Gegenstand zum Grunde liegen muss, der sie als blosse Vorstellungen bestimmt, so hindert nichts, dass wir diesem transcendentalen Gegenstande, ausser der Eigenschaft, dadurch er erscheint, auch eine *Causalität* beilegen sollten, die nicht Erscheinung ist, obgleich ihre Wirkung dennoch in der Erscheinung angetroffen wird. Es muss aber eine jede wirkende Ursache einen *Charakter* haben, *d. i.* ein Gesetz ihrer Causalität, ohne welches sie gar nicht Ursache seyn würde. Und da würden wir an einem Subjecte der Sinnenwelt erstlich einen *empirischen Charakter* haben, wodurch seine Handlungen, als Erscheinungen, durch und durch mit anderen Erscheinungen nach beständigen Naturgestzen im Zusammenhange ständen, und von ihnen, als ihren Bedingungen, abgeleitet werden könnten, und also, mit diesen in Verbindung, Glieder einer einzigen Reihe der Naturordnung ausmachten. Zweitens würde man ihm noch einen *intelligibeln Charakter* einraümen müssen, dadurch es zwar die Ursache jener Handlungen als Erscheinungen ist, der aber selbst unter keinen Bedingungen der Sinnlichkeit steht und selbst nicht Erscheinung ist. Man könnte auch den ersteren den Charakter eines solchen Dinges in der Erscheinung, den zweiten den Charakter des Dinges an sich selbst nennen.

Dieses handelnde Subject würde nun, nach seinem intelligibeln Charakter, unter keinen Zeitbestimmungen stehen, denn die Zeit ist nur die Bedingung der Erscheinungen, nicht aber der Dinge an

that which in the sensible world must be regarded as phenomenon, have in itself also a faculty which is no object of sensible intuition, but by means of which it

sich selbst. In ihm würde keine *Handlung entstehen*, oder *vergehen*, mithin würde es auch nicht dem Gesetze aller Zeitbestimmung, alles Veränderlichen, unterworfen seyn, dass Alles, was *geschieht*, in den Erscheinungen (des vorigen Zustandes) seine Ursache antreffe. Mit einem Worte, die Causalität desselben, so ferne sie intellectuel ist, stände gar nicht in der Reihe empirischer Bedingungen, welche die Begebenheit in der Sinnenwelt nothwendig machen. Dieser intelligible Charakter könnte zwar niemals unmittelbar gekannt werden, weil wir nichts wahrnehmen können, als so ferne es erscheint, aber er würde doch dem empirischen Charakter gemäss gedacht werden müssen, so wie wir überhaupt einen transscendentalen Gegenstand den Erscheinungen in Gedanken zum Grunde legen müssen, ob wir zwar von ihm, was er an sich selbst sey, nichts wissen.

Nach seinem empirischen Charakter würde also dieses Subject, als Erscheinung, allen Gesetzen der Bestimmung, nach der Causalverbindung, unterworfen seyn, und es wäre so ferne nichts, als ein Theil der Sinnenwelt, dessen Wirkungen, so wie jede andere Erscheinung, aus der Natur unausbleiblich abflössen. So wie aüssere Erscheinungen in dasselbe einflössen, wie sein empirischer Charakter, *d. i.* das Gesetz seiner Causalität, durch Erfahrung erkannt wäre, müssten sich alle seine Handlungen nach Naturgesetzen erklären lassen, und alle Requisite zu einer vollkommenen und nothwendigen Bestimmung derselben müssten in einer möglichen Erfahrung angetroffen werden.

Nach dem intelligibelen Charakter desselben aber (ob wir zwar davon nichts als blos den allgemeinen Begriff desselben haben können) würde dasselbe Subject dennoch von allem Einflusse der Sinnlichkeit und Bestimmung durch Erscheinungen frei gesprochen werden müssen, und, da in ihm so ferne es *Noumenon* ist, nichts geschieht, keine Veränderung, welche dynamische Zeitbestimmung erheischt, mithin keine Verknüpfung mit Erscheinungen als Ursachen angetroffen wird, so würde dieses thätige Wesen, so ferne in seinen Handlungen von aller Naturnothwendigkeit, als die lediglich in der Sinnenwelt angetroffen wird, unabhängig und frei seyn. Man würde von ihm ganz richtig sagen, dass es seine Wirkungen in der Sinnenwelt *von selbst* anfange, ohne dass die Handlung *in ihm* selbst anfängt, und dieses würde gültig seyn, ohne dass die Wirkungen in der Sinnenwelt darum von selbst anfangen dürfen, weil sie in derselben jederzeit durch empirische Bedingungen in der vorigen Zeit, aber doch nur vermittelst des empirischen Charakters (der bloss die Erscheinung des intelligibelen ist), vorher bestimmt, und nur als eine Fortsetzung der Reihe der Natursachen möglich sind. So würde denn Freiheit und Natur, jedes in

may be the cause of phenomena, we may consider the causality of this being in two respects, as intelligible as to its action, as that of a thing in itself, and as sensible as to the *effects* thereof, as a phenomenon in the sensible world. We should then make, with respect to the faculty of such an object, both an empirical and at the same time an intellectual conception of its causality, which take place together in one and the same effect. Such a double way of thinking to oneself the faculty of an object of the senses, contradicts none of the conceptions that we have to make to ourselves of phenomena and of a possible experience. For, as these, since they are no things in themselves, must have for their foundation a transcendental object which determines them as mere representations, nothing prevents our also attributing to this transcendental object, independently of the property whereby it appears, a causality which is not phenomenon, although its *effect* is found in the phenomenon. But every effective cause must have a *character*, that is, a law of its causality, without which it would not be a cause at all. And then we should have in a subject of the sensible world: first, an *empirical character*, whereby its actions as phenomena would stand throughout in a relation of dependence with other phenomena according to constant laws of nature, and could be deduced from them as their conditions, and therefore in connexion with them would form members of a single series of the order of nature.

seiner vollständigen Bedeutung, bei eben denselben Handlungen, nachdem man sie mit ihrer intelligibelen oder sensibelen Ursache vergleicht, zugleich und ohne allen Widerstreit angetroffen werden. Kant's *Kritik der reinen Vernunft, herausgegeben von Karl Rosenkranz.* Leipzig, 1838, p. 422. In the text I have adopted Harwood's translation with a few alterations.

Secondly, we should be obliged to accord to it an *intelligible character*, by means of which it is certainly the cause of such actions as phenomena, but which is neither itself phenomenon, nor subject to conditions of sensibility. We might also term the first the character of such a thing in the phenomenon, the second, the character of the thing in itself.

"Now this acting subject would, according to its intelligible character, stand under no conditions of time, as time is only the condition of phenomena, but not of things in themselves. No *action* would *arise* or *vanish* in it, and consequently it would not be subjected to the law of all determination in time,—of all that is changeable,—that everything which happens, meets with its cause in the phenomena (of the preceding state). In a word, the causality of the same, in as far as it is intellectual, does not stand at all in the series of empirical conditions, which render the event in the sensible world necessary. This intelligible character could, in fact, never be known immediately, because we can perceive nothing, except in as far as it appears, but it must nevertheless be thought conformably to the empirical character, in the same way as we must in general lay in idea a transcendental object at the foundation of phenomena, although we know nothing of what such object may be in itself.

"According to its empirical character therefore, this subject as phenomenon would be subjected to all the laws of determination in the causal connexion, and in so far would be nothing but a part of the sensible world, the effects of which, like every other phenomenon, inevitably flowed from nature. As external phenomena influence this subject,—inasmuch

as its empirical character,—that is,—the law of its causality was cognised by experience—all its actions must be explicable according to natural laws, and all the requisites for a perfect and necessary determination of them must be found in a possible experience.

"But this subject according to its intelligible character (although we can have nothing but the general conception of it) must still be declared free from all influence of sensibility and determination through phenomena; and as nothing *happens*, nor any change takes place, in it, in so far as it is *noumenon*, (for that requires dynamical determination of time,) consequently, as no connexion is found in it with phenomena as causes, this active being would in so far be free and independent of all natural necessity in its actions, as this is met with only in the sensible world. We should say very properly of it (the subject), that it begins its effects in the sensible world *of* itself; without the action beginning *in* itself; and this would be valid, without the effects in the sensible world needing on this account to begin of themselves, since they are always previously determined therein, by means of empirical conditions in the previous time, (but still only by means of the empirical character, which is simply the phenomenon of the intelligible,) and are only possible as a continuation of the series of natural causes. Thus then Liberty and Nature, each in its complete signification, are found in the self-same actions, co-existently and without any contradiction, accordingly as we consider them in relation to their intelligible or sensible cause."

The reader will perceive from this passage, that though I have not employed exactly the same language as Kant, I have followed him pretty closely in

three very important points. I have endeavoured to prove, first, that the whole objective side of thought and action, all in short that Kant calls phenomenon, empirical character, empirical conditions, &c. is subject to the law of causality, and does not therefore constitute the field of liberty; secondly, that the seat of pure liberty is to be found in the subject; thirdly, that the self-determination of the subject is a mediate cause in the choice of actions by its influence on the character. But there is another principle contained in the Kantian solution of the problem, which appears to me to run directly counter to our moral consciousness, and to which therefore I cannot subscribe. It is to be found in the following passages, the first two of which occur in the extract already quoted. "No action would *arise* or *vanish* in it, and consequently it would not be subjected to the law of all determination in time, &c." And again, speaking of the intelligible character, "And as nothing *happens*, nor any change takes place in it, in so far as it is *noumenon*, (for that requires dynamical determination of time,)" &c. Again[1], "Pure reason, as a mere intelligible faculty,

[1] Die reine Vernunft, als ein blos intelligibeles Vermögen, ist der Zeitform, und mithin auch den Bedingungen der Zeitfolge, nicht unterworfen. Die Causalität der Vernunft im intelligibelen Charakter *entsteht nicht*, oder hebt nicht etwas zu einer gewissen Zeit an, um eine Wirkung hervorzubringen. Denn sonst würde sie selbst dem Naturgesetz der Erscheinungen, so ferne es Causalreihen der Zeit nach bestimmt, unterworfen seyn, und die Causalität wäre alsdann Natur und nicht Freiheit. Kant's *Kritik der reinen Vernunft*, p. 432.

Die Bedingung, die in der Vernunft liegt, ist nicht sinnlich, und fängt also selbst nicht an. * * *

Aber von der Vernunft kann man nicht sagen, dass vor demjenigen Zustande, darin sie die Willkühr bestimmt, ein anderer vorhergehe, darin dieser Zustand selbst bestimmt wird. Denn da Vernunft selbst keine Erscheinung und gar keinen Bedingungen der Sinnlichkeit unterworfen ist, so findet in ihr,

is not subjected to the form of time, and consequently not to the conditions of the succession of time. The causality of reason does not *originate* in the intelligible character, or does not, as it were, begin at a certain time, in order to produce an effect. For otherwise it would be itself subjected to the law of nature of phenomena, in so far as this determines the series of causes according to time, and causality would then be nature, and not liberty. * * *

"The condition which lies in the reason is not sensible, and therefore does not begin. * * *

"But we cannot say of reason, that before that state wherein it determines the will, another precedes wherein this state itself is determined. For as reason itself is no phenomenon, and is not subjected to any conditions of sensibility, no succession of time thus takes place therein, even in respect of its causality; and the dynamical law of nature therefore, which determines the succession according to rules, cannot be applied to it.

"Reason is consequently the permanent condition of all arbitrary actions under which man appears. Each of these is previously determined in the

selbst in Betreff ihrer Causalität keine Zeitfolge statt, und auf sie kann also das dynamische Gesetz der Natur, was die Zeitfolge nach Regeln bestimmt, nicht angewandt werden.

Die Vernunft ist also die beharrliche Bedingung aller willkührlichen Handlungen unter denen der Mensch erscheint. Jede derselben ist im empirischen Charakter des Menschen vorher bestimmt, ehe noch als sie geschieht. In Ansehung des intelligibelen Charakters, wovon jener nur das sinnliche Schema ist, gilt kein *Vorher* oder *Nachher*, und jede Handlung, unangesehen des Zeitverhältnisses, darin sie mit anderen Erscheinungen steht, ist die unmittelbare Wirkung des intelligibelen Charakters der reinen Vernunft, welche mithin frei handelt, ohne in der Kette der Naturursachen durch aüssere oder innere, aber der Zeit nach vorhergehende Gründe, dynamisch bestimmt zu seyn. Kant's *Kritik der reinen Vernunft*, p. 433.

empirical character of man, even before it happens. In respect of the intelligible character of which the other is only the sensible schema, neither is any *before* nor *after* valid, and every action, irrespective of the relation of time wherein it stands with other phenomena, is the immediate effect of the intelligible character of pure reason, which therefore acts freely, without being dynamically determined in the chain of natural causes, by means of external or internal, but according to time, preceding grounds."

Now if Kant had merely intended to deny the dependence of the intelligible character (corresponding to the self-determination of the subject in the present scheme) on any causal series of phenomena, I should have had nothing to object. Indeed, in the deduction of the preceding scheme, I have particularly insisted on the self-determination of the subject being entirely independent of all objective and empirical conditions. But when he says that no change can take place in the intelligible character, he reduces the whole of human conduct within the province of liberty to a single action, and makes the multifarious in the conduct of each individual to depend exclusively on the multifarious in its objective conditions as they successively arise in time. Now I must object to this position on two grounds. In the first place, the law of causality applies only to series in time, in so far as they are objects of our internal or external sense, but not in so far as they are purely subjective, and merely known to the consciousness as its own acts. This has been proved in the section On the Grounds of our Conception of Causality. In the second place, although liberty would be saved on the Kantian hypothesis, it would be hardly worth the saving on such terms, as many phases of the moral sentiment would be based on an illusion. What, for instance, would become of remorse, repentance, or good resolutions? Unless these ideas are absolutely false and nugatory, man possesses not only a faculty by which he can produce a change of conduct, but this change takes place in precisely that element of his activity which is the seat of his liberty and the ground of his moral responsibility,—in short, in the intelligible character.

There is also another idea, namely, that of consistency of conduct, which, on the Kantian hypothesis, becomes equally illusory. For where a single free act determines the whole subjective side of human action, and a diversity of empirical conditions in time simply elicits a diversity of manifestations in accordance with absolute law, how is inconsistency possible? Every man's life, from his cradle to his grave, must be rigidly and absolutely consistent; and the impossibility of its opposite would deprive the conception of consistency of all its significance and value.

Schelling has enunciated a theory of liberty which appears to me to coincide in great measure with that of Kant, and therefore to be open to the same objections; but in the point in question he has expressed it with greater definiteness, especially in the concluding sentence of the following extract[1]:

[1] Das intelligible Wesen kann daher, so gewiss es schlechthin frey und absolut handelt, so gewiss nur seiner eignen innern Natur gemäss handeln, oder die Handlung kann aus seinem Innern nur nach dem Gesetz der Identität und mit absoluter Nothwendigkeit folgen, welche allein auch die absolute Freiheit ist: denn frey ist, was nur den Gesetzen seines eignen Wesens gemäss handelt, und von nichts anderem weder in noch ausser ihm bestimmt ist.

"As surely, therefore, as the intelligible essence acts freely and absolutely, so surely can it act only in conformity with its own internal nature, or can the action follow only from its inward nature according to the law of identity and with absolute necessity,

Es ist mit dieser Vorstellung der Sache wenigstens Eines gewonnen, dass die Ungereimtheit des Zufälligen der einzelnen Handlung entfernt ist. Dies muss feststehen, auch in jeder höheren Ansicht, dass die einzelne Handlung aus innerer Nothwendigkeit des freyen Wesens, und demnach selbst mit Nothwendigkeit erfolgt, die nur nicht, wie noch immer geschieht, mit der empirischen auf Zwang beruhenden, (die aber selber nur verhüllte Zufälligkeit ist), verwechselt werden muss. Aber was ist denn jene innere Nothwendigkeit des Wesens selber? Hier liegt der Punkt, bei welchem Nothwendigkeit und Freyheit vereinigt werden müssen, wenn sie überhaupt vereinbar sind. Wäre jenes Wesen ein todtes Seyn und in Ansehung des Menschen ein ihm bloss gegebenes; so wäre, da die Handlung aus ihm nur mit Nothwendigkeit folgen kann, die Zurechnungsfähigkeit und alle Freyheit aufgehoben. Aber eben jene innere Nothwendigkeit ist selber die Freyheit; das Wesen des Menschen ist wesentlich *seine eigne That;* Nothwendigkeit und Freyheit stehen in einander, als Ein Wesen, das nur von verschiedenen Seiten betrachtet als das eine oder das andere erscheint; an sich Freyheit, formell Nothwendigkeit ist. Das Ich, sagt Fichte, ist seine eigne That; Bewusstseyn ist Selbstsetzen—aber das Ich ist nichts von diesem verschiedenes, sondern eben das Selbstsetzen selber. Dieses Bewusstseyn aber, inwiefern es bloss als Selbst-Erfassen, oder Erkennen des Ich gedacht wird, ist nicht einmal das erste, und setzt wie alles blosse Erkennen das eigentliche Seyn schon voraus. Dieses vor dem Erkennen vermuthete Seyn ist aber kein Seyn, wenn es gleich kein Erkennen ist; es ist reales Selbstsetzen, es ist ein Ur- und Grundwollen, das sich selbst zu Etwas macht und der Grund und die Basis aller Wesenheit ist.

Aber in viel bestimmterem, als diesem allgemeinen, Sinne, gelten jene Wahrheiten in der unmittelbaren Beziehung auf den Menschen. Der Mensch ist in der ursprünglichen Schöpfung, wie gezeigt, ein unentschiedenes Wesen—(welches mythisch als ein diesem Leben vorausgegangener Zustand der Unschuld und anfänglichen Seligkeit dargestellt werden mag);—nur er selbst kann sich entscheiden. Aber diese Entscheidung kann nicht in die Zeit fallen; sie fällt ausser aller Zeit und daher mit der ersten Schöpfung, (wenn gleich als eine von ihr verschiedene That), zusammen.—Schelling's *Philosophische Untersuchungen über das Wesen der menschlichen Freyheit, Philosophische Schriften* p. 466.

which, moreover, alone is absolute freedom: for that is free which acts only in accordance with the laws of its own essence, and is determined by nothing else either in or out of this essence.

"One thing, at least, is gained by this representation of the matter, namely, that the absurdity of the fortuitous of the individual action is got rid of. So much is certain, also, in every higher view of the question; that the single action follows from the internal necessity of the free essence, and therefore itself follows with necessity, which must not, as is so often the case, be confounded with the empirical necessity that rests on coercion (but which is only the fortuitous disguised). But what is, then, this inward necessity of the essence itself? Here lies the point in which liberty and necessity must be united, if they can be united at all. If that essence were a dead being, and with respect to man something merely given to him, as the action can only proceed from it with necessity, responsibility and all freedom would be at an end. But precisely that inward necessity is itself freedom; the essence of man is essentially *his own act.* Necessity and freedom are in one another as *one* essence, which only appears to be the one or the other accordingly as it may be viewed from different sides; which is freedom in itself, necessity in form. The *ego,* says Fichte, is its own act; consciousness is self-putting,—but the *ego* is not anything different from this latter, but precisely this self-putting itself. But this consciousness, in as far as it is thought as a self-grasping or cognising of the *ego,* is not even the first moment, and like all mere cognition already presumes the true being. But this being, which is presumed prior to cognition, is no being, even though it be no cognition; it is real self-putting—it is original and fundamental willing that makes itself something, and is the ground and basis of all essentiality.

"But in a sense far more definite than the general one intended above, are these truths valid in their immediate reference to man. Man, in the original creation, is, as has been shewn, an undecided essence (which may be represented mythically as a state of innocence and original bliss prior to this life); he alone can himself decide (determine) himself. But this decision cannot fall in time; it falls out of all time, and therefore together with the first creation, although as an act distinct from it."

Now the views advocated in the foregoing pages bear a considerable analogy to those expressed in the first part of the above extract, but not to those expressed in its conclusion. As far as I understand the last paragraph, Schelling places man's freedom in a single act out of all time, by which, at his creation and once for all, man determines his intelligible essence or purely subjective character. This theory seems to me a bolder statement of that of Kant in its inevitable consequences. Liberty undoubtedly is saved in the single act out of time, manifesting itself in innumerable free actions in time, just as the same common hidden root sends up its sap and life through all the branches of a tree. But what is a liberty worth which reduces a man's conduct in all its moral relations to a single act, and allows of no internal change or motion between the various moments of his moral being? A man commits a murder, is afterwards overwhelmed with remorse, and endeavours by a total change of life to atone in some measure for his crime. But this change is a mere illusion, as it is nothing more than the exhibition of the same will under different circumstances. The crime and its repentance are both free, but they are equally determined consequences of the same free act, and are thus bound together in the fetters of a rigid consistency, an inexorable necessity. This liberty of Kant and Schelling is unquestionably to be preferred to Necessarianism; but it is utterly powerless to satisfy the conditions of the various phases of our moral consciousness.

To sum up the general result of the foregoing chapter, I object to the Necessarian liberty, because it is no liberty whatever. It consists in the isolation of certain conditions of action by the imagination, and then ignoring the others as completely as if they did not exist. I object to the Arbitrarian theory, because, as it makes liberty to consist in a faculty of giving the weaker motives the ascendancy over the stronger, it makes it consist in what, by the very hypothesis, must be an unmotived act; and such a liberty, if conceivable, would be a mere negation, and have no moral significance or value. And lastly, I object to the liberty of the single act of self-determination advocated by Kant and Schelling, because, by its being out of all time, and consisting in a single immutable act, it would make such a vast proportion of the phenomena of our moral consciousness mere illusions, that we might almost as well give up our moral sentiment altogether.

PART II.

THE RELATION OF THE WILL TO THE INTELLECT.

IT has appeared in the preceding Part, that the activity of the Will in the province of pure liberty is confined to the self-determination of the subject, and has no immediate concern with objects. This however, so far from being unfavourable to the existence of a relation between the will and the intellect, as might perhaps at first be supposed, offers the very grounds of such a relation in the form of a principle of verification of all objective cognition; for it is only where the freedom ends, that the objective can begin. The nature of this relation will constitute the subject of the present chapter.

In the brief analysis of an act of consciousness in general contained in a former section, it was observed, that we are able to fix ourselves in time. I am conscious, for instance, that "I" exist in "this present moment." The second member of the synthesis,—the present moment, *i.e.* my "now" as distinguished from my "then," was shewn to be determined empirically in the consciousness by the phenomena presented to it, and the latter again to be a particular moment in the succession taking place in some permanent subject out of me. Now to determine the nature of the other member of the synthesis, it must be observed that such a fixing in time would have but little significance or value for us,—that is, it would constitute but a very weak bond between our individuality and the external world,—if such first member were the mere formal ego, the unity by which I combine the partial phenomena into a whole, as representations in my consciousness in a single instant of time. Were it nothing more than this, the act of consciousness in each instant would be absolutely isolated, and no connected life would be possible. Every such act would thus be precisely similar to the first instantaneous thought of a man awaking from a swoon, in which he had entirely lost all knowledge of his former life. Whereas, so far from this being the case, when I say, I fix myself in this time, I attribute to this "I" not merely the form of my individuality, but a representation more or less clear of my *actual* individuality, that is, of the life I have led, and the character I have formed in it.

It is hardly necessary to dwell upon such an axiomatic psychological fact, but should the reader be inclined to dispute it, he need only consult his own experience to be convinced that he is never absolutely divested of the consciousness of a former history, which though connected by association with the objects around him, is not immediately impressed on him by them. He may perhaps for a short time be so absorbed in such objects as to render such a consciousness extremely indistinct, but some dim feeling of who he is, what he has done, and what he intends to do, is never wholly wanting. This feeling is what I understand by the *empirical ego,* or the matter of the individuality as opposed to the mere form.

The empirical ego therefore is the personal identity as it presents itself to the inner sense. It is an internal picture of myself painted in the imagination with materials supplied for the most part by the memory, and undergoing a constant change according to the accidental circumstances of place and association. These materials, only a part of which enter into the picture at any one instant, are of a very heterogeneous character. They consist, for instance, of the recollections and scenes of my former life, the representations of the objects in space surrounding the place which I occupy, (*e.g.* the appearance represented by the street in which I live,) with all of which I have only become acquainted by sensible experience. They consist further, of my inner life—the joys and sorrows that may have illumined or cast a shade over the past, the plans I have formed, the hopes I have cherished, the passions I have combated. But my present thought also contributes matter to the empirical ego. Thus the conduct I have marked out for the hour or the day, my anticipations of future events, whether hopes or fears, all constitute a part of that great composite of empirical matter which makes up my personal history, and distinguishes my actual individual life from that of every other man.

The empirical ego is thus a kind of dim biography, written on the surface of every man's consciousness; a biography, which, if it could be adequately expressed in words, would be a full and exact answer to the question, Who are you?

Now the act of the consciousness by which I fix myself in time is a synthesis, of which the empirical ego, and the complex of the sensible phenomena presented to my senses in the particular instant, form the two members. This synthesis is an act which never ceases during consciousness. For there are no conditions of consciousness under which my senses are entirely unaffected by external objects, or the picture of my empirical ego absolutely effaced. At every moment therefore both elements of this synthesis are present in my consciousness, and there conjoined in that act which constitutes the determination of myself in time.

Now in every synthesis we must be able to distinguish between the two members in order to conjoin them. The question therefore arises, by what rule or touchstone do I try the innumerable representations in my consciousness, and distinguish those which belong to my empirical ego from those which belong to my outward sense? Or the same question may be put thus: What is the principle of the division of the representations in my consciousness, by which I distinguish those of the succession of which I am myself the only permanent subject, from those the succession of which is in a permanent object out of me?

Now the empirical ego is a product of the imagination. It is the result of an activity by which I reproduce images from past experience as they were actually presented to me, or reconstruct their elements in new combinations, either as a mere play of the fancy, or as practical ends for the direction of future conduct. The imagination again is that faculty in which I am conscious of my will as one of the determinants. It is hardly necessary to add, that I am not speaking of the pure will, or the will within the province of pure liberty, as that can never be represented objectively either to the outward or the inward sense, and is confined to the self-determination of the subject. I simply assert that the activity of the imagination is one of the results of the concrete will, or the will after it has left the field of pure liberty, and partially limited itself by its union with that objective element through which alone it can give itself objective expression. The second member of the synthesis, the sensible phenomena, on the other hand, is entirely without the sphere of the will. The consciousness of the activity of the will therefore is the touchstone required.

Let us make this more evident by an example. I look at the table before me and the other objects around me, and am conscious that no *immediate* effort of my will can alter the manner in which they affect my senses. A sheet of white paper, for instance, will not change its colour to brown in consequence of any simple volition of mine. But besides these phenomena, I am also conscious of a train of thought or series of phenomena cognisable alone by my inward sense, which I can present to myself in a thousand varying forms as my fancy may direct. Among the latter must also be reckoned the recollections of past external phenomena, inasmuch as I can reproduce them in different combinations to those in which they actually occurred. Now in all these phenomena of the inward sense, which form the empirical ego, I am conscious of the activity of my own will as the regulative and constructive principle, and it is therefore through the consciousness of this activity that I distinguish between them and external phenomena.

Perhaps it may be objected here, that we are immediately conscious of the objective nature of the objects of our external sense, and that in order to recognise an external object as such, I am not obliged to try experiments with my representation of it, and endeavour, by any immediate act of will, to make it appear otherwise than it actually does. To this I would reply, that it is true that I am not obliged to exercise any act of will involving an amount of energy which is otherwise cognisable; but this arises from the fact, that the independence of the external phenomenon of the energy of the will appears at once at the limit. The very first and most infinitesimal attempt of the will to encroach on a province that does not belong to it, is so entirely without result, and the power and authority of the faculty is so unhesitatingly disallowed, that the conviction of the fruitlessness of a further attempt is immediately and instantaneously felt. No such amount of energy therefore is exerted as could be perceptible to the consciousness in any other form than in the instinctive conclusion of the presence of an object entirely independent of the will.

The above considerations have prepared the way for the solution of the problem proposed in the beginning of this chapter, namely, the nature of the relation of the will to the intellect. When we first discovered that the seat of pure liberty was only to be found in the pure subject, it was observed that this liberty did not consist in any power of the will to exercise a choice between action and inactivity, as the former was imposed on it by a fundamental law of its being. We are now able to add, that one of the laws of this compelled activity is the necessity imposed on it of maintaining a process, which from its analogy to a certain mathematical operation, may be most aptly denominated intellectual differentiation. All the representations in the consciousness are tested in the very instant of their appearance with respect to the extent of their dependence on the will, that is, they are differentiated with regard to it. Those yielding a differential coefficient = 0, those in short which manifest no change corresponding to an infinitesimal change in the will, are recognised at once as no functions of it, and therefore as of an objective character. Those on the other hand where $\frac{dR}{dW} = a$, (where R = representations, and W = will) are accepted as functions of the will, and their subjective origin is accordingly acknowledged.

That I have ascribed no imaginary office to the will in the above remarks will perhaps appear still more evident from the following considerations. If we ask ourselves what we mean when we predicate of some of our representations the actual existence of corresponding objects, and deny such a reference to objects, of other representations, we shall find that we mean neither more nor less than that the former have grounds entirely independent of our activity, of the activity in short of our wills, but that the grounds of the latter are not thus independent. Again, as the order and manner in which such objects are presented to the senses cannot, from the very fact of their being objects at all, depend entirely on *à priori* subjective laws of thought, such objectivity must be cognised empirically. Hence it follows that in the cognition of an object there is an act determining by actual experience the independence of such object of the will, and it is this act which constitutes the differentiation. For it is only by a positive comparison of the change in a representation with a change in the will, that we can empirically determine their mutual relations on the one hand, or the non-existence of such relations on the other. The infinitesimal character however of the will's operation in the process will always prevent its being an object of immediate consciousness, and may perhaps induce some persons to deny its existence. If however they will only grant that our cognition of objects is an empirical cognition of their independence *pro tanto* of the will, they will have acknowledged the above theory in all essentials, and will object only to the form under which I have symbolised it.

It appears from the foregoing analysis, that one of the most important offices of the will is the process of dividing our representations accordingly as they are functions or not of itself, into their subjective and objective elements, and thus of producing those two members whose immediate synthesis constitutes our determination in time, and our bond of union with the world in which we live. For the will, as the innermost kernel, the original essence of the pure subject, passes on through time, differentiating relatively to itself all the representations in the consciousness, and separating those which are found to be its functions from those which are none. These two classes open as it were for the instant, but are instantly reunited in the synthesis by which we determine ourselves in time, and by which they are incorporated with the rest of the matter of the empirical ego. For the perception of one instant becomes the memory of the next, and the sway of the sensible phenomenon, though still great, ceases to be absolute and irresistible in the same moment that its representation in the consciousness has passed in any degree into the province of the imagination.

Perhaps it may, at first sight, seem inconsistent that I should assert the will to be a principle of verification of intellectual operations, after having refused to acknowledge it as an intellectual faculty. The apparent contradiction however is easily explained. The intellectual differentiation of the will is not in itself a positive act of cognition, but simply supplies the object of a cognition in which it is determined whether certain phenomena have or have not an objective ground. The will therefore stands in a negative relation to the intellect. It is not itself intellect, but its activity supplies the touchstone by which the positive intellectual faculties are enabled to test the objective validity of their operations.

It is rather curious that the side of our representations, which as functions of the present will have been recognised as subjective, contains a sham objective, consisting of representations reproduced in the imagination as independent of the will of the moment to which they refer. If, for instance, I picture to myself a house that I have seen, I am conscious that the picture is merely subjective considered in relation to my present will, as I can make changes in its representation at pleasure. But in so far as I *do* fancy it of any particular form or colour, I represent it as having an objective existence independent of the will of myself or any other person beholding it. Again, when I recall such a picture to my mind's eye, I imagine the individual beholding it to have an empirical ego; for this has been shewn to be absolutely necessary to the very form of any continued act of consciousness, even when directed for the most part to sensible phénomena. Hence it follows that the subjective side of the representations in my present consciousness is again resolvable into two terms, and must be considered as consisting partly of an imaginary and sham objective, and partly of a subjective, both of which are respectively determined as such by a process of intellectual differentiation, in which an imaginary value of the will is the independent variable.

In order to avoid the frequent repetition of long and periphrastic expressions, I shall designate the two sides of my present representations by the terms, the first objective and the first subjective, respectively; and the two sides of the representations into which it appears that the first subjective is resolvable, by the terms, second objective and second subjective. I shall also call the present will the first will, and the imaginary will, by which the second subjective and objective are distinguished, the second will.

Now the first subjective has been shewn to be resolvable into a second subjective and second objective. If, for instance, I reproduce in my imagination some scene of my past life, I recall not only the sensible circumstances, but also some of the thoughts and feelings connected with it; and the latter constitute the second subjective. Now the subjective and objective of the second degree are of a precisely analogous character to the first, except that they are determined by an act of intellectual differentiation in which a merely imaginary act of the will is the independent variable. It might therefore be anticipated, that in the same manner as the first subjective is resolvable into a second objective and second subjective, so also must the latter be resolvable into a third objective and subjective, and the third subjective into a fourth, and so on *ad infinitum.* According to the mere form this is correct; but in actual practice we do not carry the process beyond a very few steps, as the imagination finds the effort of maintaining all the intermediate orders of the subjective too fatiguing, and therefore by allowing them to drop, makes representations of a higher class assume the place of a lower. That our thoughts however may sometimes carry us to a tolerably high order will appear from the following example. A young man who has been on the point of emigrating to the back woods of America, but has afterwards given up the project, writes to his friend as follows:

"I have now returned home, and am sitting in my dear old study once more. As the weather was very fine this morning, I took a walk in the woods and lay down under my favourite oak, where I passed a couple of hours in a delightful state of reverie. I felt deeply grateful at having escaped so hopeless a fate. I thought that if I had carried out my former plan, I should have already been half across the Atlantic, perhaps indeed lying ill in my berth, brooding over the dulness of a life passed in the back woods, where no pleasant thoughts would cheer the long and weary hours, except those of the loved ones I had left at home, sitting perhaps round their Christmas fire, and talking of the many happy days they had passed with their truant brother."

Now I think the reader will grant that there is nothing in the style of the above passage so extremely forced, that it could not have occurred in a letter from a young man to one of his friends under the circumstances above mentioned; and yet it contains subjectives and objectives of all orders, from the first to the sixth inclusive. It must however be confessed, that the more natural course both for the thought and its expression, would have been to break off at the fourth objective, (the dull life in the back woods), and to refer the succeeding representations either to the first or second subjective, instead of the fourth.

In the foregoing investigation I have considered the differentiation of our representations relatively to the will simply as the test by which we distinguish our sensible perceptions from the product of our imagination. The same law however has a far wider application, as it constitutes the point of contact between the will and the intellect generally, and is the ultimate principle of the verification not merely of external perceptions, but of all objective cognition whatever.

For let us ask the question, What constitutes the essential difference between a true and a false judgment? They have both existed in the mind, and consequently there must be some grounds for their existence; but the question is, What is the difference between these grounds? Now the first answer that probably will suggest itself is this: The grounds of the true judgment are objective, those of the false, subjective; and the answer is correct as far as it goes. But then the question arises, What do we mean by saying that there is an object corresponding to the true judgment, and not to the false? Clearly this: That in the former case the grounds of the judgment are entirely independent of our own will, whereas in the latter they are at the best but partially so. Judgments, for instance, are made respecting the mathematical relations of quantity, the laws of nature, and the laws of morality; and in so far as these judgments agree with such laws and relations, they are said to be true. But these laws and relations must be more than a mere passing fancy, the creation of the imagination; they must be something objective, something in themselves that will not become otherwise in compliance with a volition of ours; in short, something independent of our wills, or there would be nothing for the judgment to agree with. In order, therefore, to test the truth of a judgment, the object must be to determine whether all its grounds are independent of the will; and it is this determination which constitutes the method above described, under the name of intellectual differentiation, or the comparison of a variation in the object with a variation in the will. The difference between the two applications of the principle in its reference to the existence of sensible objects on the one hand, or to the truth of objective relations on the other, may perhaps become clearer by an example.

Suppose, for instance, I call up in my mind a purely imaginary representation of a man killing his brother in order to inherit his property. I can determine at once that the representation has no objective grounds, as it is a mere function of my will, and I can alter it at pleasure. In this case, I merely decide against the objective reality of the images presented. But now suppose the question not to refer to the reality of the phenomena, but to the truth of certain moral principles suggested by them. Let the question be propounded, for instance, Whether a man who murders his brother to inherit his property can be a good man? To answer it, I try if I can possibly represent to myself such circumstances as should make such conduct compatible with moral excellence. I find, however, that my will is powerless in the matter, *i.e.* that there are elements in the representation absolutely independent of my will, and I conclude accordingly, that such elements (which in this case are the moral laws, or practical development of the will universal) are objective, and not the imaginative product of my subjective feelings. The same formula is applicable to all conceivable exercise of the intellect in the discovery of truth.

The distinction between *à priori* and *à posteriori* cognitions may now be placed in a still clearer light than was attainable in the section devoted to that subject. It has been shewn, that in addition to the first and present will, by the differentiation relatively to which we distinguish between the first objective and first subjective, the latter also contains an imaginary or second will, by its independence of which a second objective is determined. Now *à posteriori* cognitions of objects are absolutely independent of the first will, but are conceived as falling under the dominion of the second. *A priori* cognitions, on the other hand, are those which resist the controul of any will whatever, either actual or imaginary. They are therefore recognised as grounded on the universal relations of the will in general to the faculties, and thus as referring to the general form of such faculties, and as predicable of their objects universally, and independently of all particular cases.

Perhaps it may be urged here, that moral laws cannot be annihilated in thought, and therefore that as they resist the controul of the will in its general form, they have no less claim to be recognised as *à priori* than the mathematical relations of space. To this I would reply, that the relations of space can be abstracted from all empirical cognition of phenomena, and that the proposition, for instance, concerning two straight lines not enclosing a space, is perfectly conceivable independently of all existing objects whatever. The moral laws, on the other hand, cannot be conceived except as referring to moral beings, that is to say, to objects whose existence can only be the object of empirical cognition. To whatever extent, however, we abstract from empirical matter, to the same extent may moral laws also become *à priori*. Disregarding therefore such relations as that of citizen and state, or child and parent, we may enunciate as an *à priori* moral law (but with the above qualification), the universality of the moral principle, namely, that my action must be such that no contradiction arises in supposing that all persons in similar circumstances should do the same.

Whatever may be the nature of the ultimate formula for the verification of our cognitions in general, one thing may be predicated respecting it with certainty, namely, that the formula itself is absolute, and consequently that error can only arise through its defective application. For if the ultimate appeal of the intellect in its abstract form be itself false, truth becomes an impossibility, and the very word, having no reference to anything within the reach of human faculties, loses for us at least all signification. Neither is the original seat of error to be sought for in any lower principle, that is, in any principle further removed from the most abstract form of the intellect. For if the application of the formula were as secure against error as the principle itself, it would present an infallible clue to truth, and render error impossible. Assuming therefore, in conformity with the foregoing argument, that intellectual differentiation is the ultimate formula of verification, the question arises: What is the abstract form of error, or what is the general form of that defect in our differentiation through which error arises?

As truth consists in drawing the boundary line correctly between such representations as are, and such as are not functions of the will, it might at first be imagined that two forms of error would arise, accordingly as we draw the line too much to the one side or the other, that is, accordingly as we include a part of the field of the objective within that of the subjective, or a part of the field of the subjective within that of the objective. In reality, however, it will be found that the former case ultimately resolves itself into the latter. For if I represent to myself a part of the objective as subjective, or a product of my will, this very representation (in which the error consists) is itself a subjective product of my imagination, which I assume as objective. We have therefore but one case to consider, and the general question assumes the form: What are the circumstances under which I regard the subjective, or the product of my imagination, as the objective, or as independent of my will? The problem refers to the abstract form of error in general, and strictly speaking, the solution ought to be equally general and abstract. For the sake of greater perspicuity, however, I shall treat of it in the first instance with reference to the grossest form of error, in which sensible objects are the matter of the judgments. The transition to the other cases will then be easy, as the principle is the same.

It has been shewn[1] that the first subjective is divisible into a second subjective and a second objective, which are determined by their dependence or independence respectively of an imaginary or second will. If, for instance, I form to myself the representation of a town I have never seen, I am aware that it is the product of my imagination, and as such dependent on my present will. In the representation, however, I imagine it as such that it would produce a definite impression on my senses if I were actually to behold it, and consequently as objective, or independent of my will under such imaginary circumstances, *i. e.* independent of my imaginary will.

It appears, then, that the whole energy of the first will, in the first subjective, is divided in its operation. In the first place it produces the second objective by the determination of an imaginary external world; and in the second place it produces a second subjective, or imaginary state of the empirical ego as product of a second will, by its independence of which the second objective is determined. Now two classes of cases occur, accordingly as the energy of the first will is concentrated upon the production of the second subjective, which is the activity of the second will, or upon the second objective, which is the negation or limit of such activity. Where the

[1] Page 212.

latter is the case, the first will is widely different from the second, and there is no danger that the objective or negation of the one should be mistaken for that of the other. For the change in the second objective is large in proportion to the change in the will, and consequently the consciousness of the subjectivity of this second objective proportionably great, and the danger of error proportionably small. Where, however, the former is the case, the second will, by engrossing the energy of the first will, approaches to identity with it, and thus produces a seeming identity between the first and second objectives, (which are determined respectively by their independence of the first and second wills,) by making the second objective answer approximately the conditions of the first.

These observations refer to mental phenomena of daily experience. When, in thinking of time past or future, we concentrate our whole thought, in so far as it is in a state of development or change, upon the internal sensations of such imaginary moment (*i. e.* upon the second subjective), and regard the imagined external sensations (*i. e.* the second objective) merely as fixing the time and place, then it is that this sham objective possesses for us the greatest degree of reality. Let us take an example. The more intensely a man dwells upon the feelings associated with any past scene, the greater will be the reality with which the external images connected with it are presented to his mental vision.

The state of mind called reverie is one in which the action of the will is extremely feeble, and all its energy is directed upon the second subjective, thus giving the second objective a very high degree of reality. This abandonment of the mind to the second subjective is the philosophical explanation of the fact, that a sentimental tone of thought frequently produces reverie ; and the vividness of the images connected with it arises from the identity of the first and second wills, and from the resulting error by which the second objective is confounded with the first. The disease called nostalgia is a striking instance of this state. So entirely is the mind engrossed with the feelings connected with home, that the will has no longer the energy necessary to test the objectivity of the associated images. Thus the green fields and the old village-church seem to meet the eye in every direction.

The above is an analysis of that lowest form of error in which imaginary sensible phenomena are mistaken for their realities. It offers, however, a type of error in general; and the same reasoning is equally valid with respect to those differentiations, the object of which is to distinguish the objective in our subjective representations. For whatever may be the nature of the subject matter of the error, it is nothing more than the giving objectivity to that which is subjective, or in other words, declaring that to be independent of the will which is not so. This can only arise from a want of self-assertion on the part of the will sufficiently energetic to hold its own. Through the unequal distribution of its energy over the field of the subjective, some parts are so weakly tested by the differentiating process as to appear no functions of the will, and consequently as objective. This it is which constitutes the connexion between intellectual error and our moral nature. For in any question of ethics, the real and only source of error is the feebleness of the effort of the will, by which the subjective creations of the imagination are falsely declared to be independent of the will's energy, and therefore to have objective grounds[1].

In order to comprehend the true sphere of the differentiation of the will, it will be necessary to bear in mind that the opposition between subject and object is of a different character, and is differently apprehended, accordingly as the former is understood to signify the pure or the empirical ego.

[1] If we endeavour to give the relations between the will and our representations a sensible form, by interpreting the equations as though they referred to a system of co-ordinates, we may suppose that the principle of the will corresponds to the axis of x as the independent variable, and the principle of the purely objective to the axis of y. In this case the first objective, or external world, (represented by the equation $y = a$) will be a straight line parallel to the axis of x, at every point of which it answers its distinguishing condition $\frac{dy}{dx}\left(i.e.\ \frac{dr}{dw}\right) = 0$.

The power of the will in the subjective varies every instant as our action proceeds. In a mind enjoying full moral and intellectual health, it is very great; in a mind of a weak and morbid tone, it is very small. The conscience-stricken murderer, for instance, finds it impossible to escape from the image of his crime. It will intrude upon his thoughts at the most unwelcome moments, and haunts him night and day. Now the differential coefficient $\frac{dy}{dx}\left(\text{or } \frac{dr}{dw}\right)$ is *the measure of this power*, and as it contains a variable, the equation $y = f(x)$, corresponding to the second objective, must be at least of the second degree, and the second objective itself must be represented by a curve. At the point $\left(\frac{dy}{dx} = 0\right)$ the curve takes for the instant a direction parallel to the axis of x, or to the line $y = a$, representing the objective world. Thus the second objective, by answering the conditions of the first, is mistaken for it, and error arises as explained in the text.

I should not have considered it worth while offering the reader this symbolical illustration of the activity of the imagination, if I had not been led to the above theory of error by searching for the psychological signification of the points $\frac{dy}{dx} = 0$, $\frac{dy}{dx} = \infty$ in the curve above mentioned as the symbol of our second objective.

For the pure ego contains no empirical matter in itself, and is merely the principle of the unity of the multifarious in acts of consciousness. All products of the imagination therefore, however little they may correspond to the absolutely objective world, are objective when considered in relation to the pure ego, and only fall under the category of subjective when the empirical ego is made the basis of the opposition between subject and object.

Now to prevent confusion between two different things, it must be observed that although the process of intellectual differentiation is the test by which we are enabled to distinguish between the subjective and the objective in our representations, it is not a method of distinguishing between the pure subjective and the objective in general, but on the contrary, presumes a faculty of such distinction as its own basis. For without a definite consciousness in the subject of its own activity in an act of the will, differentiation relatively to it becomes impossible, as there would be no independent variable. The problem, therefore, which alone is solved by the process in question is the following: Given certain representations and a consciousness of the activity of the subject, by means of the latter to divide the former into the two classes of the objective on the one hand, and the subjective on the other, or those in which the subject is one of the determinants. In short, the scope and extent of the process is the determination of the boundary between the empirical ego and the absolutely objective, and not between the pure ego and the objective in general.

It appears from the foregoing observations that the cognition of the objective in general by the pure ego is immediate, while that of the absolute objective, as opposed to the empirical ego, is a mediate result[1]. This distinction however must not be considered as referring to time, but merely to the fact that the cognition of the absolute objective requires the mediation of the differentiating process, and is not completed by the positive faculty of the cognition unaided by the will.

Although I have spoken of the subjective in relation to the empirical ego as objective in relation to the pure subject or unity of consciousness, yet as the opposition between the pure subject and an object in general is contained in the mere abstract form of an act of consciousness, it appears to me unphilosophical in a high degree to speak of the pure subject

[1] In Sir William Hamilton's *Supplementary Dissertation on the Philosophy of Common Sense*, there is the following passage:—"In the act of sensible perception, I am conscious of two things; of *myself* as the *perceiving subject*, and of an *external reality*, in relation with my sense, as the *object perceived.* Of the existence of both these things I am convinced—because I am conscious of knowing each of them, not mediately, in something else, *as represented,* but immediately in itself, *as existing.* Of their mutual independence I am no less convinced; because each is apprehended equally, and at once, in the same indivisible energy—the one not preceding or determining, the other not following or determined; and because each is apprehended out of, and in direct contrast to, the other." Sir W. Hamilton's Ed. of Reid, p. 747.

The doctrine in the text would have been identical with that contained in this passage, had the latter referred to the relation of the pure subject to its thought in general, instead of referring to the perceptions of the senses. My objection to regarding the consciousness of the external object in a perception as immediate, arises from the consideration, that the consciousness of its externality contains its independence of the subject. Such independence can only be determined empirically, and hence it follows, that before an object can be distinguished from a representation in the imagination, the positive deliverance of the sense must receive the seal of externality from a negative process, establishing its independence of the subject; and this process, as shewed above, is that of the differentiation of such representation relatively to the will.

as ever becoming its own object. It is true, in an act of consciousness we become conscious of the existence of a thinking subject, but there is no reason for concluding that every existence of which we become aware in an act of consciousness is necessarily an object. On the contrary, the subject is conscious of its own existence in its own activity on the one hand, and of the existence of the object in the limitation to such activity on the other. Existence therefore is not to be considered as the opposite pole or logical complement of the subject, but rather of the subject and object in their synthesis in an act of consciousness. Hence subject and object on the one hand, stand in similar relations to existence on the other, as the polar antithesis of an act of consciousness. When therefore I become conscious of my own existence, I see no reason to conclude that I have placed myself before myself as an object, but on the contrary, I believe that the consciousness of the existence of the subject arises in its own activity, and is not only simultaneous with, but absolutely involved in, the consciousness of the existence of the object; and in short, that the consciousness of the existence of the object implies in its very essence the consciousness of an existence which is conscious of such object. To assert therefore that a pure subject can ever be its own object appears to me in contradiction to the form of an act of consciousness in general, and to introduce confusion into philosophy at its very source.

The general result of the preceding analysis of the relation of the will to the intellect may be summed up as follows: knowledge, or the cognition of objects, arises where the will meets with a resistance which it cannot overcome, and the fact of this resistance is determined by differentiation. Where the resistance is only to the particular will in time, the knowledge is empirical; where it is absolute and to all imaginary wills, the knowledge is à *priori.* If we consider all objects as the operation of the Divine will, knowledge may be symbolised as the result of a collision of such Divine will with the human will; or better perhaps as the projection of the former upon the plane of the latter. This however must be understood of the concrete human will, and not of the will in the field of pure liberty, where it is the self-determination of the subject. Were the latter the case, and the position of the plane of our will entirely in our own power, we could give our knowledge an infinity of forms at pleasure; for if no element in our relations to the objective were subject to law, our faculties would be determined by our own wills. There are, however, certain laws restricting the operation of our will in determining its plane, and these laws are our faculties taken in the most general sense, that is, as all the various forms in which objects are cognisable by the subject of consciousness.

PART III.

THE HUMAN WILL IN RELATION TO GOD.

CHAPTER I.

General Statement of the Question.

IN the preceding Parts of this treatise, I have endeavoured to determine the character of the relation of the Will to Nature and the Human Intellect. In the present I propose to myself a loftier theme—the relation of the Will to God. Hitherto the members of the relationships considered, have been the thinking subject on the one hand, and certain immediate objects of consciousness on the other; and though the problem has not been an easy one, it has at least had the advantage of being concerned with our direct experience alone. Now however the case is altered. Of one member of the comparison we have no immediate experience, for no man has seen God at any time. It is true, I have attempted to shew in a former section that the moral sentiment is the innate consciousness of the relation of the individual to a higher will, which when objectivised through faith or reason is found to be the will of God; but this consciousness is a merely subjective feeling, and cannot realise its object without the aid of other faculties. The objective interpretation therefore of the moral and religious sentiments is not in any way at variance with the general proposition, that the relation of the human will to

God can never become an object of a direct and positive experience. No man, for instance, has a direct consciousness of his own creation.

It follows from the above considerations, that the conception of the relation in question must either be *à priori* throughout, as far as its Divine member is concerned, or else must start from the empirical fact of our faith in a God possessing certain attributes, without regard to the origin of such faith. In the present instance, the proofs of the existence of the Deity do not come within the scope of the work, and I shall accordingly adopt the second alternative, and assume the existence on faith. I feel moreover the less hesitation in preferring this course, as the universal faith itself appears to me the strongest argument in its own favour.

With regard to the division of the problem, I would observe that we are not at present concerned with the nature of the Deity, except in His relations to the human will. In assuming however the existence of a Deity at all, we necessarily include the assumption of certain attributes, as otherwise we should have nothing but a mere empty conception of some being in general which would offer no foundation for any argument respecting its relations. Now if we start from the absolute positive in the Divine Will in its relation to the particular positive in the human, the question arises, how can the latter, however limited, exist simultaneously with the infinity of the former, without encroaching on its sphere of possible activity; and the Divine attribute to be assumed in its consideration is that of Omnipotence. When this point however is once disposed of, and the maintenance of the human will, as a self-imposed limitation on that of the Almighty, has been accepted as true, the question arises, how such limitation, which, as an object of the knowledge of the Eternal and Immutable God, must be a fact of eternity, can have its grounds in a human action commencing in time. In the latter question, the attribute to be assumed is evidently that of prescience.

I shall now proceed to the consideration of these problems, premising however that anything like a positive solution of them appears to me to lie beyond the scope of our faculties. All I shall attempt therefore is to shew by analogy and otherwise, that however little we can comprehend the relations of the will to its Creator, there is nothing absolutely contradictory between its freedom on the one hand, and the power and knowledge of God on the other.

CHAPTER II.

Relation of the Will to the Omnipotent.

THE difficulty of conceiving the relation of the human will as free, to the will of God as absolute, arises in the following alternative. Either the human will conforms absolutely and entirely with the Divine, in which case its freedom can only be reserved by the supposition that it forms an actual part of the Divine will, and that the whole life of a man is but an emanation from God,—only one mode of God's action; or else the human will is not in absolute conformity with the Divine, but has an individual existence of its own; and in this case it appears as a limitation to the power of the Omnipotent.

The first of these hypotheses appears to me untenable for several reasons. Besides making God the immediate author of evil, it runs entirely counter to those subjective feelings, to find an object for which is the sole purport of faith's assuming a God at all. For by this absorption of man in the Godhead, the relation of the human to the Divine will is annihilated in their identity. But it is the consciousness of this relation which, in the dim region of subjective feeling, constitutes the moral sentiment, and which, when objectivised by the sum total of the faculties in their joint operation under the name of faith, evolves the conception of God, and superadds to the feeling of duty, that of religious reverence.

The difficulty of the second hypothesis is also great, but it is a difficulty of another character. It does not arise from its irreconcilability with the conception of the God of our faith, but from our inability to form any adequate conception of an act of creation.

Now emanation, or a purely positive pouring forth of the Divine activity, is a comparatively simple idea; at any rate it does not appear to involve any logical contradiction. But in the conception of creation, we have that of a created object, which, as such, must have a species of independence of its creator, and thus offer a resistance to the very will from which it has proceeded. For if it offer no such resistance, if, on the contrary, it sway here and there with the thought of its creator, it ceases to be anything in itself, and becomes a mere manifestation of the creating power without any independent result; in short an emanation from the same[1]. But then, on

[1] Aber Abhängigkeit hebt Selbstständigkeit, hebt sogar Freyheit nicht auf. Sie bestimmt nicht das Wesen, und sagt nur, dass das Abhängige, was es auch immer seyn möge, nur als Folge von dem seyn könne, von dem es abhängig ist; sie sagt nicht, was es sey, und was es nicht sey. * * * Wäre das Abhängige oder Folgende nicht selbstständig, so wäre diess vielmehr widersprechend. Es wäre eine Abhängigkeit ohne Abhängiges, eine Folge ohne Folgendes (Consequentia absque Consequente), und daher auch keine wirkliche Folge, d.h. der ganze Begriff höbe sich selber auf.

But dependence does not destroy self-subsistence, does not even destroy freedom. It does not determine the essence, and says only, that the dependent, whatever it may be, can only be a consequence of that from which it is dependent. It does not say, what it is, and what it is not. * * * If the dependent or consequent were not self-subsistent, this indeed would involve a contradiction. There would be a dependence without a dependent, a consequence without a consequent (Consequentia absque Consequente), and, therefore, no real consequence, *i.e.* the whole conception would be self-destructive.

Schelling's *Philosophische Untersuchungen über das Wesen der menschlichen Freyheit. Philosophische Schriften*, p. 413.

the other hand, this very power of resistance in which the creation as created object consists, is itself the product of the creating will. Hence an act of creation, as opposed to mere emanation, involves the conception of a double will in the creator, namely,—the positive, or the greater will which produces, and the lesser, which may be called the negative will from its being limited by the object thus produced.

This double will involves for us the principal difficulty in the conception of an act of creation. In the conception of mere *making*, we have the acting will and the resisting matter. But in that of creation, the action producing and the action resisted, or the positive and negative wills, proceed from the same being, and in the same act. And yet this relation of the double will is not quite inconceivable; at least we find an extremely analogous relation between the first and second wills in the so-called creations of the imagination. If, for instance, I represent to myself a mountain of gold, I am aware that the image, when considered positively, is a product of which my will is a principal factor; but by conceiving it at all, I give it ideally an independent existence, such an existence, in short, as resists that imaginary will, by their relation to which the second subjective and objective are distinguished from each other.

It appears therefore that the products of the imagination are termed its creations with peculiar propriety. But although they require both first and second wills in their conception, and may thus afford some insight into the nature of a Divine act of creation as far as the mere form is concerned, yet is there one difficulty referring to the matter of the conception in which the analogy does not hold. For the creations of the imagination are merely ideal, that is to say, their power of resistance is limited to the second will of that being exclusively whose first will produced them; and the second will, upon their resistance to which their imaginary objectivity depends, is ideal also. Whereas the creations of the Divine imagination, whether they be worlds or human wills, are real existences, with a power of resistance to all wills in general, and require that the second or limited will should be no less actual than they. While therefore the operations of our own minds may shew us the direction in which we have to look for the conception of creation, they cannot give us the conception itself.

Now our conception of God can never go beyond what may perhaps be aptly called a spiritual anthropomorphism, or in other words, we can never introduce into our conception of God and His operations, any elements which we have not found, in kind at least, in our own minds. To attempt therefore any further analysis of the relations of Creator and created than that with which the operations of our own imaginations present us, is simply a loss of time, as it is an attempt to go beyond the province of our faculties. Creation must accordingly be assumed as a fact.

But the hypothesis of the human will being a free centre of action in spite of its original dependence on the Divine will for its very existence, only involves the same difficulties as any other act of creation. For whether the created object be on the one hand subject to a rigid law of necessity, or on the other be absolutely free, its resistance to this second will in the Creator is still the indispensable condition to its being anything at all in itself, in short, to its being a creation and not a mere emanation. Hence it follows, that if the possibility of creation be once admitted, the objection to the second hypothesis vanishes, on the ground that the impossibility of our forming an adequate conception of it, arises from the inadequacy of human faculties to conceive an act of creation in general, in the full sense at least in which this expression is employed of the works of the Almighty.

Taking however the analogy offered by human creations as the only guide we possess for our conception of the Divine, I would represent the relation of the human to the Divine will as that of the poem to the poet. Human wills are the thoughts of the Divine Imagination. But whereas the thought of a man is a dead thing for another, until he has made it his own, these thoughts of God are in themselves centres of life and power, with a might of resistance establishing their independent individuality, and a freedom making them like the Image of their Father, and capable, in some sort at least, of fresh creation.

Whether the same can be said of all that proceeds from the Divine energy, whether in short the external world is a selfsubsistent living power, or a mere emanation, is a deep question,—one that man will never answer. For my own part I am inclined to believe that the higher form of procession from God, (that of creation as opposed to emanation,) is restricted to the free alone,—that living wills are the only new centres of power,—and that in the glory and beauty of the material world, we gaze, though through a veil, upon the Majesty of the Eternal. Not that the granite of the mountains and the verdure of the fields beneath our feet, or the blue depths and bright orbs of heaven above our heads, are the living God, but that they are the maintained manifestations of His energy, operating on the souls of all living beings. The free can surely feel subdued into reverence and awe in the presence of the free alone. Cut off the outward world, bound hand and foot as it lies before us in its causal fetters, from that first source of its existence, the free and unconditioned Cause, and what is there left in the dead machine that the spirit of a man with infinite aspirations and an eternity for their accomplishment, should feel abashed before it?

In Schelling's *Essay on Human Liberty,* already quoted, there is the following poetical passage. As the reader will readily perceive, it contains single sentences with which I entirely agree, but this is not the case with its general purport. [1] "A much higher

[1] Einen viel höheren Standpunkt gewährt die Betrachtung des göttlichen Wesens selbst, dessen Idee eine Folge, die nicht Zeugung d. h. Setzen eines Selbständigen ist, völlig widersprechen würde. Gott is nicht ein Gott der Todten, sondern der Lebendigen. Es ist nicht einzusehen wie das allervollkommenste Wesen auch an der möglich vollkommensten Maschine seine Lust fände. Wie man auch die Art der Folge der Wesen aus Gott sich denken möge, nie kann sie eine mechanische seyn, kein blosses Bewirken oder Hinstellen, wobei das Bewirkte nichts fur sich selbst ist; eben so wenig Emanation, wobei das Ausfliessende dasselbe bliebe mit dem, wovon es ausgeflossen, also nichts eignes, selbstständiges. Die Folge der Dinge aus Gott ist eine Selbstoffenbarung Gottes. Gott aber kann nur sich offenbar werden in dem was ihm ähnlich ist, in freyen aus sich selbst handelnden Wesen; für deren Seyn es keinen Grund giebt als Gott, die aber sind, so wie Gott ist. Er spricht und sie sind da. Wären alle Weltwesen auch nur Gedanken des göttlichen Gemüthes, so müssten sie schon eben darum lebendig seyn. So werden die Gedanken wohl von der Seele erzeugt; aber der erzeugte Gedanke ist eine unabhängige Macht, für sich fortwirkend, ja, in der menschlichen Seele, so anwachsend, dass er seine eigne Mutter bezwingt und sich unterwirft. Allein die göttliche Imagination, welche die Ursache der Spezification der Weltwesen

point of view is yielded by the contemplation of the Divine Essence itself, the idea of which is utterly contradictory to a succession which is not a generation, *i.e.* a putting of a self-subsistent. God is not a God of the dead, but of the living. It is inconceivable that the most perfect Being should take any pleasure in the most perfect machine. Whatever may be the manner of the succession of beings from God, which we imagine to ourselves, it can never be a mechanical one, a mere effecting or putting, in which that which is effected is nothing in itself. Just as little can it be emanation, in which that which emanates remains the same with that from which it has emanated, and which therefore is nothing of its own and self-subsistent. The succession of things from God is a self-revelation of God. But God can only reveal himself in that which is like Him, in free beings acting from themselves, for the existence of which there is no ground but God, but which are, as God is. He speaks, and they are there. If all world-beings were only thoughts of the Divine mind, they must even on that account be living. In the same manner indeed thoughts are begotten by the soul; but the begotten thought is

ist, ist nicht wie die menschliche, das sie ihren Schöpfungen bloss idealische Wirklichkeit ertheilt. Die Repräsentationen der Gottheit können nur selbstständige Wesen seyn; denn was ist das Beschränkende unserer Vorstellungen als eben dass wir unselbständiges sehen? Gott schaut die Dinge an sich an. An sich ist nur das Ewige, auf sich selbst Beruhende, Wille, Freyheit. Der Begriff einer derivirten Absolutheit oder Göttlichkeit ist so wenig widersprechend, dass er vielmehr der Mittelbegriff der ganzen Philosophie ist. Eine solche Göttlichkeit kommt der Natur zu. So wenig widerspricht sich Immanenz in Gott and Freyheit, das gerade nur das Freye und so weit es frey ist, in Gott ist, das Unfreye und so weit es unfrey ist, nothwendig ausser Gott. *Schelling über das Wesen der menschlichen Freyheit*, p. 413.

an independent power, continuing to work for itself, aye, growing in the human soul to such a magnitude, that it vanquishes and subjugates its own mother. But the Divine imagination which is the cause of the specification of world-beings is not like the human, that it gives its creations merely ideal reality. The representations of the Godhead can be only self-subsistent beings. For what else is the limiting in our representations than that we see that which is not self-subsistent? God sees the things in themselves. Only the Eternal, that which rests on itself, Will, Freedom, is thing in itself. The conception of a derived Absoluteness or Divinity is so far from containing a contradiction, that it is rather the central conception of the whole of philosophy. Such a divinity belongs to nature. Immanence in God and freedom are so little contradictory, that it is precisely the free alone and in so far as it is free, that is in God, and the not free, and so far as it is not free, that is necessarily out of God."

It is impossible to deny the eloquence of this passage in the original, harsh as it must appear in a literal translation. With parts of it I agree entirely, but not with the general conclusion, which stated shortly seems to be, that the whole creation has a free and self-subsistent existence. This is based upon two positions, namely, that the succession of things out of God is a self-revelation of God, and that God can only reveal Himself in what is like Himself, that is, in free beings acting from themselves.

Now although I have already asserted my belief that the external world is a direct manifestation of the Divine energy, yet must I pause before I can apply the term revelation in any but a highly poetical sense, where we can only arrive at a knowledge of the revealed object through the revelation, with tottering and uncertain steps, leaning half on reason, half on faith, and receiving no support from direct intuition. Besides, if there be such a thing as absolute law anywhere, surely it is in the external world. But where there is absolute law, freedom can exist in that thing for which the law is valid, only in so far as the law is self-imposed. Now if external nature is a self-subsistent being and imposes its own laws, it becomes not only free but a God. If, on the other hand, it does not impose its own laws, it ceases to be God, but it also ceases to be free, and is nothing more than a dead machine; a view of the question repudiated by Schelling, and one on which I have already commented. The only alternative, as it appears to me, which saves any form of life and freedom in the external world, anything that should account for and justify the profound sense of awe we experience in viewing the glories of the universe, without making it the very God Himself, and thus rushing at once into the grossest form of pantheism, is this,—that we should give up the idea of its self-subsistence and conceive it as a maintained manifestation of the Divine energy. But there is a wide difference between such a manifestation and a self-revelation of God; nor is there a less difference between saying "the outward world is God," and saying "that being is God, whose energy produces immediately on our souls the consciousness of an outward world."

CHAPTER III.

Relation of the Will to the Omniscient.

THE foreknowledge of God is frequently brought forward by the Necessarians as offering an unanswerable objection to human liberty. The argument founded on it consists properly of two parts, of which the one presents at least a fair subject of investigation, while the other is a mere sophism, which would hardly deserve a serious notice in a philosophical treatise, if earnest thinkers had not occasionally allowed themselves to be deceived by it. All the difficulties connected with this subject arise more or less from an incorrect conception of the various relations of modality, and it will therefore be necessary to devote a short space to their consideration.

The modality of a judgment is the peculiar nature of its relation to truth as conceived in our minds. If the matter of the judgment does not contradict the laws of thought, the judgment is said to be problematical, and the matter possible: if the matter is supplied by positive experience, it is said to be actual, and the judgment is termed assertive: if the laws of thought supply the matter of the judgment, both the judgment and its matter are said to be necessary.

Now this division into possible, actual, and necessary, is really subjective, and refers, not to objective truth, but to our manner of holding truth. We generally conceive the sphere of the possible as far greater than that of the actual, and that of the actual as greater than that of the necessary, and we are perfectly right in doing so, as long as we adhere strictly to the real force of these words, and apply them simply to our subjective point of view. If, however, we would extend their application to the objects themselves, we shall find that in the province of the conditioned, all the possible is actual, and all the actual, necessary; in other words, the spheres of the possible, actual, and necessary coincide objectively, and the distinction between them merges in their identity.

When for instance I say, it is perfectly possible that there will be a shower this evening, I mean that there are no laws of thinking which render this event inconceivable to me, and therefore that the event in question is possible *as far as my knowledge extends.* If, however, I attempt to carry the word *possible* beyond its legitimate signification, by asking whether an event be *in itself* possible, without reference to the limited powers of judgment either of myself or others, my question is equivalent to the following: Are all the conditions present which are necessary to the event? If any one condition is absent, the event is clearly impossible, or else the condition would not have been necessary. To be objectively possible, therefore, *all* the conditions must be present, and if *all* are present, the event must necessarily follow, and is thus not only possible but actual. Thus in the case of the shower, it is my ignorance of the laws of the weather that makes me speak of its possibility. If I were perfectly acquainted with all the conditions on which it depends, and the fact of their presence or absence, I should regard it either as certain or the reverse.

Now if the event be actual, it is also necessary. For if not, (as we are here speaking of necessity absolutely, with reference to the event in itself alone, and not to our limited knowledge,) the only alternative to its necessity is, that its non-existence would have been conceivable by a mind acquainted with all the conditions and the fact of their presence. But to a mind acquainted with the fact of the presence of all the conditions necessary to the existence of the object, the object itself is also equally necessary.

That the actual is objectively necessary, may also be deduced from the former proposition that the objectively possible is actual, but the proof is essentially the same as that already given. For if the actual were not necessary, its non-existence would be possible, and as all the objectively possible is actual, the non-existence would be actual, *i.e.* the non-existence of the actual would be actual, which is absurd.

This necessity however is merely a consequential not a proper necessity, that is, it is merely the necessity contained in the proposition that whatever is, must necessarily be. But it is the only species of necessity which attaches to *mere* existence, for there is no contradiction involved in the mere conception of non-existence. Or to express this somewhat differently, *if* the conditions exist, the existence of the conditioned is a necessary *consequence*, but there is no contradiction involved in the conception of the non-existence both of the conditions and the conditioned.

But then it may be asked, if all events are ultimately necessary, how is the act of liberty to escape the universal bondage? To this I reply, that the necessity of the objectively possible arises from the consideration that it requires the presence of all the conditions, and the necessary requires nothing more.

But the act of the will in the province of pure liberty is a perfectly unconditioned self-determination of the subject. Were it an object arising in the objective world, it would also depend on prior conditions. But this liberty is as it were a scintillation of the Divine essence, by which the human will quite independently of all conditions can originate an act,—this act consisting in its own self-determination relatively to the Divine will. Hence it follows that the necessity which arises in the relation between the conditions and the conditioned has no place here, as the will is unconditioned.

Thus the identity of the objectively possible, the actual, and the necessary, imposes no restriction on the wills of God and man. For this identity only exists for the things in themselves, without any reference to the limitations of our knowledge—only therefore where *all* the conditions are taken equally into consideration; and where this is the case, the free act of the will is precisely one of these conditions. The freedom therefore has been already saved prior to the completion of the conditions establishing the necessity. If then I say, such an act is possible to such a will, I mean that the *other* conditions at least are present, and only require that of the will to complete them. But the act does not become possible objectively, (that is, considered by itself as an event in the universe,) until the complementary volition also arises, and then the presence of all the conditions makes the event not only possible but necessary.

In man the free and unconditioned act terminates in the impress it gives the character. Directly the freedom is regarded in its overt results, it has ceased to be pure, as it can only objectivise itself through the passions, affections, and principles which constitute human nature. When therefore I say the act of freedom is unconditioned, I do not speak of any act that has once taken an objective form, but merely assert that the will is independent of conditions, in assuming its *status* of greater or less obedience to the inward law of the universal will; but this *status* once assumed, the objective act that results is dependent upon a great many conditions, such as prior character, education, and outward circumstances.

My object, however, in the above remarks is not to obliterate the boundary-line between the possible, the actual, and the necessary, but merely to shew that the distinction between them is really subjective, and applies to their relation to truth in our minds, but not to the things in themselves. When therefore an event is said to be contingent, or such as may or may not be, we are not expressing any quality of the event itself, but only of our conception of it, according to which the presence or absence of some of the conditions necessary to its arising, is either unknown to us, or at least not taken into consideration.

Before leaving the subject of modality, I must call the reader's attention to the important distinction between consequential necessity, and necessity proper. If I assume the truths of certain judgments A and B, another judgment C may follow from them as a necessary conclusion; but C need not on this account be necessary when considered alone, even if the premises be true. Let us take an example. All who went in the boat wore white hats. John went in the boat, therefore John wore a white hat.

This is an instance of consequential necessity; but the proposition that John wore a white hat contains no necessity within itself. But supposing I say, all polygons have as many angles as sides; a pentagon is a polygon having five sides, therefore a pentagon has five angles. In this case the conclusion is not only necessary as such, but is also necessary in its own nature, as it contains a law of our intuition of space[1].

I shall now proceed to apply the foregoing observation on the nature of the contingent and the necessary to the solution of the difficulties of reconciling the doctrine of liberty with the prescience of God. And first, let us entirely waive the question of the manner of the prescience and its possibility, assuming it as a fact that God *does* possess this attribute, but without pretending to explain it. The problem then takes this form. If God foreknows that I shall perform a certain act to-morrow, when the time comes, how is it possible that I can possess any liberty respecting it? I *must* perform the act, as otherwise I should make God to have foreknown what was not true.

This is an argument which, as I have already hinted, deserves a refutation on historical grounds alone. It is a mere quibble, quite beneath the notice of philosophy, as far as its own merits are concerned, and is based on a childish confusion between consequential necessity and necessity proper. As God cannot foreknow what is false, *if* He foreknows that I shall perform the action *A*, it follows,

[1] On the subject of the Modality of Syllogism I have treated at length in a small work entitled, *A Syllabus of Logic:* Deighton, Cambridge, 1839.

as a necessary consequence of this hypothesis, that I shall perform it, but it does not make the action *A* necessary in itself. When a future time arrives I may be perfectly free to choose between the actions *A* or *B*, the only difference being that if I perform *B*, God will have foreknown *B* instead of *A*.

An equally valid argument for necessity may be urged without introducing foreknowledge at all. It is at present true that I shall either perform *A*, or I shall not. *If* I am going to perform *A*, then, when the time comes, I *must* perform it, for if I do not, it will not have been true that I was going to perform it.

That I am not attributing this fallacy to the advocates of necessity unjustly, might be proved by innumerable passages in various authors from Aristotle downwards. This philosopher argues as follows: "But if it was always true to say that it is or will be, it is not possible that this thing is not or will not be. But what is not possible not to take place is impossible not to take place, and what is impossible not to take place is necessary to take place. It is necessary therefore that all things, that are about to be, will be[1]."

Again, Edwards has the following passage: "From what has been observed, it is evident that

[1] Εἰ δὲ ἀεὶ ἀληθὲς ἦν εἰπεῖν ὅτι ἔστιν ἢ ἔσται, οὐχ οἷόν τε τοῦτο μὴ εἶναι οὐδὲ μὴ ἔσεσθαι. Ὃ δὲ μὴ οἷόν τε μὴ γενέσθαι, ἀδύνατον μὴ γενέσθαι· ὃ δὲ ἀδύνατον μὴ γενέσθαι, ἀνάγκη γενέσθαι. Ἅπαντα οὖν τὰ ἐσόμενα ἀναγκαῖον γενέσθαι. Aristoteles, *de Interpretatione*, cap. 9. This is by no means the only case in which Aristotle has made blunders in that fruitful source of quibbles, the modality of syllogism. I have pointed out and analysed two such fallacies in the work mentioned in the last note. I take this opportunity of correcting an important misprint in that chapter. The T in p. 154, l. 6, ought to be θ in each place.

the abolute decrees of God are no more inconsistent with human liberty on account of any necessity of the event, which follows from such decrees, than the absolute foreknowledge of God. Because the connexion between the event and certain foreknowledge is as infallible and indissoluble, as between the event and an absolute decree[1]."

The fallacy in this argument is palpable. Besides the question whether two things *A* and *B* are indissolubly connected, there is another very important one to be taken into consideration, which Edwards has entirely ignored; namely, whether *A* is determined by *B*, or *B* by *A*. Now a decree determines the event, but it is the event which determines the foreknowledge. Edwards' argument may be illustrated as follows: "Where the horse has gone, the cart has gone too; and the cart has also gone the same road as the load of hay that was fastened upon it. Consequently, the direction the cart has taken has been just as much determined by the load of hay as by the horse, for both were fastened firmly to the cart, and the cart therefore could only go the same way that the hay did."

The general answer to the above piece of sophistry, whose whole claims to respect are to be derived from its age, may be shortly stated thus. I may have perfect liberty to perform *A* or *B*. If I shall perform *A*, God foreknows *A*; if *B*, He foreknows *B*.

If the Divine prescience be once assumed, its reconciliation with human liberty offers no difficulties, as the whole argument has been shewn to be a trivial quibble. The possibility, however, of the Divine

[1] Edwards, *On the Will*, Part II. sect. 12, p. 171.

prescience itself presents a somewhat more serious problem. Human foreknowledge is based on a calculation of the necessary sequence of cause and effect, according to empirically discovered laws. It is not, therefore, unnatural that in the first instance we should be inclined to attribute the same character to Divine prescience. But if a future act of the will is only foreknown as the result of a preceding chain of events, it is clear that it must be absolutely determined by such events, and human liberty is impossible. We must therefore either give up liberty, or base the Divine prescience on other grounds.

Now, as it is absurd for man to pretend to determine the nature of the Divine knowledge, the only arguments that can avail against the possibility of a Divine prescience not based on causality, one therefore of intuition, must tend to shew that the conception contains a contradiction in itself. This has accordingly been attempted by the Necessarians in various ways.

"To suppose," says Edwards, "the future volitions of moral agents not to be necessary events; or, which is the same thing, events which it is not impossible but that they may not come to pass; and yet to suppose that God certainly foreknows them, and knows all things, is to suppose God's knowledge to be inconsistent with itself. For to say, that God certainly, and without all conjecture, knows that a thing will infallibly be, which at the same time He knows to be so *contingent*, that it may possibly not be, is to suppose His knowledge inconsistent with itself, or that one thing, which He knows, is utterly inconsistent with another thing that He knows[1]."

[1] Edwards, *On the Will*, Part II. sect. 12, p. 169.

Now, the whole of this argument is based on the supposition that contingency can be a quality of the events in themselves, and that it does not refer simply to the limitations of our knowledge. I have already explained this fallacy in my remarks on modality. To God, who knows all things, no event is contingent, because He knows all the conditions necessary to their occurrence; but then among these very conditions is the free act of the human agent. How God foreknows what this free act will be, we cannot pretend to say. All for which I am now contending is, that the foreknowledge of our future actions contains no contradiction on the score of its being a certain knowledge of an event contingent in itself. In short, the action is not necessary to the man, because all the conditions, exclusive of his will, are not sufficient to determine it. But the action is not contingent in itself, or for the knowledge of God, because He foresees the complementary condition supplied by the human will.

Priestley's arguments on this subject are equally fallacious. "To all minds," says that philosopher, "the foretelling of a contingent event is equally a matter of conjecture: consequently, even infinite knowledge makes no difference in this case. For knowledge supposes an object, which, in this case, does not exist, and therefore cannot be known to exist[1]." Here again we find an event considered as contingent in itself. But perhaps the weakest sentence in the above quotation is the last. In the first place, to object that the object of a faculty of *prescience* does not exist *now*, is equivalent to objecting that it does not possess an accident (that of

[1] Priestley, *On the Doctrine of Philosophical Necessity*, sect. 3.

present existence), which would make it impossible to be the object of that faculty. In the second place, if knowledge supposes the *present* existence of its object, not only is *all* foreknowledge impossible, but also all knowledge of past events; and memory falls with prescience. And if it should be urged that memory has a present object in the representation in the mind of past events, it may be answered, that in like manner prescience also has its present object in the representation in the mind of the prescient being of future events.

But the most important consideration in this question is the nature of time. Do what we will, we can never give any definition of it (not already involving the conception) which shall be essentially different from this: that it is that form of human consciousness in which the events of the world within and without are doled out to us in portions. It is in short the subjective form of the most abstract conception of limitation. Now on what grounds are we obliged to assume that God's own universe is apportioned out to Him, as He thinks right to apportion it out to us? With God one day is as a thousand years, and a thousand years as one day. Why then should we imagine that His knowledge of the future is at all a less immediate intuition than that of the present? We see the universe and its events piecemeal, as in a moving panorama; God sees the whole stretched out at once and for ever before Him. We see the effect follow the cause; God may see how the effect which is to follow has predetermined the preceding cause. Omniscience is surely as far beyond our grasp as prescience; and if we assume the former, it is absurd for us to pretend to determine the forms of the Divine consciousness. If the reader should feel sceptical as to the possibility of an intuitive prescience, I would ask him to consider the following conversation which a friend of mine once had with a learned native of the Island of Typhlia.

The friend in question had been wrecked on the above-mentioned island, and on reaching the shore and recovering his senses, was astonished to find that the country was inhabited by a race of men entirely destitute of the sense of vision, but in other respects like the rest of mankind. Before he came among them they had never met with a man who could see, and had of course no conception of what sight was. After a residence in the island of some years, he succeeded in acquiring a perfect knowledge of the language spoken there. The Typhlians have their philosophers, like the rest of the world, and on one occasion my friend had the following conversation with one of their first scientific men.

Typhlian. I have not been very well lately, and I think a good long walk would do me good. Are you disposed to join me?

Englishman. I shall have much pleasure in doing so.

Typh. Where shall we go?

Engl. As you talk of a long walk, I propose that we explore the conical hill on the other side of the forest. It must be several thousand feet high, and the rocks near its base assume very wild and romantic forms.

Typh. (*with evident astonishment*). A conical hill! I know of no such place, and had no idea that you had ever been even as far as to this side of the forest. When have you visited this hill, that you seem to know so much about it?

Engl. I have never been there in my life.

Typh. Who then told you that we should find such a hill?

Engl. Nobody.

Typh. You speak in riddles! You propose that we should walk to a hill which you have never yet visited, and the very existence of which no one has ever hinted to you! How can you know that we shall come to such a place as you describe?

Engl. Trust yourself to my guidance, and I will convince you that there is such a hill. But it will be two or three hours at least before we reach it.

Typh. You English must be very remarkable people. You seem to have a most extraordinary knowledge of what we are going to experience in the future. The other day you cautioned me to be on my guard, as I should probably stumble over a stone. A minute afterwards I did stumble, and yet the stone was on my side, and I am sure you could not have touched it. Neither had you ever walked in that direction before. Can you explain to me this miraculous faculty of foreknowledge?

Engl. I saw the stone lying in your path.

Typh. That is to say, you knew it would be there and that I should run up against it, for sight and seeing are evidently the English words for foreknowing. But in what manner did you attain this knowledge?

Engl. I was immediately conscious of it by my sense of sight.

Typh. (*musing*). Sense of sight! What words are these! You allow that you did not touch it, and yet you knew it would be there. Sense of sight! Yes, it must be so. The sense of sight is evidently a faculty of foreknowledge. You English have extraordinary reasoning powers, and by your knowledge of the laws of nature you were able to conclude from something you trod upon as a cause, that I must tread upon the stone directly after as an effect. We Typhlians can also reason in a similar manner. When I pass through my garden-gate, I know that I shall feel the door of my house soon after. But then I have often been there, whereas you had never walked in that direction before, and yet you could foretell the stone. Ah, I am afraid our natural science falls far short of yours; you evidently reason from cause to effect.

Engl. No, that was not the way in which I became aware of the stone. I did not reason about it at all, but knew at once that you would stumble against it without ever having known of the existence of the stone till a minute before.

Typh. Excuse me, but that is absurd. You may be gifted with other faculties than myself, but all knowledge must have an object. Now when you spoke, there was no object. No,—I am sure that you foretell events by reasoning on the laws of nature you have observed. You must know, perhaps, that after walking over so much grass and so much sand, one must come to such a sort of stone. But as to any immediate faculty by which you can foreknow such an event,—the thing is absurd,—it is a contradiction.

The reader will easily perceive the conclusion I would draw from the above dialogue. A future event is no immediate object of human faculties, but who shall say that it is no object of the Divine? To say that a future event is no object for any conceivable faculty, because it is no object for us, is to judge of a Divine faculty of prescience from our knowledge of other faculties. Now this is as absurd as the judgment of the Typhlian, who concluded that there was no object for any faculty, because none was presented to his sense of touch. It is true, we must not invent faculties for God at pleasure. But there are reasons of a moral and religious character for believing that God possesses the attribute of foreknowledge, there are also reasons for believing in man's freedom, and the intuition of space suggests by analogy a way of reconciling the seeming contradiction between them. Hence I arrive at what appears to me an irresistible conclusion, namely, that God looks through time as we look through space, and that for the Divine mind all that has been, is, or ever shall be, is an ever-present fact.

BOOK II.

THE WILL DIVINE.

CHAPTER I.

The Divine Government of the Universe.

THE will of God may be considered generally under three relations, namely, those to the will of man, to the Universe, and to the Divine Nature respectively.

The first of these subjects has been already considered, but only with reference to the possibility of reconciling the liberty of a created soul with the omnipotence and omniscience of its Creator.

The relation of God to the Universe involves two principal questions, referring respectively to the creation and the government of the world. I have already treated of the former, briefly indeed, as I believe that it lies for the most part beyond the grasp of human faculties. I shall now address myself to the consideration of the latter.

The problem may be stated thus. If God has determined certain immutable laws for nature, and also leaves the human will free, how is the Divine Government possible? For the laws of nature being fixed, the course of events must vary with the human wills, which constitute the only remaining element in their determination.

Now there are but two conceivable hypotheses. Either God has given the above elements only a partial independence, and interferes miraculously when He thinks fit, or else He has made such original dispositions that the whole result shall conform absolutely with the Divine scheme.

The first hypothesis may again be divided into two others, accordingly as we consider the interference to take place in nature or the human will. On the first assumption, God governs the world by miraculous interference with the laws of nature. Now it is a matter of fact that such interferences do not take place with the direct knowledge of man. If therefore they take place at all, it is in secret. A midnight act of malice has placed a stone upon the rail, that the train may be upset, and lives destroyed. But such a catastrophe does not lie within the scheme of Providence. Under the cover of the darkness therefore the stone rolls off as if moved by an invisible hand, the passengers hurry on their way, and reach their destination in safety. The laws of nature have been suspended; a miracle has been performed, but no man has seen it.

The second hypothesis is, that God works no miracles in external nature, but that He suspends human liberty by a secret miraculous act, influencing man's will, and thus making it an unconscious instrument of the Will Divine, when, if its freedom had been left unfettered, it would have resulted in an opposite line of conduct.

Let him who can believe in this patchwork providence of miraculous interference. It contradicts every lofty conception of the Divine character. The stealth, the falsehood, the imperfection of a scheme requiring shifts and artifices even for beneficent ends, are in the highest degree repugnant to all those subjective grounds in our nature on which our faith in God rests.

All special providence, strictly so called, must assume one or the other of the above forms. Those who believe in it, fondly imagine they are glorifying God by attributing to him a perfect knowledge of expedients. But an expedient, in its very idea, is a mode of escaping from some form of imperfection. Now as the idea of God is that of the absolute original of all things, imperfection in him is not to be rejected merely on the grounds of the religious sentiment, but rather as a logical absurdity. For every form of imperfection implies in its conception a perfection somewhere, as the form or rule, by its falling short of which it is declared to be imperfection. But this norm can be sought for nowhere else than in the first absolute ground of all things, that is, in God.

Before I leave this question, I must add a few remarks in anticipation of an objection which may perhaps be raised by some persons to the doctrine of the non-interference of Providence with the human will, on the grounds of its irreconcilability with that of Divine grace. What! will it be asked, do you deny that God acts directly on the human heart in answer to a prayer for grace, and that he thus influences human conduct? To this I reply, that I by no means deny such influence; on the contrary I fully believe it. I only deny that it is *special*, *supernatural*, or *miraculous*. I think it may be taken for granted that he who makes this objection will not hesitate to allow that God has not only created him and nature, but that both are sustained by the Divine power. Nature therefore is no less the result of Divine energy than the supernatural or miraculous, and the only difference between them is, that the former is the Divine energy working according to a self-imposed law, while the latter is the same energy stepping out of these laws in a special and isolated act. Now I maintain that grace falls under the category of the former and not of the latter.

But perhaps my imaginary adversary may object to this, that when he is under the influence of Divine grace, he is immediately conscious, not only that it is a direct, but also a special and supernatural influence from God on his heart, and thus on his will.

That it is direct, I have allowed. But if he asks me to believe in his immediate consciousness of its being *special,* I must pause,—because he virtually asks me to believe that he is immediately conscious of a negation, that is, of the absence of this influence in others; as that alone would make it special.

I am inclined to think that few persons would advocate the doctrine of a special grace, if they were fully aware of what it means. I would address the man who holds such opinions as follows. Do you, who have prayed for grace and received it, believe that God will grant it to you again and in like measure, if you pray for it again under similar circumstances and with like fervour? Again, the circumstances being similar, do you believe that God would grant his grace to the prayer of another as readily as to your own? I am sure you will answer both these questions in the affirmative. But even if the circumstances are not quite similar,—supposing for instance you meet a man who has been a great sinner and has never experienced the benefits of grace, will you not counsel him to pray for it too, and will you not have full faith that if he does pray for it earnestly, he will obtain it, with such difference only as will have a reasonable ground in the difference of the cases? Do you not in short believe that God is no respecter of persons?

If these questions should be answered in the negative,—if God be supposed to send his grace to one man and refuse it to another, or to grant more to one man than another in exactly similar cases, or if in different cases the difference in the measure of his bounty is not determined by some fixed principle or law, then are God's dealings with mankind the sport of an arbitrary chance, and this too in precisely the most solemn of all concerns, in man's spiritual life. It is no argument against this view, to say that God has his *reasons* for the preference, for a *reason* would presume some principle, and by bringing the act of preference into conformity with some general rule or law would rob the grace of its special character.

But God is a God of reason, not of unreason, and the last supposition must be rejected as irreconcileable with the Divine nature. It is impossible therefore to escape the conclusion that God sends his grace to men in conformity with certain principles, in other words, that God's dealings with mankind in spiritual matters are no less regulated by self-imposed laws, than the manifestations of his energy in the physical world, and that grace instead of being special or miraculous, is granted according to the general laws which regulate our spiritual nature. In a certain sense indeed nature itself is supernatural, as it is the action of a God who is above nature. But this epithet can only be applied to grace in the same sense as to nature in general, unless we are prepared to regard the distribution of God's most precious gift, as utterly fortuitous and quite irrespective of all reasonable grounds. It is not however my wish to shake any man's conviction of the immediate influence of God on his soul in grace, but rather to establish for it that universality which makes it reason in God, and nature for man. I see the hand of God in every phenomenon of the natural world, and in grace I can do no more. I do not therefore depreciate grace, but I raise nature, which is only general for man's discursive reason, but for God is immediate and individual.

If then we reject all special or miraculous interference either with external nature or the human will, the only remaining hypothesis by which we can save the Divine government is this: that God has made such original dispositions that the whole result of his own and man's agency shall conform absolutely with the Divine scheme. How is this conceivable?

Now as the problem before us is the reconciliation of the conception of a Divine scheme with human freedom, it is clear that we must regard each of these elements in it as given constants, and as independent of each other. That is to say, in the same manner that the human will is not to be made to vary in accordance with the Divine scheme, which would destroy its freedom, so is the latter again to be consideders a independent of the human will, for otherwise the world would be subject to human and not Divine government. But the Divine scheme considered objectively, is the product of the human will and nature. Hence the reconciliation between these two independent elements, can only be effected by considering nature as the variable. But nature regarded in time is determined. Hence its variation is to be sought for in the original creation of the universe, and the problem to be solved was the determination of such a system of nature, that in co-operation with the foreknown will of man, the grand result should be the scheme as predetermined in the Divine reason. In short, the human will being known, nature was determined as the complement necessary to the fulfilment of the Divine will[1].

Perhaps a general idea of the nature of this problem and the form of its solution, may be given through the medium of a mathematical analogy. Let us consider it then as a vast equation in which the universe considered as a function of the human will and of nature forms one member, and the Divine scheme the other. So that

$$\text{Divine scheme} = \text{human will} \times \text{nature}.$$

or if S = Divine scheme, w = will, n = nature,

then $$wn = S.$$

Now as, by the hypothesis, the liberty of man is to be saved, and the course of events to conform absolutely with the Divine scheme, it is clear that w and S are

[1] Either the doctrine propounded in the text, or something very similar to it, appears to have been entertained by William von Humboldt:—"For in the terrestrial alone" writes Humboldt "nothing can be free, and in the superterrestrial, nothing bound. The opposition is only to be explained on the supposition that the whole province of liberty exercises a dominion over the whole province of the dependent, a dominion which we cannot conceive in detail, but which so guides the concatenation of things from the primæval beginning that it must correspond to the free resolves of the will."

Denn im Irdischen allein kann nichts frei, und im überirdischen nichts gebunden sein. Der Widerstreit ist nur dadurch zu lösen dass es eine Herrschaft des ganzen Gebiets der Freiheit über das ganze Gebiet der Abhängigkeit giebt, die wir nur im Einzelnen nicht begreifen können, die aber die Verkettung der Dinge vom Uranfange so leitet, dass sie den freien Beschlüssen des Willens entsprechen muss. Humboldt's *Letters*, Vol. I. p. 191.

to be considered as constants for the determination of n.

Hence, $$n = \frac{S}{w} \cdot$$

This equation being interpreted, signifies that nature is originally determined by the relation which the Divine scheme bears to the human will as foreknown by God.

This analogy however is in so far imperfect, as we have considered the human will and nature as single quantities. Let us now assume two human wills w_1 and w_2 respectively, and nature as involving two variables n_1 and n_2 respectively. We shall then have the following equation

$$(n_1 + n_2)\ (w_1 + w_2) = S.$$

But here again, as the scheme of providence is not only a general result, but also particular in its relations to individual wills, we shall have some additional equations between n_1, n_2, S, and w_1 and w_2 taken separately. Now to arrive at a just conception of the form of these equations, it will be necessary to observe that the relation of the wills to nature considered purely as law, must be the same for each individual will, as the laws are equally valid for all. If, therefore, the natural world contained no other element but law, these additional equations would involve the individual wills homogeneously. But the natural world contains not only laws but also particular collocations of concrete substances to which these laws refer. The individual wills moreover, through the medium of the body, have also particular relations in space, and therefore to the collocations. Hence it follows that the relations of the different individual wills to nature generally are by no means the same, and the equations expressing them will not be homogeneous. And for the above argument what a collocation is in the external world, the innate character of the individual derived from the parents will be in the world of mind.

Having then once established that these particular equations will not be homogeneous with regard to w_1, w_2, as my sole object is to give the general form of the problem, I need not introduce any new symbol for the collocations, but may consider the various values of n_1, n_2, either as arising from variations in the laws, or in the original collocations. If c represent a collocation generally, and l a law, we shall then have for the parts of nature either

$$n_1 = c_1 l, \quad n_2 = c_2 l, \text{ \&c. } \quad n_m = c_m l,$$

or,

$$n_1 = c l_1, \quad n_2 = c l_2, \text{ \&c. } \quad n_m = c l_m,$$

and as far as our present argument is concerned, each set of values is equally admissible.

The equations required will then assume the form

$$(n_1 + n_2)(w_1 + w_2) = S \ldots\ldots\ldots\ldots (1),$$
$$\phi(n_1, n_2, w_1) = \alpha S \ldots\ldots\ldots\ldots (2),$$
$$f(n_1, n_2, w_2) = \beta S \ldots\ldots\ldots\ldots (3),$$

where there will be of course a conditioning equation between α and β, which will make (3) identical with (1) and (2).

Here then we have the two equations (1) and (2) for the determination of n_1 and n_2, and the same form may be extended to any conceivable number of wills, only observing that there must be a corresponding number of variables n_1, n_2, &c.

The general solution of the problem of the Divine Government, which I offer on the above consideration, is as follows :—

God, foreknowing all human wills through all time, and unwilling to infringe on their liberty, created such a world, and subjected it to such laws, that the grand resulting product of the wills and the nature should agree exactly with that scheme of the course of events, which he in his infinite wisdom had predetermined. But a system of nature which might exactly suit the Divine scheme, considered with relation to a single will, might not suit such scheme with reference to another, and still less with reference to the wills of all mankind. Hence, the only system which would suit for all wills had to be obtained by elimination from a number of equations equal to that of all the human wills of all ages, in which the laws of nature, and the collocations of their objects constitute the unknown quantities.

To prevent the possibility of misconception, it may be as well to add, that I by no means intend to assert that God ever really solved such an equation as the above, for what man can only arrive at by reasoning, is known to God intuitively. But what I do mean to assert is this: that the above equations represent the only system of mutual dependencies for the elements of the problem of Divine government, by which we can save at once and entirely the absoluteness of the Divine scheme of government, human liberty, and the laws of nature.

Though the above theory of Divine government includes both the conceptions of a predestination and a harmony, it has nothing in common with the predestined harmony of Leibnitz. That philosopher, unable to conceive the possibility of any causal relations between mind and matter, believed that God had established such a system of laws for each, that the respective series of their phenomena should exactly agree with each other in the parts of time. In the scheme, therefore, of Leibnitz two objective series are to be brought into harmony. In the theory at present under consideration, no attempt is made to explain the causal relations between mind and matter, but on the contrary such relations are assumed. The harmony, however, which I have attempted to explain, is that between the conception in the Divine mind of the Divine scheme considered in its results, on the one hand, and, on the other, the actual course of the universe considered as the product of nature and of human liberty.

But although the above theory does not in any way correspond to the pre-established harmony of Leibnitz, yet has it some outward similarity to the doctrine which that philosopher has suggested, in the concluding pages of his elaborate Essay on the Goodness of God, Human Liberty, and the Origin of Evil. Leibnitz first gives, in the form of a dialogue, the substance of a passage from the work of Laurentius Valla against the fifth book of Boethius *de Consolatione* (the object of which passage is to reconcile the foreknowledge of God with the liberty of man), and then adds a sequel of his own. The whole dialogue is too long for insertion here, and I shall therefore confine myself to a sketch of its philosophical contents.

Laurentius having endeavoured to explain to a young Spaniard, Antonius Glarea, some of the difficulties connected with foreknowledge and freewill, concludes his remarks with the following fable by way of illustration.

Sextus Tarquinius consults the Oracle of Delphi, and there learns that he will be banished from Rome. He complains to Apollo of his hard fate, but the god replies, that although he knows the future, he does not make it, and that if Sextus feels himself aggrieved, he must apply to Jupiter and the Fates. Sextus thinks that Jupiter has treated him very hardly, and that he is not free. Apollo answers, that the gods make every being such as it is,—the wolf murderous, the hare timid, the ass stupid, and that Jupiter has given Sextus a wicked soul, and will punish him according to his deeds.

Leibnitz does not seem quite satisfied with this argument, and indeed it would be difficult to imagine how he should be; for although it does not make the act to be determined by the foreknowledge, it makes at least the external determination of the act a necessary condition to the foreknowledge,—a view which is just as fatal to liberty as the other. He accordingly supplies a sequel to the story for the purpose of vindicating liberty. Sextus leaves Delphi for Dodona, and after having offered the usual sacrifices, asks Jupiter why he has condemned him to such an unhappy fate. Jupiter answers, that if Sextus will renounce Rome, the Fates will spin another thread for him, and that he will then be a wise and happy man. Sextus however cannot make up his mind to give up a throne, goes to Rome, and is banished.

Theodorus, the high priest, has listened to the conversation, and unable to reconcile Jupiter's decrees with his justice, observes very respectfully, that Sextus must now ascribe his destruction to his own wicked will, but adds that he should like to know why Jupiter could not have given him another and a better will. Jupiter refers the priest to Minerva, who in a dream conducts him to a magnificent building, which she informs him is the palace of the destinies, and of which she has the charge. "In this palace," says the goddess, "not only is there a representation of everything that happens, but also of everything that is possible. When before the beginning of the actual world, Jupiter considered all possible events, he arranged them in an infinite number of worlds, and then chose the best * * .

I have only to speak a word, and we shall behold a complete world which my father could have created, and in this manner we shall learn what would have happened if this or the other possibility had actually occurred. And if the conditions are not sufficiently determined, there will be as many worlds as we like, all of which will correspond to any particular case in every conceivable manner. Like all other well educated youths, you have studied geometry. You are aware therefore that when the conditions do not sufficiently determine any required point, they all fall into a *locus*, as the geometricians call it, and that this locus at least, which is often a line, will be determined. In the same manner you may represent to yourself a regular series of worlds, all of which contain the present case, and merely introduce variations in the circumstances and their results. But if you assume a case which varies from the actual world in a single definite thing and its results, only one definite world will answer the conditions. All these worlds are here, in pictures or in ideas. I will shew you some in which, indeed, there is not precisely the same Sextus whom you have seen, (that is impossible, for he has always had that in him already, which he gradually becomes) but very similar Sextuses who have in them all that you know of the real Sextus, but not all that is really in him, and consequently, not all that is yet to happen to him. You will find in one world a very happy and noble Sextus, in another a Sextus who is contented with a subordinate position,—in a word, all sorts of Sextuses."

Upon this she conducts Theodorus into the palace, each room of which represents a possible world. In one of these he sees Sextus settled at Corinth, where he buys a small garden, digs up a treasure, and dies at a good old age, one of the most beloved and respected of the inhabitants of that city. In another world, Sextus goes to Thrace, marries the king's daughter, and succeeds in the government. These rooms, however, are all arranged in a pyramidal form, and become more and more beautiful as they approach the apex. At last Theodorus enters the last and most perfect room, in which he recognises the actually existing world, and sees Sextus as the wicked king of Rome.

"You see," says Minerva, "how Sextus goes to Rome, sets everything in confusion, violates the wife of his friend, and is banished with his father. Had Jupiter taken a happy Sextus at Corinth or a king in Thrace, it would no longer have been this world; and yet he could not do otherwise than choose this one, as it surpasses all the others in perfection, and forms the apex of the pyramids.

"You see that my father has not made Sextus wicked. He was so from all eternity, and indeed freely and unconstrained. Jupiter has only given him the reality, which his wisdom could not refuse the best world. He has taken him out of the land of possible things and placed him in that of the actual."

The above passages are quite inadequate to enable the reader to appreciate this fable as a work of imagination, but I believe they contain all that is essential to the comprehension of its philosophy. The objections I shall offer to it may be easily anticipated from the theory of Divine Government enunciated in this chapter. According to Leibnitz human wills stand in a relation of such absolute causality with the course of events, as predetermined in the Divine Mind, that the quality of the former must be predetermined too, as otherwise the Divine scheme could not be carried out. Jupiter therefore finding that he wanted a wicked Sextus for his scheme, created him at the fitting moment. Leibnitz has thus made the character of the will to be determined by the scheme, and destroyed its freedom. To say that Sextus as a possible being was wicked from all eternity, and that Jupiter merely gave him reality, is nothing more than to say, that Jupiter had from all eternity conceived a wicked Sextus, and created him when he wanted him.

Now according to the scheme of Divine Government propounded in this treatise, God creates wills such that they are unconditioned self-determinants as far as their allegiance to the will universal is concerned, and therefore free; but foreknowing what their self-determination will be, he places them in the midst of such a natural world, both moral and physical, that the grand result is the scheme which he has preordained from the beginning.

To make my meaning plainer, I will state shortly the change that would be necessary to make the fable of Leibnitz suit the above theory. Instead of the Sextuses in the other possible worlds being like the real one in certain externals, but differing from him in essentials, I would conceive them as exactly the reverse, *i.e.* as having the same intrinsically bad will but manifesting it under other circumstances. After having shewn Theodorus the apparently happy and respected Sextus at Corinth, Minerva would then have given him an insight into his real life. Theodorus would thus have learnt that the happiness and prosperity of Sextus were a mere illusion. He would have seen how in the possible world Sextus would have acquired the garden and its hidden treasure by unjust means, and that he would be living in the daily fear of detection, disgrace and ruin. It would then have appeared that Jupiter, having made a Sextus with a power of self-determination, the latter had chosen for himself a bad will, and that Jupiter, foreknowing what this will would be, and wanting an instrument to bring about the liberty of Rome, had merely arranged his world in such a way that the circumstances acting on this bad will should cause it to manifest itself in the form of a lascivious and tyrannical king.

Mr Plumer Ward, in his novel of Tremaine, has referred to the above fable with unmixed approbation, and without pointing out its defects. His own solution however of the problem of Divine Government agrees in great measure with that proposed here; but it contains an ambiguity on one very important point, and is incomplete in another no less important. Evelyn says, in an argument with Tremaine, "So determined might the Deity be to leave man perfectly free, that, in casting the scheme of his dispensations when he originally created mankind, he might, according to my theory, from foreseeing what every man would do in given circumstances have originally shaped His own government of nature accordingly."[1]

Now, in the first place, "the scheme of God's dispensations" is a phrase which would generally be understood to include God's moral government, and in the above sentence it would appear that Evelyn makes this scheme dependent on the individual wills. If this interpretation of the passage be correct, Evelyn makes the human and not the Divine will the ultimate determinant in the course of events, and the Divine *government* to be little more than Divine *obedience.*

Secondly, although it is evidently beyond the reach of human faculties to attempt to obtain any insight into the matter of the Divine decrees, yet is the whole problem concerned with their formal relations to nature and to human liberty. Unless therefore we arrive at some system in which the mere logical interdependencies of its various elements are determined, and the possibility of their harmony demonstrated, but little has been accomplished. Tremaine however might have answered, "If the human wills are left free, perhaps Omniscience may be able to find such a form for nature, as would bring a million wills into harmony with the Divine scheme; but how do we know that the reconciliation of the other wills may not offer a logical contradiction? Now the object of the above symbolical solution is to answer this question by proving, that the problem offers no difficulties on this score, so long as the variables arising in the possible collocations and laws of nature is supposed equal in number to the human wills.

[1] Vol. II. p. 304, Colborn's *Standard Novels.*

According to the above view of the Divine Government the most minute circumstances have all been not only foreknown, but planned by God, and form a part of his eternal scheme. The attempt to exclude any existence in the world of mind or matter from the interest of God on the ground of its minuteness or unimportance, is simply one form of that common error, which would attribute the limitations of our knowledge of objects to the objects in themselves. Nothing can really be more absurd than for man to pretend to draw a line between the important and the trivial for the Divine intellect, or to assume that even the position of individual grains of sand has no significance for Divine wisdom. Is the interest of the Creator in his works to be measured by yards and inches? Where are we to draw the line between a grain of sand and Mont Blanc? Besides, the position of a single grain has its influence on the centre of gravity of the world, and thus on the solar system; and such effect, ever increasing through time, may eventually exercise an immeasurable influence on the destination of our planet. If we were to see a man sitting quietly in a room with a piece of wire in each hand, what would be more natural than for a casual spectator to regard it as a very indifferent matter whether he held them apart or brought them together? There is only an interval of a few inches between them, and by a slight movement of one hand he at length places them in contact. A few seconds afterwards a deafening report is heard, and the earth trembles, as if shaken by an earthquake. A fortress of granite has been hurled from its foundations; what a minute before was a beautiful city with its theatres and its palaces and its temples, presents now but an unsightly heap of ruins, and thousands of human beings that had thronged its streets in the fulness of life and strength, now complete the scene of devastation with their blackened corpses. Such effects as these come within man's knowledge of the possible; and who shall dare to say, that to God, who sees and knows all things, a deviation from their appointed place of any two grains of sand may not be known to involve even far greater consequences?

The moral bearings of this doctrine are very grand. He who believes in it, learns to regard himself as an essential link in the mighty chain that is to bind the whole creation into that perfect unity[1], which has made it find favour with the Creator. Each man has his work to do; each man does what is to be done by him and no other. Each has moral liberty, and can determine for himself the moral elevation of his mission; but the task to which God will set him has been preordained through God's perfect knowledge of what such self-determination will be.

Perhaps the above scheme may at first be considered as derogatory to God, on account of its making his determination of nature in any way dependent on the will of each individual man. But it must be re-

The absurdity of the doctrine that denies this unity, by exchanging the grand doctrine of a particular Providence for the very narrow doctrine of a partial Providence, has been wittily exposed in the following passage.

"A perpetual curate told a lamentable tale of the upsetting of a boat on the river. * * * There were two men, he said, in the boat,—one was providentially saved.

"'And the other, Sir,' interrupted Barker sharply, 'the other, I suppose was providentially drowned.'

"The perpetual curate looked aghast.

"'Don't you think,' pursued Barker, with acrimony 'that Providence had as much to do with the drowning of the one, as with the rescue of the other?'" *Bachelor of the Albany.*

membered, in the first place, that the Divine scheme is completely saved; and secondly, that under any circumstances it is only man's discursive reason that generalises, but that to God every human soul is individual.

The above view must not be confounded with that weak superstition, the offspring of a morbid imagination and an overweening self-complacency in spiritual matters, which recognises a special call to a particular line of conduct on innumerable trivial occasions. A special call would be a direct revelation to a particular individual, informing him of the peculiar task which he was destined to perform. It would in short be a miraculous interference with his will, to which doctrine I have already expressed my objections in my remarks on the nature of grace. All that I here contend for is, that every human action has its significance in the eye of God, and contributes its share to the universal scheme.

Thus it is that all of us,—sinners as well as saints, are in some sort soldiers in God's army, and carry out his operations. But it is an army in which there are no privates. Two hundred men without individual distinction are not set to do this, and two hundred others to do that, but each man has his special and distinctive task. Each has his particular position to occupy or post to storm, and does not, like a private soldier, rank as a mere unit in a crowd of others, but rather as an officer; and a firm faith in this fact will enable him to bear himself bravely in the world's campaign, and establish by the greatness of his accomplishment the loftiness of his mission.

The difficulties respecting the efficacy of prayer vanish at once before the above view of Divine Government. The laws of the nature both of mind and matter having been once determined in the great equation of the Universe, and the Divine scheme and human liberty having both been saved inviolate, such answer to each prayer as God shall see fit to grant, has also been saved as a part of the scheme, without any interference with the uniformity of nature. And here, let it be observed, I have only attempted to bring to the distinct consciousness of reason, a conviction which is absolutely indispensable to our faith, if our prayers are to be more than a hollow mockery. For to pray to God to save the life of one who is dear to us, with the thought lurking in our hearts that the Divine decrees are quite irrespective of such prayer, to pray therefore in unbelief, and merely in the hope of obtaining some sort of consolation from the general tone of the feelings produced, is to make the prayer a pitiful equivocation, and to rob it of all efficacy for ourselves as well as others. If we are ever to be true, surely we must be so in our heart's communion with Him who is all truth.

There is another phasis of the above scheme of Divine government which gives it to my mind an unspeakable majesty. The causality cognized by human faculties, leading from the present to the future, and based on the limitations of time, appears in it only as one side of the higher and all comprehensive causality in the Divine reason, which recognises no such limitations. The universe through all eternity and all space is thus knit together into one great harmonious whole, and the future is found to determine the past, just as the past determines the future.

CHAPTER II.

The Divine Will the absolute Principle in the Divine Character.

HAVING considered the Divine will in its relations to the human will and to nature, in the creation and government of the universe, I shall now proceed to examine its relation to the Divine nature. The form which the problem assumes is the following question: Is the Divine will co-ordinate with the Divine nature, or is it the ground of such nature? Or it may be stated thus: Are the laws constituting the Divine nature imposed upon the Divine will, or freely assumed by it in its own act? The question is an important one, for it involves that of God's perfect liberty, and therefore of his omnipotence.

Now a very little consideration will suffice to shew that the former alternative is incompatible with the idea of God. For if the Divine nature be not self-assumed, it must have a ground in some energy out of the Divine will. But if we adopt this hypothesis, we have virtually deposed the God with which we have originally started, for we cannot refuse to acknowledge the higher claims of this energy, as a still higher principle, to be enthroned in his place.

Or the same argument may be stated thus. The nature of a being is the complex of the conditions of its activity. All conditions presume a higher will imposing them. Consequently, every nature presumes a higher will as its ground. The conception of God excludes every will superior to, or collateral with his own. Consequently, the Divine nature has no other ground than the Divine will.

The above conclusion by no means denies the eternity of the Divine nature, or presumes a time when God was not infinitely good. It merely states that the Divine will has from all eternity made the Divine character, and that God has assumed the goodness freely, and not found it imposed upon him by any form of necessity; and from this conclusion it is impossible to escape. For directly we make the least attempt to evade it, and endeavour to conceive God with a certain opaque kernel of attributes, and the Divine will as limited to certain modes of action by laws not originating in its own act, we must look for some higher energy which has imposed these laws; in short, we must look for a God above God as the ultimate ground of his having such a nature.

I will here anticipate an objection to this position. Perhaps it may be said that this doctrine lowers the conception of the Deity, by making him in his essence a mere force,—infinite no doubt,—but still a mere force, and thus robbing him of all those high attributes which command our veneration and our awe.

Now the real bearings of the above view of the Divine nature are diametrically opposed to this result. In the first place, the conception of a will is necessarily logically prior to that of a moral law. For *can* is perfectly conceivable without *ought*, but *ought* presupposes *can*. In the second place, it is precisely the opposite doctrine which would destroy all claim on the part of the Deity to the love and reverence of mankind. A *necessarily* good being is a contradiction in terms; for a *necessarily* good being is simply not good, inasmuch as necessity at once removes an action from the sphere of morality[1]. The feelings of love and awe would, therefore, be utterly misplaced on the supposition that there is a necessity of goodness in the Divine essence, not subject to the Divine will, for these feelings only acquire their full significance when we have completely grasped the conviction of the absolute and unconditioned liberty of God in the determination of his own attributes. Why should we feel grateful to God for his loving-kindness, if such loving-kindness were an attribute not chosen by himself, but one of which he could not divest himself if he would?

It follows from the foregoing considerations that the ultimate principle of the moral law is the will of God; in other words, that God has made morality,

[1] The moral perfection of the Deity consists, "not in having no power to do ill, otherwise, as Dr Clarke justly observes, there would be no ground to thank him for his goodness to us, any more than for his eternity or immensity; but his moral perfection consists in this, that when he has power to do everything*, a power which cannot be resisted, he exerts that power only in doing what is wisest and best." Reid's *Essays on the Active Powers*, Essay IV. Chap. IV.

On the above passage Sir W. Hamilton has the following note.

* "To do everything consistent with his perfection. But here one of the insoluble contradictions in the question arises; for if, on the one hand, we attribute to the Deity the power of moral evil, we detract from his essential goodness; and if, on the other, we deny him this power, we detract from his omnipotence." Hamilton's *Reid*, p. 609.

In the above passages Reid's text seems to me to contain a sounder view than the commentator's note. The power to do evil does not detract from the goodness of the Deity as long as it remains unexercised, any more than my power to kill a man makes me at all the worse morally, provided I never attempt it. But if it be urged that the power to do evil detracts from His *essential* goodness, meaning thereby, goodness that is necessary, and not chosen freely in preference to evil, then I would observe, that such moral goodness is neither man's nor God's, as freedom is essential to all moral goodness.

not found it. But this position must not for an instant be understood to imply, that morality first sprang into being in time through a fiat of the Almighty, in the same manner as we may conceive the creation of a planet. Moral perfection is eternal,—as eternal as the All-perfect God; but it is a Divine attribute freely adopted by his will, not imposed upon it; for necessity in any form is its death.

Still it may perhaps be argued, that morality, as one form of eternal truth, must be independent of the will of any being, even though that being should be the Eternal God. Now let us consider the soundness of this objection. Supposing God had never created a reasonable or even a sentient creature, where would the moral law have been then? In the mind of God, perhaps will be the answer. Good; but now suppose there never had been a God or any other reasonable being, where would the moral law have been then? Moral perfection, or any other principle, however eternal it actually *is*, presupposes a reasonable mind as its abiding place. If, however, we contemplate an absolute void without either God or man, and still maintain morality as an eternal principle, it is merely as a possibility which is first to come into existence on the creation of reasonable beings. But a mere possibility is objectively absolutely nothing. A possibility is the conception of what may take place without violating the laws of thought of the conceiving being, and in assuming the possibility we have thus assumed the conceiving being, and therefore the mind in which the morality, by the necessary laws of human thought, appears as one of its phases. In other words, the speculator has not succeeded in the impossible problem of producing an absolute void, as he can never annihilate the speculating mind that endeavours to conceive it.

The whole objection may be shortly answered thus. Whenever we think an imaginary state of things, or rather of nothing, we think at least a thinking subject, and, therefore, the moral law has already found a resting-place. But as this moral law has no significance except for thinking beings, we are justified in saying that if none such had ever existed, there would have been no moral law; though we can never represent such a void by any effort of the imagination, as that faculty cannot annihilate itself.

It has been attempted by Cudworth to adduce an argument for the independence of the principles of morality of the Divine will from the necessity of other formal laws of thought. Could God, for instance, have made the square of the hypothenuse greater than the sum of the squares of the other sides?

Now this argument involves precisely the same fallacy as the last. In conceiving the supposed principle, the possibility of whose falsity is in question, we have already assumed the conception of space, and with it all the laws of that form of intuition as they have actually been given us; and, consequently, we take the truth of the principle as a starting-point for the question in which we demand whether its falsity be possible. To make the cases really analogous, the question should be couched as follows: Is it conceivable that God could have created minds without the conception of space at all? I think there can be no hesitation in answering this question in the affirmative.

The analysis of the moral principle given in a former chapter leads to precisely the same result as that at which we have arrived in this. I there endeavoured to shew that this principle consists in the entire subjection of the human will to the will universal, thus making the latter the ultimate standard of the moral law. And here we arrive at the true ground of our conviction of the necessity of the moral perfection of the Deity. The will of God *must* agree with itself; and here we have the necessity of the Divine perfection, but merely as a necessity of consequential modality. That, however, the will of God should have been precisely what it has been, there was no antecedent necessity; and here we have the free and unconditioned causality of the Divine will as the absolute original of all things.

The above views of the relation of the Divine will to perfection, answer at once all the difficulties arising in an optimism from its supposed limitation to the Divine liberty. Some writers, Leibnitz for instance, speak as if God had found so many plans proposed to his mind as possible, with different degrees of perfection, and chose the best. But who determines which is this best? If he *found* so many first best, and so many second best, there must have been a God above or before him to determine the standard which determines the best. But he who created the universe, is he alone who gave a meaning to the word *best*.

In the first book of this treatise I have endeavoured to establish the position of Cudworth, that the human will is the last thing in the human soul. The goal I have at length arrived at in the second book, but without the sanction of Cudworth's authority, is the extension of this principle to that Divine energy, the absolute ground of all things in heaven and in earth, in time and in eternity. Neither morality nor religion will ever find a surer basis than a living faith that the Divine will is the last thing in the Divine mind.

And now in conclusion, I will repeat my innermost conviction, that the existence of freewill, in man as a fact of the consciousness, in God as an object of our faith, is the cardinal point on which all that is sound in philosophy or true in religion ultimately turns. Banish it from heaven and earth, and men become nothing more than the petty wheels in the vast machine of which God is the involuntary motive power. But the engineer is absent, and he whom we then call God is bound in the trammels of a merciless necessity,—no object of love, for he cannot hate, no object of prayer, for he cannot aid, no object of praise, for he is a tool in the hands of a higher fate. Morality then sinks into a calculation of pressure and leverage, and nice adjustment of screws and cogs; reverence is but the yielding of the various parts to the primary force; the spiritual finds no resting-place, and the material has undivided sway. Restore freewill, and where all before was death and darkness, all now becomes life and light. Then indeed does God cease to be the omnipresent automaton, the dead God of the dead, and becomes a spirit and a power, and the living God of the living. Then, indeed, are love, and prayer, and praise his just meed and our high privilege, for of his own freewill and of no necessity is he a gracious God and merciful, slow to anger and of great kindness, and his tender mercies are over all his works. For of Him, and through Him, and to Him, are all things; to whom be glory for ever.

APPENDIX A.

Burthogge's anticipation of Kant.

Bishop Berkeley is generally regarded as the first English writer who propounded any form of idealism. This opinion, however, is incorrect. Berkeley may have been the first who made idealism the subject of a long treatise, but a far more sweeping form of it had been enunciated in an earlier work. *An Essay on Reason and the Nature of Spirits,* by Richard Burthogge, M.D., was published at London in 1694, sixteen years, therefore, before the appearance of the Bishop's treatise on human knowledge, and when Berkeley was only ten years old. This work is now extremely rare, but possesses considerable interest, as it contains numerous passages expressing in clear and unequivocal language the general theory of Kant's Criticism of the pure reason, as far as the understanding alone is concerned. I do not mean by this that Burthogge has hit upon Kant's exhaustive method of deducing the categories by an analysis of the form of a judgment, but he repeatedly asserts that the conceptions of substance and accident, cause and effect, whole and part are not anything in themselves, but are only notions of the understanding under which it apprehends its particular objects, or as he sometimes calls them *modi concipiendi.*

As Burthogge's work is very rare, it is highly probable that the reader has not met with it, and I therefore subjoin a few extracts by way of establishing the correctness of the above statement respecting it.

In Chapter III. Sect. I., having described a notion as 'any conception formed by the mind in reference to objects' (p. 52), he proceeds (at p. 56) as follows:

'But besides the former sense of the word (notion), there is another which is more restrained and limited; in which a notion is *modus concipiendi,* a certain particular manner of conceiving; a manner of conceiving things that corresponds not to them but only as they are objects, not as they are things; there being in every conception something that is purely objective, purely notional; insomuch that few, if any, of the ideas which we have of things are properly pictures; our conceptions of things no more resembling them in strict propriety, than our words do our conceptions, for which yet they do stand, and with which they have a kind of correspondence and answering: just as figures that do stand for numbers, yet are no wise like them.

'To make this clearer, it must be considered that the eye has no perception of things but under the appearance of light and colours, and yet light and colours do not really exist in the things themselves that are perceived and seen by means of them, but are only in the eye. Likewise the ear has no perceivance of things, as of a bell, of a lute, or of a viol, but under sounds, and yet sound is only a sentiment in the ear that hears, and is not, or anything like it, in the bell, or viol, or lute that is heard. For as the eye has no perceivance of things but under colours that are not in them, (and the same with due alteration must be said of the other senses,) so the understanding apprehends not things, or any habitudes or aspects of them, but under certain notions that neither have that being in objects, or that being of objects, that they seem to have; but are, in all respects, the very same to the mind or understanding, that colours are to the eye and sound to the ear. To be more particular, the understanding conceives not anything but under the notion of an entity, and this either a substance or an accident; under that of a whole or of a part; or of a cause, or of an effect, or the like; and yet all these and the like are only entities of reason conceived within the mind, that have no more of any real true existence without it, than colours have without the eye, or sounds without the ear. Every person that hath the least understanding of the way in which we do apprehend things, will yield this to be true as to whole and part, to cause and effect, and to all the notions which are commonly termed by logicians the second; and it is as certainly true in reference to substance and accident, to quantity, quality, and those other general notions under which the understanding apprehends its objects, though commonly they are called first ones, and in comparison of the others, are so.

'I have laboured the more to make the notion that I have in this business plain and easy, because much of what is to be said hereafter will depend upon it; and now taking for granted that my meaning is *intelligible*, what remains is to evince *true;* and this I shall do, from the very nature of cogitation in general, (as it comprehends sensation as well as intellection), since that the understanding doth *pin* its notions upon objects, arises not from its being *such* a particular kind of cogitative faculty, but from its being cogitative at large; let us then reflect again on the nature of cogitation at large.

'It is certain that things to us men are nothing but as they do stand in our analogy, that is, in plain terms, they are nothing to us but as they are known by us; and as certain, that they stand not in our analogy, nor are known by us, but as they are in our faculties, in our senses, imagination, or mind; and they are not in our faculties, either in their own realities, or by way of a true resemblance and representation, but only in respect of certain appearances or sentiments, which, by the various impressions that they make upon us, they do either occasion only, or cause, or (which is most probable) concur unto in causing with our faculties. Every cogitative faculty, though it is not the sole cause of its own immediate (apparent) object, yet has a share in making it: thus the eye or visive faculty hath a share in making the colours which it is said to see; the ear or auditive power a share in producing sounds, which yet it is said to hear; the imagination has a part in making the images stored in it; and there is the same reason for the understanding, that it should have a like share in framing the primitive notions under which it takes in and receives objects; in sum, the immediate objects of cogitation as it is exercised by men, are *entia cogitationis*, all phenomena; appearances that do no more exist without our faculties in the things themselves, than the images that are seen in water or behind a glass, do really exist in those places where they seem to be.

* * * *

'And as for substance and accident, which yet are the first steps we make toward a distinct perceivance and knowledge of things; what are they but likewise *modi concipiendi?* Entities of reason, or notions, that (it is true) are not without grounds, but yet that have themselves, no formal being but only in the mind that frames them; there being no such thing in the world as a substance, or an accident, any more than such a thing as a subject or an adjunct; and yet we apprehend not anything but as one of these, to wit, as a substance or as an accident; so that we apprehend not any at all, just as they are, in their own realities, but only under the top-knots and dresses of notions, which our minds do put upon them, p. 64.

* * * *

In truth, neither accident, nor substance hath any being but only in the mind, and by the only virtue of cogitation or thought.'—*Essay upon Reason and the Nature of Spirits*, by Richard Burthogge, M.D., London. Printed for John Dunton at the Raven in the Poultry. 1694. Chap. III. Sect. I.

APPENDIX B.

Cudworth's Letters, while a Student at Cambridge.

THE quotation from Cudworth, at page 239, is taken from the first of the two following letters. The originals are in my possession. Neither of them has any date, but as Cudworth was born in 1618, and took his degree about 1639, the first was probably written about 1638; and the other appears to have been written about the same time. The matter of these letters is so very interesting, as shewing the tone of Cudworth's mind while a student at Cambridge, that I shall offer no apology for subjoining them at length. The Dr

Stoughton to whom they are addressed was Cudworth's step-father.

To the right wo[ll] *my very loving father,* D[r] STOUGHTON, *at his house in Aldermanbury, these with speede.*

DEARE AND MUCH HONORD FATHER,

Hoping of yours and my Mother's healths in the Lord: I came the last night from Seaton to Cambridge, and find the state of things here unpleasing to me: Understanding the departure of our Ministry which wee enjoied under Mr Hall and Mr Goade: To thinke of stay here rellishes not my thoughts: and therefore I am much troubled and unpleasingly affected with my Tutor's violent importunity towards me, to sitte the next weeke for a fellowship, as soon as I come cras-ingupon me: as far as I understand of your minde, your loving councell is not, I should goe on that way: Mine owne Spirit is for the present averse: and I shall no way satisfy my Tutor unlesse it may please you this weeke to write a Line or two to me to this Effecte, that your advice is, that at leaste for this present, I should not meddle in that kinde, but suspend upon Considerations best known to your selfe: if this be as I thinke your judgment: in submitting to which and no other way can I inoffensively deny to satisfy my Tutor's desire: for however, if I were affected that way, it seems fond to mee, to put forth myself to no purpose at such a time, when there are 4 besides my selfe, all my seniors and 3 of them Masters of Arts: I desire I hope seriosly not in the least to prejudice the spirituall advantage and elevation of my soule towards my God and the pretious knowledge of Christ Jesus my Lord: which if I mis-take not myselfe when my soule is calme and composed within itselfe I account my chiefes Treasure: I would looke upon my Being as one entire whole thinge drawne out and continued from one end of time to the length of eternity like a continued Line having only that little knot of Death in it: and seriosly provide for my selfe and love my selfe in Lineâ not in Puncto: comprehensively taking up all the successive moments of my selfe in one Generall View and prospect: Sir

Fran. Bacon speaks of Idola Specus. I thinke this to bee one when a man looks round upon himselfe bounded and limited within the horizon of time here, as in the walls of some narrow cell, and lets not his ingenuous soule have a free prospect upon the whole compasse of its immortality: I desire to caste the Dy of my Being, my time and eternity upon my God: studying only to grow in divine Life, in elevated and truly noble Communion with his blessed selfe, thro Christ Jesus my glorious Saviour: O the happiness that souls, spirits feel when they come to mingle with the father of Spirits, to roll themselves in the bosome of the ever-living God, drinking of those Streams of immortality that flow from his right-hand: his bosome is ἀληθὴς ψυχῶν πατρὶς as the Platonists speake, and hee is the end of all knowledge and learning, the beholding of him the End of all Philosophy saith Plato, tanquam ἐπόπτεια τῆς τελετῆς: to which that divine Heathen thought to sublimate his soule by Mathematicall Abstractions, but wee have a glorious Ladder to that blessed Divinity, for so hee himselfe interprets Jacob's Ladder in John, Christ Jesus, whose humane Nature doth as it were γεφυρῶσαι τὴν γῆν καὶ οὐρανόν: in an unspeakable Mysterious Manner: I am perswaded all true knowledge if our understanding were right, would end in the Practicall Loving and closing with God: Tis an excellent speach of Aristotles which Plutarch often remembers in his Moralls, I remember not the Greek readily, concerning Alexander: Hee may Glory saith he, that is Conqueror of the whole world, and yet another may glory as well as hee, that knows how to thinke of the Gods what hee ought: Certainly hee that is the End of all Being would bee the End of all knowing, knowledge doth but ἀναμετροῦν τὰ ἴχνη τοῦ ὄντος: And as they say well, Nihil debet esse in Globo Materiæ quod non habeat Parallelum in Globo Chrystallino vel Intellectus, so then is our knowledge right when the Pictures in the little world of the soule, for so are they called in the Hebrew, have the same order that the things themselves in the great world abroad: God being the ultimate close of all: Certainly I cannot phanzy that to bee truly called knowledge which is in animâ but tanquam in Vase, and doth not alter and change the soule: and most of that which the world calls knowledge, as Plutarch speakes of the Philosophy of his time, 'twas but καπνὸς φιλοσοφίας, so our Tounges and jangling Arts, are to that which is true knowledge and wisdome: Wee cannot see true Wisdome for the Cloths of it and the stuffe about, in which since man's fall it is wrapt and mufled up: and which wee mistake for knowledge itselfe: So much I thinke I know, as truth and good are married together within my soule: not how much I fill my soule but change the crasis and Complection of it: The will is the Last thing in the soule, and the ultimate resolution of all others: I thinke my understanding and apprehension should bee but like Jupiter's Doves, to bringe in Nectar to feed my will and affections: A man that is αἰσθητικὸς καὶ δεκτικὸς τῶν εἰς φιλοσοφίαν φερόντων may certainly in all studies and knowledge find that which will carry in his Love to the bosome of his God: I pray pardon my present bodily distemper if I have troubled you with confused writing: I hope you will not faile to send a word or two to free me from this matter of the fellowship however at this time: and if you meet with any place in the country or the City which you should thinke fit for mee, I care not how soone, to commend mee unto it. I wrote to you concerning mony but afterwards I heard from Mr Theobalds: Thus hoping of your health allso of my little sister I leave you to the Protection of Christ Jesus,

Your ever humbly engaged Son,

R. CUDWORTH.

I pray let this Letter bee sent to my Unkle, because I have too much neglected him.

To the right wo[ll] my very much honord father, D[r] STOUGHTON, *at his house in Aldermanbury these.*

DEARE AND LOVING FATHER,

I am glad to heare of your and my Mother's safe returne from the Country which I did the laste weeke by Mr Man: And I presente you with my thankfull remembrances for your invitation of mee by Mr Coxe to goe with you: but besides other things, his Letter came too late to mee according to that time which it afterward informed mee of: Tis a noble thinge to walke in the beams of divine light, in St John's Phrase ἐν τῷ φωτὶ περιπατεῖν: Our soules, as the substance of them is cloistered up within the thicke walls of the body, so their apprehensions are much bounded and imprisoned within the darke dungeon of sence; and because all their actions are from sence and thro sence, like pure Sunbeams, that receive a Materiall Impression of color if they passe thro colord glasse, so they by percolation thorough the body have a grosse and earthy tincture: and indead have allso lost their owne primitive purity. The highest excellency of our Nature is in the deepe apprehension of God's infinite Majesty and glorious transcendent excellency to become nothing in ourselves in the deepest degree of holy annihilation, being swallowed up in him, and loosing the little drop of our owne being in the vast ocean of our eternall God, making him in the Lord Christ, the fountaine of all in humble acknowledgment, the Centre of all in Motion and Tendency. Moving towards him by faith, for faith in Christ is our προσαγωγὴ to God, and it is somewhere in the Scriptures defined by a coming to God, and then moving and rolling in him by a circulation of holy Love: No such wonder in the World as that God which is all in every thing and πλήρωμα πάντων as the Platonists call the soule, should bee loste and by so few fully discerned: What a little thing is heard of him, saith divine Elihu, when hee had reckond up all his workes. Nay our soules themselves are so narrow and their highest thoughts so unworthy, that when they graspd with all their might, to reach after him and lift themselves up towards him, they fall downe in the midst of a thicke darkenesse: And perhaps therefore the Holy of Holies called God's Throne in the Revelation was not only Negatively darke, because it had no windows, but there was allso a Cloud there, and moreover the Priest never went in but hee was to make a Cloud before him by his Incence: in imitation of which the Gods in Homer never went any whither but wrapt up in a Cloud: But the best is, in Heaven our soules shall bee filled with him, and not only as

Buckets drawne full out of Well, but as open Vessells swimming in the Ocean: Wee shall bee baptized in God, I thinke the expression may bee used, for so both Casaubon and the Greek Scholiast expound that in the acts, βαπτισθήσεσθε ἐν πνεύματι ἁγίῳ, Domus enim in quâ hoc peractum erat Spiritu Sancto fuit repleta, ita ut in eam tanquam in Κολυμβήθραν quandam Apostoli demersi videantur, elegantly. But I trouble you with tediosnesse: Thus with my duties to my Mother, and my Brother and Sisters best remembrances to you both I leave you to the Protection of the Lord,

Your much obliged Son,

R. CUDWORTH.

Mr Genua promised to send a Copy of your Letter which I much desire, but wee here not of it.

THE END.

CAMBRIDGE:
PRINTED AT THE UNIVERSITY PRESS.

www.ingramcontent.com/pod-product-compliance
Lightning Source LLC
LaVergne TN
LVHW020246110826
845151LV00003B/1027